# Selecting, Preparing and Developing the School District Superintendent

T0316183

# Dedication

This book is dedicated to the Fellows of the Cooperative Superintendency Program at the University of Texas at Austin — past, present and future.

# Selecting, Preparing and Developing the School District Superintendent

David S.G. Carter
Thomas E. Glass
and
Shirley M. Hord

Routledge
Taylor & Francis Group

LONDON AND NEW YORK

First published 1993 by The Falmer Press

Published 2005 by Routledge
2 Park Square, Milton Park, Abingdon, Oxfordshire OX14 4RN
711 Third Avenue, New York, NY 10017

First issued in paperback 2016

*Routledge is an imprint of the Taylor and Francis Group, an informa business*

**A catalogue record for this book is available from the British Library**

ISBN 13: 978-1-138-99600-7 (pbk)
ISBN 13: 978-0-7507-0170-9 (hbk)

**Library of Congress Cataloging-in-Publication Data are available on request**

Jacket design by Caroline Archer

Typeset in 9.5/11pt Bembo by
Graphicraft Typesetters Ltd., Hong Kong

# Contents

Contents

# Preface

In marked contrast to the intensive scrutiny of the principalship by academics, researchers, representatives of professional bodies, politicians and the public at large, the superintendency has remained relatively immune from the glare of the spotlight, until recently that is. In our view this is a somewhat anomalous situation, if only because there are some 15,000 school districts each headed by a superintendent, as well as other senior executives of equivalent status or above in central education agencies. Collectively, they operate a budget derived from the public purse of quite mind-blowing proportions. Until recently we have known relatively little about them — who they are, what they do and to what effect — except to say they are now the subjects of close scrutiny given that there is today a widespread public dissatisfaction with the quality of schooling across America. What are their needs now and in the future? What makes an effective school system leader and how can potential executive leaders be screened, selected, prepared and further developed? Recent conceptualizations and research focussed on these sorts of question, have provided the motivation for this book.

In the recent past a considerable intellectual effort has been applied to the solution of problems that have emerged from a series of official reports that are commonly referred to in professional circles. Frequently their substance is clouded by media hype. The intellectual effort, however, to problem find and problem solve, has not been uniform across the country. Rather, it has tended to occur in pockets in a somewhat desultory fashion. There are now signs, however, of a consistent body of research and practice emerging that is innovatory in nature and scope. This new knowledge base provides us with a more optimistic view of the nature of the superintendency than that which was evident during the last decade. It can inform us about what needs to be done to regenerate and revitalize the superintendency. We consider a dynamic research base to be a vital adjunct to the successful reform of the American public schools and school districts on which the well-being of the nation ultimately depends.

One of the centers of excellence for research and exemplary practice that is probing the substantive nature of the superintendency, supporting the development of superintendents in the field and assisting with their selection and preparation is located at The University of Texas at Austin. This book is the result of collaborative efforts by researchers based mainly at The University of Texas at Austin, and funded by the Meadows Foundation of Texas.

The focus of their work was identifying and mapping out the needs of senior

educational executives and evolving a system for their ongoing and further professional development in the field. This research and development has taken place
under the auspices of the embryonic National Executive Development Center
(NEDC) established by the American Association of School Administrators
(AASA).

New findings, stemming from the considerable efforts of the Meadows Project
Team, and supported by a growing number of dissertations, prompted us to
disseminate this body of research to the academic and professional community
as a matter of some priority. This book, however, is but part of that effort. A
monograph addressing instructional leadership and a series of papers have been
prepared and are in press or published in the relevant journals. This volume
represents a coherent synthesis of some intense research activity that is now
beginning to appear in journals in a piecemeal fashion.

Shirley Hord opens the account in Chapter 1, taking research on the principal
as instructional leader as her model and inspiration, and partialling out the implications and relevance of this for the complementary but distinctive role of
superintendents. It is fashionable to talk today of leadership forces. It seems not
unreasonable from this standpoint, to infer that it is the interaction of these forces,
represented by those who fulfill the roles of principal, superintendent and school
board official, as being instrumental in providing the needed vision, guidance and
leadership for the achievement of desired educational ends. Each player can learn
off the other in this regard.

The focus becomes more narrow in Chapter 2, and in Chapter 4, where Tom
Glass distills a selected body of research, chosen for its pioneering nature in initially contributing to a map of the superintendency territory, with no claims for
comprehensiveness. In Chapter 3, he takes an unashamedly normative stance in
considering current practices and realities in the light of what ought to be, to
achieve and maintain excellence in the superintendency. Just what are the characteristics of superintendents who have been designated as being 'exemplary'? Surely,
these are the successes of the profession and those preparing future superintendents should look hard and carefully at the profiles of these individuals.

In Chapter 5, Shirley Hord and Nolan Estes examine the highly problematic
area of superintendent selection by school boards. The premise of this chapter is
that preparation of superintendents must be configured to, at least partially meet,
the needs and perceptions of the consumers, namely, the school board. In Chapter
6, David Carter and Ben Harris consider some conceptual and empirical problems
related to the diagnosis of executive knowledge skills and competencies, as well
as the potential use of highly focussed diagnostic data for professional growth
planning.

The use of assessment methods for selection and screening and, rather uniquely,
for personal development plans in which executives retain control over their own
self-energized assessment data, is treated by Judith Loredo, Ben Harris and David
Carter in Chapter 7. Judith Loredo and David Carter extend this perspective
to the selection and preparation of administrators for senior executive roles in
Chapter 8.

In a text such as this, one might expect a chapter entitled *Leadership for
Learning — Learning for Leadership* to open the dialogue. Instead, we have pre-
ferred to leave this until the end of the book in Chapter 9. In this chapter David
Carter synthesizes and integrates the knowledge base developed at The University

of Texas at Austin with what we know about the nature of leadership and its much needed transformative power to realize the reinvigoration of American education.

As a research team, we felt the need to include an epilogue. As well as looking retrospectively at the work already done and currently underway, we also wished to project ahead, to present a future of what has yet to be accomplished and the infrastructure being put in place to facilitate this. From early beginnings centered around the Texas pilot site, the still-evolving National Executive Development Center is embodied in various sites across the nation. A decentralized approach with a suitable division of labor was conceived expressly to research and develop packages and processes in an open way for the ongoing professional development of superintendents. The form, nature and organizational arrangements to achieve this goal are presented by David Carter and Tom Glass, last of all in Chapter 10.

If we have accomplished the task we set out to do, it should leave the serious reader with a sense of what has been completed thus far, what remains to be done and the magnitude of the tasks involved. Above all, from our perspective, we would like to impress readers with a sense of *how* a high quality, diagnostic and action-oriented, professional growth system that meets the present and future needs of the superintendency might be achieved in a realistic fashion.

This manuscript has been completed in several locations ranging from Texas and Illinois to England and Australia. We would like to thank especially Angela Smith and Kathleen McDaniel at the University of Texas at Austin for word processing early sections of the manuscript; Sheena Carter, Laurie Coonan, and Jayne Piscioneri at the University of Notre Dame Australia for important middle-stage revisions; and Lori Kitchens and Lonne Parent, on staff at the Southwest Educational Development Laboratory, Austin, who produced the final copy for publication. All contributed and participated so competently and cheerfully.

Finally, we have had colleagues and graduate students too numerous to name individually, who have read and constructively commented on sections of this book. We are most grateful for the advice and commentary they gave. Any deficiencies in the final product, however, are of our own making — not theirs.

# List of Acronyms

AACTE   American Association of Colleges of Teacher Education
AASA    The American Association of School Administrators
AFT     American Federation of Teachers
ASCD    Association for Supervision and Curriculum Development
CAI     Competency Analysis Inventory
CEO    Chief Executive Officer
CSP     Cooperative Superintendency Program
DECAS   Diagnostic Executive Competency Assessment System
EAEP    Educational Administrator Effectiveness Profile
ESC     Education Service Center
GRE    Graduate Record Examination
ISD     Independent School District
LEAD    Leadership in Educational Administration Development
MBO    Management by Objectives
NASE    National Association of School Executives
NAESP   National Association of Elementary School Principals
NASSP   National Association of Secondary School Principals
NCATE   National Council for Accreditation of Teacher Education
NCEI    National Center for Educational Information
NCSI    National Curriculum Study Institutes
NEA    National Education Association
NEDC    National Executive Development Center
NPBEA   National Policy Board for Educational Administration
NSBA    National School Boards Association
PAL     Peer-assisted Leadership
PDP     Professional Development Program
PPBS    Performance-based Appraisal and Program Budgeting
REDS    Regional Executive Development Satellites
TAI     Task Analysis Inventory
TASA    Texas Association of School Administrators
TEA     Texas Education Agency
UCEA    University Council of Educational Administration

*Chapter 1*

# Smoke, Mirrors or Reality:
# Another Instructional Leader

*Shirley M. Hord*

The current interest in, and attention to, leadership appears to be unprecedented in this nation's history. Not only is the analysis of corporate executive officers' 'leadership' the focus of much of the television and other media coverage, but leadership at all levels is being recognized and publicly applauded: the high school sports team leader, the community's women volunteer leaders, even 8-year-old cub scouts are singled out and valued for their demonstrated leadership. In this milieu educational leadership has not escaped attention. The surfeit of national commission reports are all clear in their demands for a new view of educational leadership that will solve current problems and bring new visions to address pressing societal concerns both now and for the future. There are those who believe that the role of the school, and of those leading the school, is tied inexorably to the common 'good', and that preparing young people to function successfully and to contribute maximally to an improved social order will benefit all citizens.

High-sounding rhetoric! Nonetheless, it is not over-dramatic to assert that the nation's economic and cultural survival and hopes for the future ride in large measure on the shoulders of our schools, and thus *inter alia*, on the leadership of school superintendents. Such a relationship suggests a requirement for superintendents who are looking beyond buildings, buses, and bonds to students and instructional improvement. Thus, the superintendent's priority attention is on the schools' thirteen-year student 'product' and 'consumer', and on how each student is prepared to fit as an effectively functioning adult now and in tomorrow's society. Some contend that such administrative leadership is a critical factor in effective schools. For example, Coleman (1986) maintains:

> This component (administrative leadership) has emerged from virtually all the effective school studies as critical, even when the initial expectations did not include it as a factor. Any consideration of school district processes necessarily must include leadership as a primary linking mechanism. (p. 93)

What is bold leadership? While the concept is developed in Chapter 9 of this book, a simple definition characterizes leadership as guidance for movement from an existing to a preferred state. Assuming that to be the case, a vision of the preferred state is required, as are change strategies for inducing the organization to move toward the preferred state. What is known about superintendents operating in these modes? Not very much, but a knowledge base is evolving as is made clear in this chapter and elsewhere in this book. The role explication of the effective, improvement-oriented principal has been the focus of much study and consequently a burgeoning research base. Unlike the study of principals, disciplined inquiry into the superintendent's effectiveness is still in its infancy (Hord, 1990; Muller, 1989); there is a lack of models to support such intellectual work. Can the instructional leader principal serve as a model prototype paralleling the role of the superintendent in this area?

Utilizing the emerging research base that examines superintendents' problem-solving processes and roles in effective districts, this chapter explores the evolving literature and the underlying imperative of superintendents' leadership both now and in the future.

The chapter is organized in three sections:

(i)   the first provides a brief review of the chief education officer's various publics and their current expectations for superintendent's performance;

(ii)   in the second section, the new findings emerging from research on effective superintendents are presented; two paradigms that portray the effective principal are introduced, and the 'fit' between superintendents' findings and principals' frameworks is explored;

(iii)   finally, for increasing the effectiveness of instruction district-wide, the relationships between superintendents and principals are examined, noting the implications for the education of the school board and community and for the continuing professional development of superintendents.

### Finances and Facilities vs. the Future

Depending on just who is responding, the role definitions of superintendents vary widely. Those who occupy the role adhere to differing definitions from those outside the office — school boards, school staff, and the public at large. The chief education officer is a resident in the ever-widening contexts of these constituents. How the latter perceive the role and what they value most about it can significantly influence the way it is exercised by incumbents, but let us look first at the CEO's views.

### The Superintendent Looks at Herself/Himself

Mirror, mirror on the wall,
Just what am I, after all?

Such might be the query of many superintendents currently active in the position. In a study to learn if gender influenced the superintendent's view of his/her role (Youngs, 1988), it was discovered that half of the men and half of the women sampled viewed themselves as leaders, while the other 50 per cent of each group perceived themselves as managers. Furthermore, age was the factor that served to differentiate most between the different views across the study sample. Men and women under the age of 45 saw themselves as leaders while those over 45 viewed themselves as managers. Much attention and space has been given in the literature to differentiating management from leadership (see Chapter 9). Suffice it to note here that, as already suggested in the introductory passages, leadership can be thought of as entailing a visionary or symbolic dimension that addresses movement and change, while management is seen as securing an orderly *status quo* or the smooth operation of routines.

Additional studies addressing superintendents reported that aspects of their role identified as most important to them involved financial issues, building a positive climate to support and facilitate the work of staff and students, and an effective curriculum (Collier, 1987). How superintendents are influenced by self-perceptions of their careers and role(s) may be characterized by the place-bound and career-bound categories of superintendents: the place-bound superintendent, who does not see him/herself moving onward and upward or in leading the district forward, curbs change and maintains the *status quo*; the career bound or upwardly mobile superintendent, conversely, guides the system in new ways through the development and adaptation of new policies and practices (Crowson, 1987).

Given the disparate views of the role held by superintendents, it is not surprising that boards, also, differ among themselves and in contrast to the chief education officer. Of special significance is the influence the board can exercise on the superintendent's role. Such divergent perceptions impact and create tensions when superintendent role perspectives compete with the board's. It is instructive to consider, then, what views are characteristic of boards?

### The Eye of the Board

One-hundred-and-fifty school board presidents representing districts of various size, geographic region, and amount of wealth, were studied by Pringle (1989), who found that board presidents agreed 'skills considered most critical for selection and contract renewal . . . (were) those of providing information to board members and building a relationship of trust and respect with the board' (p. vii). Other areas deemed important (beyond the boards' self-interests) were those of professional staffing and evaluation, together with attention to the ways in which central office staff were organized. In Pringle's study, board presidents were found to be less concerned about operations and auxiliary services, results that differ from other studies of boards and their views of the superintendent. Pringle reported that the literature available for review reflected priority roles for the superintendent in the areas of 'finances, facilities, operations, personnel management, board relations and community relations'.

In contrast, narrative responses solicited in his study revealed that board presidents were also interested in the instructional-related abilities of superintendent-as-candidate and superintendent-as-incumbent. In a concurrent review of the literature, Hord (1990) also found boards' interest in superintendents' capabilities to manage finances and personnel to be a high priority consideration. At the same time, it appears that boards generally are not in agreement about the area and degree of the superintendent's license to demonstrate leadership, thereby providing the potential for superintendent/board conflict (making it easy to understand why boards prefer superintendents who 'build a relationship of trust and respect'). Alvey and Underwood (1985) described a 'tug-of-war going on in many school systems (with) board members . . . and superintendents . . . each trying to edge more responsibility . . . especially concerning personnel'. Hentges (1986), however, reported a balance of power with the superintendent's role predominating on internal policy issues where his/her professional technical expertise is of importance, and boards taking a stronger decision-making role in external policy issues.

### And Others

The advent of politics and the emergence of militant action-oriented interest groups have significantly impacted the superintendent's activities. The politics of community groups with particular interests to pursue, and the district's influential professional staff associations and unions, have had a profound effect on policies and practices in some school systems. This 'politicization' of public education (Lupini, 1983) has resulted in more than the usual active involvement of board members and others, further complicating the superintendent's role. How all these activities play out in the public press on a slow news day is easily observed.

On a more positive theme, there are some, like Tucker, who propose that superintendents adopt a role of managing people who think for a living as distinct from those who are just told what to do and expected to get on with it as directed (Tucker, 1988). With this view, Schlechty and Joslin (1986) maintain that knowledge work will be the most dominant occupation of our country, with teachers undertaking a decision-sharing role, requiring the redesign of authority relationships in a school system. In describing this new model, Schlechty and Joslin portray 'the superintendent . . . as the chief teacher . . . who defines problems and inspires others to solve them. Leadership, then, is more important than managerial skill, though managerial skill is not to be discounted'.

In summary, school boards as instruments of public policy have articulated roles and expectations for their superintendents to perform in certain ways. In addition to the way superintendents and boards view the role, others outside or peripheral to the confines or restraints of the school system promote extensive lists of skills, tasks and responsibilities they consider should accrue to the superintendent's role. The efforts of community interest groups and political action add further to the demands placed on the chief education officer for performance and accountability. In short, the modern superintendent is required to be all things to all people.

These multiple and frequently competing perspectives, role expectations, and demands do not bode well for the person in the 'catbird' seat. With mixed perceptions, an unrealistic array of expectations, and multiple role definitions abounding, it is not surprising that the art of politics has taken precedence over the craft of instruction in the superintendency. If instruction is to be accorded the highest priority by our schools, it would seem important at least to discover which role requirements of superintendents relate most powerfully to effective instruction — a topic to be examined in the next section.

**Effective Leaders**

There is an extensive research base on effective principals (Duttweiler and Hord, 1987) but a critical lack of much research-based knowledge about the effects that superintendents have on their districts that relates to student outcomes, the presumed focus of district programs. Wimpelberg (1988), Leithwood and Steinbach (1989), and others (Hord, 1990) have called attention to this fact, exhorting researchers to contribute to a much needed research base. Modestly and increasingly, study findings are accumulating, and though the quantity of results is still relatively small, they commonly exhibit a great potential to increase understanding about superintendents' effects on instruction. See for example, Harris and Wan (1991) and Muller (1989).

*Superintendents: Their Work in Effective Districts*

Most of the recent studies reported here have gone beyond the short self report survey method and have employed multiple data collection techniques including interviews with subjects, colleagues, subordinates, and community members; examination of documents; ethnographic field studies to observe the subjects *in situ* and so on. Further, most of the subjects and samples studied have been identified on the basis of their *effects* on district policies and practices and, more specifically, on student academic outcomes. Such study samples, though small, stand in contrast to those selected on the basis of 'reputation' by persons not in direct contact with the district and its daily operations. The work of these subjects, superintendents in effective districts, has been examined and reported by several researchers and a brief review of their findings follows.

In a series of three reports of twelve effective districts, Hallinger, Murphy and Peterson (1985, 1986, 1987) provided clear information about the role of the superintendent in district effectiveness. According to Murphy and Hallinger (1986), the superintendents of these twelve effective districts were characterized as setting goals and establishing expectations and standards, selecting staff, supervising and evaluating staff, establishing an instructional and curricular focus, ensuring consistency in curriculum and instruction, and monitoring curriculum and instruction.

Some of the superintendents collected products of the schools' work and used meetings of various sizes, formats, and composition to investigate implementation of instructional processes. They inspected curriculum and instruction in operation through visits to schools. Student achievement results were used in teacher and principal evaluations by two-thirds of the superintendents. They were, in a word, seen as being directly involved in the technical core operations of their districts (Murphy and Hallinger, 1986).

Murphy, Hallinger and Peterson's paper (1985) added that the superintendents were also engaged in culture building: communicating with staff; developing team activities, showing concern, and building morale; and resolving problems, cutting through paperwork, and securing rapid solutions to pressing problems. They were the primary actors in linking schools and district offices, promoting closer relationships between district and site administrators, and mandating administrator staff development that focussed explicitly on curriculum and instruction. The superintendents' message was 'every child can learn', and principals were expected to realize this ideal in practice (Murphy, *et al.*, 1985).

Peterson, Murphy and Hallinger (1987) reported that superintendents in effective districts did not believe that 'instructional technologies are totally idiosyncratic, evanescent and unspecifiable' (p. 18); therefore, they specified instructional models and teaching methods to improve student learning outcomes. To ensure that instruction was attended to, they communicated the expectation that the identified models would be used. They established goals and standards for evaluation, and they put in place support structures through ongoing staff development activities and the allocation of budgets to support these initiatives. They signaled in powerful ways that curriculum and teaching were important (*ibid.*).

In comparing two small rural districts with similar communities, the characteristics and activities of the District B superintendent appeared to be significant to the district's success (Jacobson, 1986). For example, to improve student performance, teachers' performance was nurtured through professional development, and monitored. If teachers did not perform in accordance with expectations, they were dismissed, pressured into retirement, or denied tenure. In turn, teachers were supported in student achievement efforts through a strictly enforced code of student discipline by the administration. The improved student behavior contributed to improved teachers' working conditions.

Teachers were encouraged to work collaboratively to address problems and to experiment with the curriculum. The superintendent regarded faculty as the agents of change and held them accountable for improvement. To facilitate this initiative, he supported staff as they upgraded course offerings, materials, facilities, and their own professional development. In this small district, the superintendent worked directly with teachers, rather than with principals. Gains in student achievement was the goal of the superintendent and he pursued this outcome aggressively even at the risk of faculty and community opposition (Jacobson, 1986).

Coleman and LaRocque (1988) examined the activities of superintendents in high-performing districts and contrasted them with superintendents in less successful districts. They concluded that the superintendent's leadership was the single most important factor in creating a positive district ethos, with both cultural elements and technical factors contributing to its success. In explaining district ethos, they identified six activity and attitude 'focusses' that were given attention: learning, accountability, change, caring, commitment, and community. For each focus, the superintendents emphasized being accountable, and being improvement and adaptation-oriented. In addition, they consistently established and followed through on their expectations.

The superintendents influenced staff by reference and adherence to the dominant norms of accountability and collegial responsibility for declared objectives. In the high performing districts the superintendent established a consensus through using committees as consultative bodies, accessing teachers through principals, and using principals as reactors to ideas. The superintendents were perceived by the researchers as a presence in the schools and community, modeling energy and effort for the staff and demonstrating accountability to, and on behalf of, the community. Their overall effect was manifested through the 'creation and maintenance of a positive district ethos' (*ibid.*, p. 33). Ethos in this respect may be thought of as the pervading climate or culture.

Superintendents, reported by Pollack, Chrispeels, Watson, Brice and McCormack (1988), were regarded by district and school level administrators as key players in setting and guiding improvement goals. They were also regarded by themselves and others as modeling instructional leadership, especially in a symbolic sense through the image they projected as they visited schools on a regular basis. They played an active role in monitoring change and improvement efforts, focussing on curriculum issues as the fulcrum for planned change.

Again, direct control over principals' behavior was exercised through selection, supervision and evaluation, and through enhancing professional socialization by means of training and staff development. Indirect influence on principals and improvement efforts occurred through setting goals, allocating resources, developing curriculum and evaluating instruction, and by analyzing test data. This form of district control was not seen by subordinate staff and the broader community to be denigrating of principals who were themselves generally accepting the directives they were given, and being supervised in a developmental and nurturing way. The superintendent's role with principals included setting goals for change, articulating the district's goals, and modeling priorities for change through visibility, proximity and monitoring. They also provided support through staff development, on-site assistance and resource provision.

The cultural characteristic typical of the improving districts was the belief that educators in the schools *could* increase student achievement (*ibid.*).

In identifying the superintendent's role in reform, sixteen district leaders were studied by Paulu (1988), and several generalizations from the results were reported by the investigator. First, the superintendent created an expectant atmosphere where reform flourished by encouraging staff to share ideas and take risks and by rewarding those who initiated change. Fundamental to creating such an atmosphere was to build trust with all staff before the introduction of change efforts. Establishing ties with all constituents was also important, but the relationship between superintendent and principal was identified as particularly critical to outcome success. Also cited was the development of credibility with minority group members and building trust with the media.

Second, superintendents' initiatives for their districts' improvement required a comprehensive vision-based plan. While the superintendent introduced the plan, other participants molded it through their work in committees charged with the development of a fully articulated vision and long-range plans congruent with the shared vision.

Third, communication of the plan was the responsibility of the superintendent, and was done in a variety of ways in order to reach all people who would be directly and indirectly affected by the plan. Because they may be a step ahead of those they lead, successful superintendents communicate plans carefully and in convincing and persuasive ways to their multiple audiences.

Fourth, after plans were made they were executed. Thus, superintendents provided for the training of staff and all those involved in implementation. They delegated responsibilities but remained, however, actively involved in monitoring events. If plans did not proceed as intended, modification or elimination of some elements was considered by the superintendent and/or others responsible for implementation. In other cases, barriers had to be eliminated. These sixteen superintendents were reported to be at various stages in their reform efforts, and they remained optimistic about their expected results (*ibid.*).

In a study of big city school districts' improvement efforts, Hill, Wise and Shapiro (1989) selected six districts for investigation: Atlanta, Cincinnati, Miami,

Memphis, Pittsburgh and San Diego. A key finding was that 'No improvement effort can succeed without an active school superintendent . . .' (p. v). In explaining the contributions of these specific actors to the process of improvement, the researchers concluded that 'The school superintendent is usually the single most important actor in the improvement process, whether that person is the initial architect or an indispensable member of a coalition of improvement-oriented groups. No improvement effort that was studied caught fire without an active superintendent willing to interact with community forces to attack the school system's inertia' (p. 20). What did these six superintendents do?

First, they worked with their boards and the community to establish a public mandate of goals and priorities to guide the policies of the school system. The resulting goal statements were broad and general but meaningful guides for actions, providing agreement on direction and focus. Superintendents created these mandates in various ways, but they reflected 'public needs and aspirations' and granted greater authority than would normally be the case to the superintendent.

Second, these superintendents almost guaranteed results, but did not promise overly-ambitious short-term outcomes. Thus, they helped the community to understand that change and improvement would take a long time to achieve.

Third, the superintendents strove to assure that the improvement effort would be continuous and would not disappear if the current administrator moved or was replaced. By cultivating and nurturing younger administrators in the philosophy, processes and intermediate effects of the change efforts, its continuity might be assured.

Fourth, relating to the community at large, which is necessary for any district-wide improvement, means meeting the politics of race, income and ambition head-on. The superintendent's race was a factor to be reckoned with in these large, urban communities and these three black and three white superintendents did just that, in addition to addressing in a personalized way the needs of all children regardless of their race or family income.

Fifth, while the preceding four areas represent external issues, there was the internal dimension to be dealt with. Inside issues focussed on three strategic factors: information, principals and professional expectations. First, the information flow during change efforts was increased, and the media used to keep priorities and emergent needs up-front in the public mind. Second, a common means for managing change, identified by five of the executives, was to manage principals. They did so by reorganizing and eliminating organizational structures to make their relationships with principals readily accessible. 'Under new arrangements they (principals) reported to area superintendents . . . and through them to the superintendents . . . the line relationship between principal and superintendent re-emphasized the idea that the principal, responsible for the whole school, reports only to administrators with comparably broad concerns' (pp. 25–6).

To address the third issue, these superintendents spent major parts of their time in schools, treating teachers and administrators as professionals, yet leading them by articulating priorities and providing guidance and exemplary role models. Their symbolic actions — classroom visits, participation in principals' performance reviews or a school award ceremony — conveyed what was important. To make their expectations for quality performance absolutely clear, four of them paid unannounced visits to schools to deliver ultimatums for improvement if needed, and firing of principals as necessary. Principals were used as the instruments for inducing and facilitating change, and were also the focus of change and improvement in the direction needed (*ibid.*).

Muller (1989) investigated the relationship of superintendent instructional leadership competencies and elementary principal effective instructional leadership behaviors to school effectiveness. He found that superintendent competence in the area of organizing for instruction was the best predictor of campus and district effectiveness. According to Muller eleven tasks are included in this area, namely:

(i)    The executive understands instructional design;
(ii)   The executive establishes priorities among the district's instructional goals and objectives;
(iii)  The executive adopts instructional methodologies that facilitate the efficient delivery of the district's curriculum;
(iv)   The executive develops an instructional and resource management system that implements the district's instructional philosophy;
(v)    The executive develops goals and objectives that guide the district's instructional philosophy;
(vi)   The executive provides an instructional evaluation program that accurately monitors the instructional program;
(vii)  The executive monitors student achievement through feedback from the instructional evaluation program;
(viii) The executive maintains a system for instructional change;
(ix)   The executive maintains a system of instructional improvement that seeks to upgrade the process of student learning;
(x)    The executive ensures that the district incorporates varied and diverse instructional methodologies that allow for a wide range of learning styles that exist in a multi-racial student population;
(xi)   The executive stipulates that homogeneous ability groupings within classrooms do not segregate students into racial or other inappropriate groupings. (p. 127)

While this study does not suggest a causal relationship between superintendents' tasks and district effectiveness, it reports a significant correlation between these variables (*ibid.*).

From a descriptive study of forty-nine reputationally nominated superintendents, Buck (1989) identified seven most frequently described transformational leadership behaviors. The results are reflected in Buck's research-based behavioral definition of a transformational superintendent leader. According to Buck, such a leader uses leadership that goes beyond merely managing the system to helping the system achieve its next stage of evolution; sharing a vision that becomes the fused purpose of the organization; and communicating this vision, formally and informally in order to provide up-to-date information to different audiences regarding the status of the organization.

The leader accomplishes the district's mission based on the vision by initially conceptualizing a specific future; engaging in appropriate risks to bring about change; involving others in goal setting and decision making; empowering others; and communicating the vision to every level of the organization. The leader concerns herself/himself about the individual, is committed to quality development of others, and seeks to move followers to becoming self-actualized. He/she demonstrates a positive attitude and a strong value system that includes being a strong advocate of quality education for students and educational reforms; demonstrates and models the directed learner, continually seeking to improve and develop skills personally and professionally; and portrays an enjoyment of his or her work and profession (pp. 201–2).

From this concise review of recent studies, an emergent picture of the effective superintendent is forming. Do superintendents exhibit a unique set of behaviors or is there a parallel to school-based leaders, i.e., principals?

Leithwood and Steinbach (1989) examined the problem-solving processes of superintendents in order to better understand what they do. With minor refinements, they used a methodology for their sample of 'expert' and 'typical' superintendents, similar to that which had proven successful in their previous studies of expert and typical principals. An information-processing orientation to problem solving that was employed in their research on principals was used as a framework for the study of superintendents. Leithwood and colleague referred to Schwenk (1988) who judged such a perspective in understanding the strategic decision making of senior executives to be appropriate and relevant. From Leithwood and Steinbach's report, it seems reasonably easy to infer that the researchers were satisfied with the results of transporting the methodology they had devised for the study of principals to that of superintendents.

There were similarities as well as differences in the results obtained from expert principals and superintendents. Expert superintendents, for example, demonstrated an undeniable air of self-confidence; this same posture of certainty was expressed by expert (but not typical) principals. Some of the differences between expert principals and superintendents seemed to be a 'function of work context'. For example, superintendents had significantly more problem solving resources, such as instantly available and accessible information. The researchers hypothesized that differences between superintendents and principals may be attributable to the expanded experiences of superintendents in the broader, more diverse environment in which they operate.

On balance, therefore, while superintendents' and principals' work environments differ, it seems not unreasonable to consider the use of common methods and structures for investigating and analyzing both principals and superintendents — not only their problem-solving processes but also the components of what they do in their jobs, leading a school and leading a district.

### Principals: Their Work in Effective Schools

Two frameworks used in describing and explaining effective principals appear useful in considering the role of the effective superintendent as well. One identifies components that distinguish between effective principals and others, and the second addresses three principal styles of facilitating change, with one style more characteristic of effective principals. These frameworks are presented, and the body of recent research summarized above on superintendents is then examined for its fit with these models.

As already noted, there is an abundant literature on the principal as an instructional leader and the results of research on principals' leadership appear quite

*Table 1.1:* Relationship of principal leadership to successful change

| Effective Principal | Effective Change |
| --- | --- |
| Vision | Innovation Configuration |
| Goals and Expectations<br>Supportive Environment | Developing Supportive<br>Organizational Arrangements |
| | Training |
| Monitoring | Monitoring and Evaluation |
| Data-Based Interventions | Providing Consultation<br>and Reinforcement |
| | External Communication |

*Adapted from:* Hord, S.M., Rutherford, W.L., Huling-Austin, L.L., & Hall, G.E. (1987). *Taking Charge of Change.* Alexandria, Virginia: Association for Supervision and Curriculum Development.

consistent. As an example of one summary, Rutherford (1985) explicates five factors of effective principals, or five components of their roles, namely, they:

(i) have clear, informed visions of what they want their schools to become — visions that focus on students and their needs;

(ii) translate these visions into goals for their schools and expectations for the teachers, students, and administrators;

(iii) establish school climates that support progress toward these goals and expectations;

(iv) continuously monitor progress; and

(v) intervene in a supportive or corrective manner, when it seems necessary. (p. 32)

Not surprisingly the actions of these improvement-oriented school-based leaders parallel the types of interventions found to be associated with successful school change. This alignment is depicted in Table 1.1.

Not only has the research on principals revealed *what* they do, reported briefly above in the five-factor framework, but studies have also illuminated our understanding of *how* they do it. Hall, Rutherford, Hord and Huling (1984), drawing on intensive studies of principals engaged in improvement efforts with their faculties, identified three different ways that principals work. The three do not pretend to encompass all the ways all principals work, but the essential features of the styles have been confirmed in cognate studies (Leithwood and Montgomery, 1982; Thomas, 1978; Trohoski, 1984; Schiller, 1988).

Drawing on Hall, Rutherford, Hord and Huling (pp. 23–4), the three styles and their definitions (characterizing superintendents) are as follows:

1 **Initiators**

Initiators have clear, decisive long-range policies and goals . . . they have very strong beliefs about what good schools and teaching should be like and work intensely to attain this vision . . . they have strong expectations for students, teachers, principals, and themselves; they convey and monitor these expectations through frequent contacts with principals and clear explication of how the school is to operate and how principals are to provide guidance and manage improvement . . . they solicit input from staff and then make decisions in terms of school and district goals and what is best for students.

2 **Managers**

Managers represent a broader range of behaviors. They demonstrate both responsive behaviors . . . and they also initiate actions in support of the change effort . . . work without fanfare to provide basic support to facilitate principals . . . keep principals informed about decisions and are sensitive to principals needs. They will defend their principals from what are perceived as excessive demands.

3 **Responders**

Responders place heavy emphasis on allowing principals and others the opportunity to take the lead. They believe their primary role is to maintain a smooth running district by focusing on traditional administrative tasks, keeping principals content and treating all constituents well. They view principals as strong professionals who are able to carry out their work with little guidance . . . This seems to be due, in part, to their desire to please others and in part to their more limited vision of how their school district and all personnel should change in the future.

These paragraphs describing the normative approach typical of each leadership style summarize the concerns, motivation, and behaviors of the three styles. The initiator principal has been identified through research studies as the effective principal (Rutherford, 1985) and the initiator description resonates closely with the descriptions of superintendents in effective districts reported above.

### Does the Shoe Further Fit?

Using the five-factor effective principals' framework, the findings on superintendents are discussed and a composite of the five-dimensional superintendent is described from a synthesis of the study findings (Table 1.2). These data are collectively powerful and provide a lens through which to look at the superintendent, as well as principal, as instructional leader.

### Vision

Overall the studies do not report much about superintendents' visioning. This may be a function of the study methodologies, i.e., did the study questions actually address superintendents' vision-making? It is to be expected that the goals and expectations espoused by superintendents come from some view they hold of the future, though it is equally possible to believe that their goals represent more short-range needs than those implicit in reflecting futuristic scenarios. Paulu reported that planning for what they want their districts to become is an important activity for superintendents. Others in the district may be solicited for their ideas on molding and developing the plan for the future. Buck cited the superintendent as sharing a vision that drives the organization to achieve its 'next stage of evolution'. While little is reported about vision, much was revealed about goals and expectations, the next factor for consideration.

Table 1.2: *Five factors of effective principals and findings on roles of superintendents*

| Five Factors of Effective Principals | | | Findings on Roles of Superintendents | | | | | |
|---|---|---|---|---|---|---|---|---|
| | Hallinger, Murphy, Peterson | Jacobson | Coleman, LaRocque | Pollack, et al. | Paulu | Hill, et al. | Muller | Buck |
| *Vision* | | | | | Paulu | | | Buck |
| *Goals/Expectations* | Hallinger, Murphy, Peterson | Jacobson | Coleman, LaRocque | Pollack, et al. | Paulu | Hill, et al. | Muller | Buck |
| *Supportive Environment/Climate* | Hallinger, Murphy, Peterson | Jacobson | Coleman, LaRocque | Pollack, et al. | Paulu | Hill, et al. | | |
| *Monitoring* | Hallinger, Murphy, Peterson | Jacobson | Coleman, LaRocque | Pollack, et al. | | Hill, et al. | Muller | |
| *Intervening* | Hallinger, Murphy, Peterson | Jacobson | Coleman, LaRocque | Pollack, et al. | Paulu | | | |

## Goals and expectations

All the researchers reported superintendents' involvement in setting goals, communicating them to the public and articulating specific expectations to the district's professionals. Specifically, Hallinger, Murphy and Peterson characterized superintendents in effective districts as setting goals and establishing expectations and standards, especially focussing on curriculum and instruction, to the point of even identifying models of instruction to be used. The superintendents clearly signaled the high priority they gave to teaching and learning (Hallinger, Murphy, Peterson, Coleman and LaRocque).

Jacobson's effective superintendent similarly articulated goals and the means for acquiring gains in student achievement. Pollack *et al.* reported district perceptions that viewed the superintendent as the *key* person in setting, articulating and guiding improvement goals. Paulu's sixteen superintendents widely communicated their plans and goals to all school and business constituents, and in various ways they communicated carefully and convincingly so the goals would be understood by multiple stakeholders.

Establishing a public mandate of goals and priorities to substantiate agreement on the direction to be taken was one of the activities of successful urban superintendents in effecting change (Hill *et al.*). Muller reported similar findings on the effective superintendents that he studied. The urban superintendents, according to Hill, spent time in schools articulating their priorities directly to school personnel. Buck suggested that this sort of communication is done both formally and informally by exemplary superintendents, as a matter of course.

## Supportive environment/climate

Developing a district 'ethos' (the climate/culture) was a strong thrust of the superintendents studied by Coleman and La Rocque. In the study's high performing districts the superintendents established consensuality as a norm, by employing collegial committee work and consultation with staff in order to produce positive attitudes toward planned change. Hallinger, Murphy and Peterson reported the effective district superintendents' role in culture building: communicating with staff, developing teams, demonstrating concern and building morale. The superintendents established support through budget allocations and staff development — a phenomenon confirmed also in the Pollack study. In Jacobson's study of two small, rural districts, teachers were supported in their improvement efforts by the administrative enforcement of discipline policies with students.

Paulu's findings described superintendents as creating an atmosphere 'where reform can flourish' by supporting idea sharing by staff, encouraging staff risk taking, building trust and rewarding change initiators. This building of an 'expectant' atmosphere was done before change was introduced. Hill cited treating teachers and administrators as professionals by the superintendent as an important aspect of climate.

## Monitoring

A critical factor in successful change in schools is that of monitoring progress. Likewise, the effective transfer of new learning in the staff development process that supports improvement is greatly enhanced by monitoring behavior and skills change. It is noted that effective principals are characteristically 'quality control' monitors, which also was a dominant aspect of the work of superintendents monitoring schools in effective districts (Pollack *et al.*; Hill *et al.*), and in monitoring classrooms (Jacobson; Hill *et al.*). Hallinger, Murphy and Peterson reported that superintendents monitor personnel (principals), and curriculum and instruction (also Pollack study). Some superintendents collected the products of students' work as exemplars of achievement. In meetings they inquired about implementation. Student achievement scores were used as monitoring and accountability indices for formative purposes (cited by Coleman and La Rocque; Pollack; Muller).

The superintendents of effective systems did not assume that once the plans for improvement were in place realization of the vision was assured. Quite the contrary, continual formative monitoring of progress was done to make certain that the implementation of change was happening and was on track. Monitoring was also used to access data for providing support and assistance when and where it was needed — the last of the five factors.

*Intervening*
The companion to monitoring is intervening with actions that will influence staff to continue their efforts toward instructional effectiveness and improved student outcomes. Interventions can reinforce what is being done, can cajole or coerce staff movement, and/or can assist with trouble-shooting or problem-solving about the impact of the change process. Intervening can take the form of inhibiting inappropriate behaviors or celebrating positive progress. Some superintendents, reported Hallinger *et al.*, Pollack *et al.*, and Paulu, provided and mandated staff development for all players, a large scale intervention. They also provided on-site assistance (Pollack). Jacobson found that teachers' performance was monitored and when performance was not as high as expected, interventions by the superintendent included dismissal, pressure to retire, or denial of tenure. Coleman and La Rocque, and Pollack *et al.*, discussed superintendents who modeled instructional leadership energy and effort for the staffs. If effects didn't materialize as was envisioned and planned for, then superintendents modified or eliminated some or all aspects of the plan accordingly (Paulu).

Clearly, an analysis of the superintendent's work in effective districts, using the factors characterizing effective principals, indicates that effective superintendents are engaged in a similar range of activities. As the Hill *et al.* study reminds us, unique findings related to the superintendency are found in the broader district context, seen as a highly political realm that the superintendent must interact with in order to effect improvement. While the principal has responsibility for the school's public relations and political harmony on a smaller scale, it is likely to be more homogeneous, and thus, logically less demanding, than the diversity to be found within a larger district context.

Yet classroom, school, and district activities are nested, with classrooms embedded in schools, and schools in districts, thus making it probable that district level leaders can act in ways paralleling the activities of principals to affect district outcomes. Murphy and Hallinger (1986) make a strong statement, proclaiming 'there are substantial parallels between the findings on the principal as instructional leader and the role of the superintendent as instructional leader'. What is common from this body of research then, is the possibility for two variables focussed on effective instruction: the role of principal as instructional leader and the role of superintendent as instructional leader. The interaction of these two variables, however, constitutes a third factor in district effectiveness plans. This interaction is examined and discussed in the final section of the chapter.

## A New Relationship: A New Alliance

There can be no denying the powerful influence of the site-based administrator, the principal, on instructional improvement at the school level. The leadership of the principal has been consistently cited as the most significant factor in the success of campus change efforts. These efforts, however, thrive or die, supported or otherwise, in the wider school district setting. Thus, for more powerful and pervasive instructional leadership and improvement, attention has begun to focus at the district level.

### Superintendent as Developer

Several issues demand a district focus. One of these is the obvious need for more improvement simultaneously on more 'fronts'. One school at a time is a theme frequently heard, but such a pace or frequency is unacceptable in the light of today's needs and tomorrow's demands. A second issue stems from the needs of principals themselves who have been called upon to personally adopt and implement a new professional role (instructional leader and school improvement facilitator) — new to 50–70 per cent of them (Hord, 1988). This constitutes an innovation for most principals and requires for this school building administrator the same support, training, and technical assistance and coaching as any new practice or skills acquisition. In most districts, this presents something of a dilemma: who will provide the assistance and coaching for the ongoing development of the principal? The principal's support and development needs originate in the challenge to improve student learning, and are logically linked to the superintendent in effective districts via a chain of reasoning as follows.

For children to learn more successfully, teaching practices must change to become more effective. Teachers require help in implementing new practices — who will provide this assistance? The principal has been identified as the person responsible for providing such help. This role demands new skills and behaviors of principals. To implement the role, the principal requires help — who will provide this assistance? The superintendent?

A number of the studies reviewed in the previous section identified the superintendent as this 'nurturer'. For example, Pollack *et al.* (1988) reported that the superintendent exercised direct control over principals' development through his/her supervision and evaluation, and through enhancing principals' professional socialization by training activities and other methods. They used indirect influence through setting goals jointly with principals and selectively allocating resources. Principals generally accepted being indirectly directed in this nurturing manner, to grow in the ways envisioned by the superintendent. Murphy *et al.* (1985) revealed that superintendents took a primary role in mandating staff development for administrators that focussed on curriculum and instruction, thus, preparing them for their role in improving teaching and learning. In the Hill *et al.* study (1989) superintendents cultivated and nurtured younger administrators (principals) in the philosophy and processes of the reform effort to assure its continuation.

As good managers of personnel, superintendents were providing the support counterbalanced by gentle pressure, for helping principals acquire new skills. Some superintendents, however, were viewed as taking a more comprehensive and direct role with principals, using principals as their instruments for promoting and effecting change and improvement.

### Superintendent as Strategist

Paulu, in summarizing the role of superintendents as actors in reforming their districts, cited the quality of the relationship between the superintendent and principal as being particularly critical to the success of school and district change efforts. Hill *et al.* described the superintendents as managing change through managing principals. They made the development of relationships with principals much easier by removing organizational structures such as layers of personnel that intervened between the two levels of administrators. After reorganization, principals reported only to area superintendents and through them to the district superintendent. The clear message from this change was that the principal who was responsible for his/her entire school would interact and report to administrators with similarly wide-ranging responsibilities.

The superintendents made regular visits to schools for the purpose of working with principals, identifying their priorities and modeling behaviors they wished in turn to have emulated. These executive leaders used principals to carry their message to schools, to implement their shared visions in schools, making reality out of their dreams. By working directly with the principals and coaching them in their new roles, they developed allies who would work with them to realize their goals and objectives. Superintendents shared decision making with principals (under particular circumstances), thus further enhancing their relationship with each other. Once new norms were established, these teams of district-level/school-level instructional leaders provided a powerful impetus and greater facilitation for increasing instructional effectiveness at the campus and district levels.

### Concluding Remarks

In the USA, teaching and administering have become divorced from one another (Cuban, 1988), and schools have come to be viewed by administrators as corporate enterprises, rather than as centers for learning and growth (Gibboney, 1989). This may be true generally, but it certainly does not come through the effective superintendents' stories described in this chapter. It is widely believed, however, that administrative behavior derives from its context; therefore, significant reforms in administrative behavior will occur when school system reform occurs (Crowson and Hannaway, 1989). Exhortations for better performance, behavioral prescriptions for managerial success and externally-generated regulations will have little value within existing structures *(ibid.)*. Thus, at least two issues are basic to changing what most administrators do or don't do. They are:

(i) **The school board**
   Studies of school board's preferences for superintendent competencies have identified managing finances, facilities, operations, personnel, and

board and community relations as high priorities (Hord, 1990; Pringle, 1989). These appear to be typical manifestations of the values held by those who hire the superintendent — the school board. Because school boards formulate policy, thereby shaping the district context, the board members become either the naysayers or the supporters of an expanding superintendent role. Boards seem to disagree about the extent of that leadership to be exercised by the superintendent specifically for instruction, although in Pringle's study, board presidents were interested in hiring and retaining superintendents who had instruction-related abilities. Pringle advocated follow-up research to identify components of instructional leadership deemed necessary for successful superintending.

Educating the school board and community to understand and appreciate an instructional leader superintendent is basic to the board's development of a district context wherein superintendent leadership can flower. It has been suggested that the superintendent 'teach' the board and community about alternative role definitions, an interesting 'chicken and egg' problem. If the superintendent doesn't have the knowledge base and competence in district-level instructional leadership, how can he/she teach it? And if the board is not knowledgeable, how can they provide the means for the superintendent to learn? Which leads to the second issue.

(ii) **Superintendents' professional development**

Both preparation programs and professional development activities have been targeted as means for improving the skills of superintendents. Also targeted is the improvement of these programs and activities in order that they do a successful job, a case of building an airplane and flying it simultaneously. Muller's study (1989) reported a relationship between superintendent instructional leadership competencies, elementary principal effective instructional leadership behaviors, and school effectiveness. From his findings, Muller suggested that the preparation and continuing development of superintendents should include instructional design theory, goal setting, strategies for planning, evaluation of instruction, strategies for change, and methods of instruction.

While the call for reform of administrator preparation increases, McCarthy (1987) found that few educational administration professors thought important changes were needed in their programs — a view at odds with that of many others, practitioners and researchers, for example (see also Chapter 3).

The National Policy Board for Educational Administration released its report in 1989 concerning upgrading the training of school administrators. In it, *people* were addressed (both candidates for programs as well as faculty of programs), *program* structure, duration, and content were recommended, and assessment *provisos* were stipulated. Already, action has been mounted to address these issues, some of which are described in Chapter 6. Thus, there is good reason to be optimistic that superintendency programs in the future will be more effective in preparing individuals for this important post of district instructional leadership.

Is the 'new' model of instructional leader superintendent smoke, or mirror, or reality? Is it possible that district executives have the opportunities or take the opportunities to study achievement data, articulate priorities, review principal performance, model desired behaviors, and monitor progress toward desired outcomes? It is clearly a reality in those districts cited by the reports referenced in this chapter.

The researchers who conducted the set of studies reviewed here concluded that significant change required the active and enlightened involvement of super-intendents, and this involvement typically included direct functional relationships with principals regarded as the other instructional leaders. From the work conducted to date, it is evident that working together comprehensively and collegially, these instructional leaders can more effectively serve the needs of children — the most important of any nation's resources and our hope for the future.

*Chapter 2*

---

# Through the Looking Glass

---

*Thomas E. Glass*

Any field of research is concerned with some aspect of reality, the delineation of which defines its territory. Ideally, research in a new area aims at the creation of an increasingly refined map of its territory and, typically, research in a new field begins with a description of its territory (Kallos and Lundgren, 1975). It is approximately only five to ten years ago that research efforts were directed, in any concerted manner, beyond the building principal toward senior executives in school districts and their equivalents in central office agencies. From being an under-researched field, the American superintendency has now become a focal point for numerous studies, a selection of which is referenced in this book. These studies have advanced and refined our knowledge of the territory as well as providing us with directions for its further unfolding.

We started to circumscribe the boundaries in the first chapter, drawing parallels between what we know about the considerable research conducted on the principalship, with implications from the findings for the cognate area of the superintendency.

In this chapter, the focus is narrowed in order to review a small group of studies, conducted since the mid-1980s, and selected because of their pioneering nature in helping to establish and crystallize the research base on the superintendency.

In this chapter, studies have been selected for the light they shed on the nature, scope, form and function of the superintendency; and on the role requirements of superintendents *vis-à-vis* knowledge, competencies and skills in order to be effective. For the purposes of this book, the superintendency has been conceived as a cadre of senior executives charged with two major tasks. The first is the routine management of schools and school systems at the district level. The second is the not-so-routine challenge of envisioning and transforming these systems in response to changing national priorities and the aspirations of local communities.

The chapter also addresses what the research has to say about aspiring to the superintendency through career paths analysis, in addition to holding a mirror up to practitioners to reflect what they themselves regard as being important to the nature of their work. A similar perspective is provided on the professoriate. Collectively, the findings can illuminate the preparation of administrators although the issues raised are addressed more fully in Chapter 8. It is, however, of more than passing interest to establish the degree of congruence, or lack of it, between what practitioners and those who prepare them regard as being important, using common criteria.

The record shows that much of the early innovative work, notably under the umbrella of the American Association of School Administrators (AASA), has been conducted by researchers in Texas. Today there is an increasing and widespread interest in this field from both a research and a professional development perspective (Murphy and Hallinger, 1989; Murphy, 1991). The compelling need is to understand better the nature and scope of the field, including its numerous and varied elements. Clearer understandings could drive much needed changes in the screening, selection, preparation and ongoing development of senior school district executives. While our focus is primarily on the superintendency, other key players tasked with leading the nation's schools and school systems into the next century are also included in the research base. That aside, there are still many gaps in the emerging body of research, as yet to be closed by another generation of researchers.

In 1982, the AASA produced a document describing a set of guidelines for the preparation of public school administrators, i.e., superintendents. The guidelines included performance goals, and were compiled by a joint committee of professors of educational administration and practitioners in the field. The relevance of the performance goals was investigated by McClellan (1983) using a sample of practicing superintendents who verified them as being basically appropriate to the demands of their role(s). The AASA also commissioned John Hoyle, Fenwick English and Betty Steffy to translate the guidelines into leadership skills considered necessary for school executives to achieve the performance outcomes specified in the AASA Guidelines (Hoyle, English and Steffy, 1985).

Early research verified the appropriateness of the performance goals and competencies in terms of requisite preparation and training for the role(s) of a superintendent. It had not confirmed, however, their validity. Do actual on-the-job behaviors of superintendents correlate with emerging theoretical conceptions of the role(s)? It is fairly self-evident that, if sets of performance goals, competencies, and skills are deemed to exist in theory, they obviously need to be verified in a field setting to confirm and evaluate their relationship to job performance. In other words, what superintendents are trained to do must at least relate to executive effectiveness in the performance of their duties.

In attempting to establish congruence between theory and practice, the first investigation into the operational use of performance goals and competencies contained in *Guidelines for Preparation of Administrators* (1979) and *Skills for Successful School Leaders* (1985) was undertaken on a national basis in 1986. The study was directed jointly by the AASA and researchers at the University of Texas at Austin. Later, in 1987 and 1988, companion studies were initiated on a statewide basis in Illinois and Texas; and a second national study was conducted in a contiguous area in 1989. In the latter investigation, a sample of professors of educational administration was drawn to discover the perceptions of academics concerning the appropriateness of the previously identified performance goals and skills to superintendent effectiveness. In concert, the general conclusions to be drawn from this group of studies was that some goals were more directly relevant to performance than others. Also, there can be no sustainable generic view of the superintendency because of, among other things, its temporal and context-bound nature. What emerged from the research was an excellent typology of approximately five types of superintendents — each requiring a different range and level of skill and placing individual emphases on previously identified performance areas.

During this period a seminal study was conducted by Susan Sclafani, focussed on the occupational content of the work of superintendents. Its purpose was to establish whether the AASA guidelines, developed initially from the (then) extant literature, formed a valid framework for the preparation of superintendents. It also sought to prioritize those performance goals and skills considered by practicing superintendents to be important for effective performance in the field. Sclafani's sample was drawn from the national population of practicing school superintendents, including a sub-set specifically nominated as 'effective superintendents'. For the purpose of analysis the groups were then sub-divided along demographic lines such as size of district, geographical location of district and enrollment features of the district, and other social factors such as minority populations, for example. The initial seven performance areas of the AASA were increased to eight after a review panel recommended more emphasis on finance and budgeting skills than had been previously given to this area. The eight performance areas (goals) were as follows:

(i) Establishes and maintains a positive and open learning environment to bring about the motivation and social integration of students and staff;

(ii) Builds strong local, state and national support for education;

(iii) Develops and delivers an effective curriculum that expands the definitions of literacy, competency, and cultural integration to include advanced technologies, problem solving, critical thinking and cultural enrichment for all students;

(iv) Develops and implements effective models/modes of instructional delivery that make the best use of time, staff, advanced technologies, community resources, and financial means to maximize student outcomes;

(v) Creates programs of continuous improvement and evaluation of both staff and program effectiveness as keys to superior learning and development;

(vi) Undertakes responsibility for the management of all school finance issues within the school district;

(vii) Skillfully manages school system operations and facilities to enhance student learning;

(viii) Conducts and utilizes research as a basis for problem solving and program planning of all kinds.

The set of skills contained in the AASA *Skills for Successful School Leaders* (1985) was matched to the eight performance areas and a composite list of fifty-two skill statements was developed for use in the main data collection phase of Sclafani's study. Pilot trials showed a single instrument to be too unwieldy and the fifty-two skills were reorganized into four sets of thirteen in each. By this means four discrete and potentially less intimidating instruments were created to improve the chances of an acceptable return rate. For the purpose of analysis the collation of demographic questions also allowed for the ready allocation of respondents to groups according to district characteristics.

Each respondent was invited to address the eight performance goals/areas in relation to:

(i)    their contribution to effective on-the-job performance as a super-intendent;
(ii)   their degree of influence on the preparation individuals had received prior to their entry to the superintendency;
(iii)  their self-perceived areas of greatest and least strength.

Next followed the list of fifty-two skills. Superintendents were asked to indicate which eight they thought were the most and least important to being successful, according to the following criteria:

* Which performance goals/areas do superintendents indicate are most important to effective performance as superintendents?
* Which skills do superintendents indicate are the most important to effective performance as superintendents?
* Are there significant differences between the levels of importance ascribed to particular performance goal areas by superintendents identified as 'effective' and those in the random sample of superintendents?
* Are there significant differences between the levels of importance ascribed to particular skills by superintendents identified as effective and by a random sample of superintendents?
* Are there significant differences between the levels of importance ascribed to particular performance goal areas and skills by superintendents of districts with different demographics such as size, ethnicity, type of location or geographic area?
* Are there significant differences between the levels of importance ascribed to particular performance goals/areas and skills by superintendents with different educational backgrounds, such as highest degree earned, or different certifications or different numbers of years of experience in the superintendency?

Sclafani used a sample of 1800 superintendents randomly selected from a list of public school K-12 districts throughout the United States. Since there is approximately double that number of districts potentially available outside of metropolitan areas, selections continued to be made until 600 metropolitan districts and 1200 non-metropolitan districts had been drawn. The returns included 1011 superintendents in all who had satisfactorily completed the four instruments that collectively captured the skills identified by the AASA (1985).

The sub-sample of 'effective superintendents' was drawn using criteria provided annually by the National School Board Association (NSBA) to select the 100 best superintendents in the country. The nomination process used by the National School Boards Association (NSBA) is conducted by Chief State School Officers and executive directors of state professional organizations. The sampling procedure was used concurrent with NSBA selection to identify a sample of 140 effective superintendents for the purpose of the survey.

A cross-sectional design was used employing descriptive, inferential and non-parametric statistical analysis techniques. Analysis of variance was performed for each dependent and independent variable while Chi square was also used to examine relationships between selected variables.

## Discussion of Sclafani's Findings

To reiterate there were two main purposes of this study. The first was to query superintendents as to what performance areas and skills they considered to be most important to effectiveness in their role. The second purpose was to examine their priorities with respect to selected demographic characteristics of school district types, in addition to profiling their personal backgrounds.

An overall acceptable rate of return of survey instruments was achieved which included 35.7 per cent from the metropolitan sample and 64.5 per cent non-metropolitan. The rates proportionately reflected the ratio of metropolitan to non-metropolitan districts within the USA. The largest single group of districts was rural (53.7 per cent) followed by small city (18.5 per cent). In terms of enrollment size, the largest group was that containing districts of 1000 to 5000 students (44.4 per cent). Districts under 5000 comprised 82.2 per cent of the sample. Very few districts were multicultural and 75.3 per cent of those sampled were entirely Anglo in their make up. The personal backgrounds of the respondents showed that 40 per cent held doctoral degrees; tenure as superintendent averaged about ten years; and, as an occupational group, superintendents were very active professionally outside their districts as well as participating in numerous community activities within them.

## Level of Importance of Each of the Eight Performance Areas

The performance area which both groups of superintendents (i.e., 'national' and 'effective') indicated to be of highest importance was that of climate. Climate was conceived as the establishment and maintenance of a positive and open learning milieu engendering motivation and bringing about the social integration of students and staff. This was followed in importance by the performance area encompassing district finances. The development of an effective curriculum was ranked third, and in fourth place was the creation of programs of continuous improvement including program evaluation and the appraisal of staff effectiveness. Management of district operations was ordered fifth while in sixth place was the delivery of an effective means of instruction. Building up strong local, state and national support for education came seventh and, finally, conducting and utilizing research in problem-solving and program planning was ranked eighth.

The resultant prioritized sequence of the perceived importance of performance areas is not entirely surprising. Most of the relevant literature to date discusses in some detail the central role of the superintendent as that of social engineer or architect of the school district's profile. Lay boards do not routinely participate in district management and the teaching service is perhaps the most isolated of all major professions. Change of the status quo is considered unlikely by many in the professional community of interest. This leaves the onus on the superintendent and his/her administrative team to take actions which directly impact the organizational climate of the school, affecting in turn how it is perceived and responded to by the public. Sclafani's data confirms that, for superintendents at least, development of climate is the most important performance goal according to their own estimation.

The second important performance area, finance, was clearly contingent on the variables of district size and geographic location. Rural superintendents indicated this was *the* most important performance area/goal for them. On reflection this is largely to be expected since they do not possess business office staff to assist them in the routine work of paying bills and overseeing the general management of district finances.

Curriculum, evaluation and instructional performance areas were also recognized as important adjuncts to effectiveness by both groups of superintendents. Concerns in this area are more pervasive today since the drive for improving instructional leadership across the board became a national priority. There are comparatively few studies which guide and inform the role and actions a superintendent might take in order to be an instructional leader, develop curricula and provide instructional models.

At the opposite end of the scale the most lowly ranked performance areas were management of district operations, building support for education and utilizing research in problem-solving and management. Again, it comes as no real surprise that the research utilization performance area was placed last. Surveys over the years have always indicated that practicing superintendents, for the most part, leave research perspectives on the front step of the college or university program they last attended. While this finding may be viewed as undesirable, it does seem to make a statement about the way superintendents perceive themselves in relation to the nature of their work and the utility of research findings in guiding and informing it. Further reflection on this suggests they regard themselves as 'hands on' managers more than visionary executives constantly seeking for alternative ways in which to make their school organizations more effective. The ingrained adage 'let's not reinvent the wheel' often appears to create a climate militating against creativity and risk taking.

Sclafani also determined the importance practitioners assigned to each of the fifty-two skills. Respondents were asked to identify what they considered to be the most important skill, followed by the two next important skills. Data from this set of items showed the two most important skills to be those of (i) using a broad array of leadership skills; and (ii) using sound principles of personnel management. Other skills, ranked in order of importance were (iii) financial planning; (iv) effective school and community public relations; and (v) effective evaluation of teacher performance. The second tier consisted of (vi) sound program budgeting; (vii) use of motivation techniques; (viii) conflict mediation and coping with controversy; (ix) valid performance measures for instructional outcomes; (x) principles of sound curriculum design and instructional delivery systems; and (xi) using an array of human relations skills.

Matching the skills against performance areas/goals was not difficult, and it can be seen quite readily from Sclafani's data that superintendents do regard their jobs as architects of climate and themselves as day-to-day managers of business and instruction. In many respects, tensions exist in the adequate fulfilment of these role expectations, explaining some of the difficulties some superintendents experience in meeting the expectations of very different client groups in school-system and district communities. A large number of rural superintendents are represented in the priority ranking of managerial skills, unlike superintendents in larger school districts who usually have more diverse populations with which to deal and with the facility to devolve their authority to subordinates if they become overloaded. Many rural superintendents work in social and cultural environments that are homogeneous with respect to parental expectations and cultural milieu. But in general, all of the groups or 'types' of superintendents do regard their role as one of being a 'people person'. They have been stereotypically characterized in some ethnographic studies as typically moving from one type of human communication or encounter to another all day long.

Technical skills and knowledge are also regarded as being important to functionality. It is likely that, if not well grounded in this area, the superintendent could experience great difficulty in moving beyond the technical dimension to deal with those human interaction tasks deemed necessary in order to create a productive organizational climate. Schools have to remain open, buses must operate, food must be served; employees must be paid and buildings have to be cleaned as basic minima for the instructional program to be routinely effected. The evidence shows that, while superintendents value climate building more than technical skills, their views in the first instance are firmly embedded in the real world of keeping the district functioning smoothly.

## The Profile of 'Effective' Superintendents

As previously mentioned, a group of 'effective' superintendents was identified for detailed study. The profile of the group selected varied from the national sample as far as demographic composition was concerned. Urban superintendents, for example, represented 23 per cent of the total sample; another 20 per cent were from suburban districts and rural superintendents comprised only 24 per cent; whereas, in the national sample, they comprised 52 per cent of the total. Of the 'effective' superintendents 55 per cent had earned a doctoral degree.

In the rankings of performance areas, 'effective' superintendents numbered five out of eight performance areas quite differently compared to the national sample. They also indicated that climate development and motivation of staff were of the highest importance to them. This group ranked the development of instructional delivery as significantly more important to their effectiveness than did those included in the national sample. School financial management was of lesser importance than instruction to this group. Similarly, the effective superintendents group considered management of school system operations and facilities to be of lower importance than did the other group. Since the sub-sample of 'effective' superintendents basically appeared to work in large districts with comprehensive central office staffs, this might explain why day-to-day operations were perceived to be of minor importance to the overall level of effectiveness of this group of superintendents. It should not be construed, however, that the listed tasks are not important simply because they do not appear to be directly relevant to current effectiveness in the role. In many cases the superintendents performed them at some point in their careers and now supervise others who carry them out on a daily basis on their behalf.

## Importance of the Fifty-two Skills

Skills considered to be quite important by the 'effective' superintendents were 'communicating articulately' and 'projecting previously agreed platforms persuasively at forums on behalf of the district'. Also cited as important was 'using the mass media effectively in shaping and forming public opinion'. It is noteworthy that finance and budgeting skills were ranked higher by superintendents in the national sample than by the 'effective' superintendents. The same was true for instructional delivery systems and models. Throughout Sclafani's analyses, the influence of demographic features on the ranking of both performance areas and skills is persuasive. The smaller the district, the more managerial the emphasis. With increase in district size, there is concomitant executive emphasis. In addition, some regularities can be seen in the typical suburban district that typically emphasizes curriculum and instructional skills and performance goals.

School board and community expectations, as well as the socioeconomic status of communities, seem to play a significant role in attracting the type of executive who is eventually hired by a particular district. An example from the data illustrates this point. For urban areas, the performance goal of garnering support for education was found to be much more important to school boards than was the case for those in more affluent suburban districts.

When interpreting these findings, the most obvious criticism to be levied at Sclafani's study is that the interval scale she uses does not strictly relate to the ordering of the eight performance areas. Because the constructs are not equivalent it could be argued that a 'pure' ranking cannot be strictly achieved, but, in the practicalities of the real world, where resources and time are limited, decisions have to be made regarding what is of the highest priority and what will be attended to first. Superintendents, being very practical people, would be the first to recognize this reality.

Sclafani found the most important performance areas/goals to be environment and curriculum, both of which are of major public concern in the current climate of reform. Managerial areas such as finance and operations were found to be of greater importance to the 'effective' group in both small and rural districts. Acquisition of a broad array of leadership skills and utilizing good personnel skills also had a strong measure of overlap with the two highest rated performance areas, while, once again, sound financial planning and cash flow management emerge as priority areas in the minds of superintendents located in the smaller sized districts.

That the 'effective' group came mainly from larger districts when compared with their 'national' counterparts is evident in the data. The former agreed with the majority of their peers concerning the importance of climate and curriculum, but disagreed as to the relative importance of finance and other managerially oriented performance areas. What the data showed consistently, and can be readily appreciated from the foregoing account, was that to regard the superintendency as a unitary monolithic entity is at best untenable and at worst simply incorrect. Similarly, the effectiveness of the superintendent and the nature of the role(s) cannot be viewed independently or otherwise existing separately from the context of the school district itself. As an area for further research, a question that needs to be addressed is, do superintendents in their ongoing professional development pass through a range of administrative positions of different types in which they acquire the skills and competencies necessary for *future* effectiveness in alternative settings? Another important research question in our opinion is, what are the different criteria which need to be met for superintendent effectiveness across rural districts, suburban districts, small city districts and/or urban districts?

What *does* the research tell us therefore about the superintendency that is of concern to those who develop pre- and in-service preparation and training programs. Extrapolating from Sclafani's findings, it is possible to differentiate educational administration programs according to the type of career path chosen by a prospective superintendent. It also appears that qualifications, assessment, and prior experiences need to be properly weighed when making the appointments of prospective superintendents to particular districts. It would be useful if pre-service preparation programs would align course content and learning activities carefully to the world of practice — although this seems to us currently to be an exception rather than the norm.

## Partial Replication in Illinois

Another study seeking to verify the appropriateness of the AASA performance areas was conducted in Illinois in 1989. Drzonek, a doctoral student at Northern Illinois University, conducted his investigation after receiving prior permission from AASA, and subsequently, from Sclafani to use her prototype instrument. He then slightly modified it to make it more amenable for use by Illinois superintendents.

The design employed by Drzonek was to survey all 982 practicing public school superintendents in the state of Illinois. The Sclafani instrument was abbreviated according to recommendations made from feedback using a stratified random sample of superintendents in the pilot phase of the study. Drzonek decided, however, to have each superintendent respond to all of the fifty-two skills in a single instrument instead of using the four different versions of the questionnaire (each containing thirteen skills) as it was initially developed. This unwieldy document probably accounts for a low return rate of 32 per cent. Another likely factor contributing to the low response rate was the large number of previous doctoral dissertation surveys, together with surveys from other organizations and groups, targeting school districts in recent years. Illinois superintendents, under pressure of time and task complexity, have become less and less cooperative as a consequence of 'survey overkill'.

Once completed, however, the returned questionnaires did proportionally reflect the different types of school districts to be found in the state but the findings are necessarily tentative. Illinois contains nearly 1000 school districts of varying size and diverse geographical locations. Small rural districts predominate and most of these are located outside the Chicago metropolitan area, even though some are situated quite close to the city limits. It is generally not well known, but there are more rural small school districts to be found in Illinois than in any other state in the USA, with the possible exception of Texas.

The responses of the 300 superintendents who participated in Drzonek's survey reflected the overall trends found in the research referred to earlier in the chapter using a national sample. The most important prioritized performance goals reported were finance, then climate. Other local factors peculiar to Illinois, besides size of districts, probably contributed to the high scores given to finance and in managing budgets competently. There is no system of agencies in Illinois, such as intermediate school districts, to assist small districts with their budget and finance tasks. A district of less than 200 or 300 students generally has an individual with the combined role of superintendent/principal at its head, and typically an untrained bookkeeper who might also double as a school secretary.

Recently, the state education office has directed more of its time, attention and resources to regulatory rather than service functions. This places additional burdens on the superintendents of small districts who, while reorienting themselves to this development, have had to cope with the implementation of state-wide reforms. Given the pervasiveness of turbulence in education today, there is no reason to believe that the situation of small school district superintendents in Illinois is any different from that occurring in other states.

Illinois superintendents administering larger districts responded very similarly to those in the national sample, and markedly so in terms of the priorities they gave to climate and curriculum. They differed to the extent that they placed a much higher priority on the evaluation performance goal than either of the national or 'effective' samples reported in Sclafani's study. Similar to the national sample, 'research', and 'gaining support for education' were ranked lowest and 'the delivery of instruction' ranked sixth which was lower than the ranking accorded to this construct by the national sample of superintendents.

In summary, and within the limitations imposed by a low return rate, the Illinois superintendents responded in a broadly similar fashion to those in the national sample. Rural superintendents acknowledged that finance and budget skills were the most important priorities, the reality in their day-to-day work. Superintendents in larger districts, especially those in the metropolitan area surrounding Chicago, regarded the climate performance area as *the* most important with curriculum and finance in second and third place respectively.

There were, however, some important differences between the Illinois superintendents and those in the national sample. Illinois superintendents prioritized the evaluation performance goal and managing school district operations more highly than did either the national or 'effective' superintendent samples in Sclafani's study. This necessarily relegated curriculum and instructional delivery performance goals lower in the rankings. To account for these differences, they are likely to be attributable to the current emphasis, in Illinois, on the 'school report card'. To elevate the importance of curriculum and instruction, recent legislation has been introduced mandating that all principals spend a substantial part of their working day on tasks directly associated with instructional leadership.

The prioritization of skills was referenced, not only to the national sample, but also to the performance goal priorities. Here the two most highly regarded sets of skills were associated with leadership and good personnel practices. Evaluation of program development appeared third while school community relations was fourth. The latter did not do so well in this case as it did in the national sample.

Nevertheless, outcomes of the Illinois study are largely congruent with the findings of the national study. They also draw attention to other in-state factors that are of importance in the determination of the most necessary or essential skills for the superintendent in a given state.

### Further Confirmation of Earlier Findings in Texas

In 1987, a further doctoral study, similar in design and nature to those of both Sclafani and Drzonek, was undertaken at the University of Texas at Austin by

Collier. Mirroring the Illinois study, the sample Collier drew included all superintendents in the state of Texas. Collier used a similar process to that of Drzonek for her instrument development but reverted to using four different versions of the instrument. It was mentioned earlier that Texas, like Illinois, has a large number of small districts, mostly in rural localities, so that one outcome of Collier's study, like that of Drzonek's, was influenced by the idiosyncratic geography of the State.

In the performance goals, finance was ranked first as might have been expected. Climate was listed a close second, while curriculum and management performance goals were ranked third and fourth respectively. Texas superintendents also considered the two skill areas subsuming a broad array of leadership skills and personnel administration to be the highest contributors to effectiveness in their role.

Superintendents in the larger districts perceived finance and management performance areas as being less important when compared to those in small districts. This once again shows a similar pattern to that evidenced by the national and Illinois samples. It is quite clear, comparing the data from all three studies reported above, that there is a measure of agreement between superintendents who administer widely different types of school districts in geographically discrete parts of the nation regarding what is important to their job success. This convergence of views attests to what must be learned, known, and routinely demonstrated in the field to be regarded as an effective superintendent. The moot question at this point is whether a school district can be considered as 'effective' in the absence of a superintendent to lead it? Also, what obverse effect does the essential quality and ethos of the district have on the self-perceived effectiveness of its superintendent?

From the research findings summarized thus far, the importance of the superintendent as the primary developer of a climate that promotes learning and social development has been verified from multiple sources. It is also clear that leadership skills are considered to be very important, and that most of the individuals surveyed thought leadership skills were synonymous with 'people' skills. These findings correlate well with the earlier ones regarding AASA's climate performance area. The current national preoccupation with reform and accountability requiring value for money lends credence to the perceived importance of the performance areas of finance and curriculum. This too was of paramount importance in the studies reviewed in this chapter.

### The Career Paths of Superintendents

In order to further illuminate our understanding of the contemporary role requirements and the attendant professional development of superintendents, the relationship between career path aspirations and professional development is addressed. An investigation into career paths pre-, during, and post-individuals' appointments to the superintendency shows that a sequence of positions and experiences tends to occur in a logical and ordered progression of positions of increasing responsibility and complexity. A small proportion of superintendents, especially women, have been observed to deviate from this somewhat 'natural' progression. But, considering that a professional, over a period of some ten to fifteen years, acquires sets of behaviors through the process of tenure, some variation in career from the norm is not unexpected. Some behaviors, skills and competencies are acquired and developed through formal training at the pre- and in-service level, but much of what superintendents (and principals) learn is internalized through on-the-job training and practical experience. It then becomes part of their tacit knowledge and is incorporated over time into a repertoire of craft-related competencies.

The fourth study summarized in these pages builds on the Sclafani study and its replicated variants as previously described. In this study, Burnham, at the University of Texas at Austin, investigated superintendents' career paths in light of the formal training they had undertaken to prepare themselves for senior roles and responsibilities at a later point in their career. For the purpose of her study, career path was defined as the actual educational positions held by a person for a set length of time over the course of an individual's career. Specifically, Burnham (1989) enquired of subjects, both in the previously identified national and 'effective' superintendent samples, to ascertain the composition of their formal graduate preparation. She also investigated non-formal professional experiences they might have acquired extending beyond the field of education, and the progress of their careers upon entering the world of professional education. Non-formal types of preparation include those activities that do not attract credit and/or occur outside of normal university classrooms.

The investigator was particularly interested to establish whether a specific pattern of respondents' graduate preparation emerged, regardless of whether they featured in 'effective' or national samples. She also wanted to discover whether the 'effective' sample respondents had participated in more internships than had those in the national sample. There was a concern about the extent to which people from the two groups participated differentially in these activities. A further issue was whether the two groups were professionally active in organizations that could be conceived as existing primarily for the benefit of their peer groups. These might include, for example, the American Association of School Administrators and its state affiliates.

Three aspects that characterize a career were analyzed, namely, the paths followed, the specific educational positions held in sequence by incumbents and their length of service as both teachers and educational administrators. The findings confirmed that effective superintendents participated more actively in both formal and informal preparation programs than did their counterparts in the national sample. Second, more of the effective superintendents (68 per cent) held doctorates than did those in the national sample (37 per cent). Third, the 'effective super-intendent' group was underrepresented in small rural school districts, which are in the majority in the USA. Burnham also found that, in general, superintendents' educational profiles align with the certification requirements of most states.

In a majority of states, superintendents are currently required to have the equivalent of an educational specialist degree (thirty semester hours beyond the masters degree). The masters degree itself is required for a principal's credential in all states. With the median age of superintendents approaching fifty years, however, one could anticipate some 'grandfathering' of certification requirements in some instances. Burnham's study confirms earlier findings that superintendents who head up larger metropolitan districts are more likely to possess a doctorate than their rural or small city peers, but whether this makes them a better operator is open to question.

*Thomas E. Glass*

Surprisingly, only 18 per cent of the effective superintendents' sample had participated in a formal internship compared with 26 per cent of the national sample. This finding is now somewhat incidental in its policy implications because most states require either credit hours in an internship, a practicum or completion of a National Council for Accreditation of Teacher Education (NCATE) approved program, in which the latter also includes provision for an internship. Just how well structured and purposeful internships might be is uncertain at this stage. The National Policy Board of Education Administration (NPBEA) considered that many internships were composed of rather cursory and superficial experiences conducted on a spare time basis rather than fulltime during formal release away from the district. According to this professional body, the internships in most programs are not embedded in model or exemplary schools, or otherwise in districts where interns can receive professional experiences of validated high quality. Superintendents, as an occupational group, according to these data, were also socially interactive in the public arena which is to be expected when the essence of their role requirements is fully appreciated.

The nature and type of school districts studied had particular implication for these data. Metropolitan superintendents of larger districts who supervise a central administrative team have more time, opportunity and most likely certain board expectations to represent their district at many civic meetings as well as membership of community-based organizations in order to pursue their district's interests. In rural districts similar expectations and activities frequently atrophy because of reduced access to and availability of civic organizations, less travel money available for state and national meetings and fewer central office staff to perform the necessary routine duties in the district. This necessarily constrains the superintendent's time and availability for extra-mural work.

Findings confirm that superintendents are very active in supporting their communities and professional organizations, and that their position is by no means insular. This finding contrasts with the stereotypical portrayal of the superintendent filling a rather 'lonely' position, which is only true to a limited extent. Opportunities for interaction with individuals and groups in the community as well as with other superintendents occur frequently. Nevertheless a certain ambivalence exists concerning the extent to which and to whom informality can be accorded and the inner self publicly revealed. A superintendent leads a professional life both in and out of the school district. While social interaction is a feature of this professional life, fostering close personal relationships with subordinates is not conventionally regarded by peers and significant others as constituting good practice.

Burnham analyzed the career paths of 185 superintendents from the national 'effective' superintendents sample. From these she subsequently constructed a typology of eight readily identifiable career paths. A Chi square analysis was conducted to ascertain whether significant differences might exist between the 'effective superintendents' and those in the national sample. An additional Chi square was performed to explore gender differences between the career paths of female and male superintendents. All but ten of the 185 superintendents' career paths fitted one of the eight groups. The latter were subsequently and further reduced to four.

The most conventional career path followed by the largest number of superintendents (28.6 per cent) was to commence work as a teacher, move to principal

32

(assistant principal) and thence to superintendent. Only 12 per cent of the 'effective' group, however, followed this pattern. One modification of this progression included taking up a position in central office before assuming the rank of superintendent. A limitation of the study was that the researcher did not acknowledge that, in many states in order to become a superintendent, the individual must have previously acquired several years of administrative experience beyond the building level, and this automatically requires a central office position. Again, with the mean age of superintendents calculated at fifty years, most are more than fifteen years removed from their building level experience and have been a state certified superintendent for a protracted period of time. It is likely that, in future, in almost all 'post-reform' states, superintendents will be required as a matter of course to have internships and central office experience, and almost certainly building level administrative experience too. In this regard it is noteworthy that some states are currently making distinctions between line and staff experience in determining the needed prerequisites for candidates aspiring to the superintendency.

The majority of superintendents had secondary teaching and administrative experience, which is consistent with data from states such as Illinois. Burnham's respondents indicated that only a third of their previous experience was as a teacher/coach. In an average school district (3500 students) with six competitive sports at the junior high and eight at the high school level, at some point in their career almost all teachers are expected to coach.

A significantly higher proportion of the 'effective superintendents' had previously served as central office administrators prior to becoming superintendents. It should be remembered however, that the majority of the 'effective' sample was drawn from metropolitan areas where there are larger, more complex districts, necessitating that the superintendent supervise a number of central office specialists in areas such as personnel, curriculum and finance. It is difficult for chief executives to supervise these administrators credibly if they themselves have not had prior experience in similar roles. Moving directly from the building level to the superintendency is evidently a common feature in small rural districts, especially where the superintendent is also the building principal. With respect to gender, women superintendents are more likely to have served as elementary principals and directors of instruction/curriculum than their male counterparts.

Across the sample as a whole, the mean number of years of classroom teaching was 8.5, while the total number of years of administrative experience before becoming a superintendent was 9.5. The mean figure for superintendency tenure for 1008 superintendents was just over thirteen years, together with eight years of teaching, nine-and-a-half years of building/central office administrative experience and thirteen years in the superintendency itself (assuming that the superintendent entered teaching aged 22). The mean age of nearly 50 years for group members was close to the population's age statistic.

Differences between the 'effective superintendents' and the national sample were not great. Individuals in the 'effective' group had spent two years less than the others at the building level, and had moved into the superintendency in less time than those in the national sample. Individuals in each group had, on average, held 1.7 superintendencies. Women superintendents had more years experience in the central office than males and, overall, had held a greater number of appointments than male superintendents.

To summarize, the history of career paths taken by superintendents indicates 75 per cent of their time is spent in building level administration. For a majority, career progression to the superintendency is via the central office. When a superintendent is 50 years old, he/she has spent approximately twenty-eight years in the profession including eight years as a teacher, eight as a building level administrator and twelve to thirteen years in central office or in the superintendency. Most superintendents have the equivalent of a specialist's degree, are active in their professional organizations, have taken part in a reasonable number of non-formal training activities, have been a superintendent in two districts and have a doctorate if they serve in a fairly large metropolitan school district.

## A Professorial View of the Superintendency

Professors of educational administration, historically, due to circumstances affecting state certification for principals and superintendents, have exerted quite an influence in shaping administrator roles and behaviors in terms of their context, content and process requirements. It is possible to say that the professoriate in many respects created the modern day superintendent, beyond the first quarter of this century. Cubberly, Serars, Strayer, Bobbit, and Judd, for example, were extremely successful in placing their graduate students in key superintendencies across America. They also participated in numerous surveys conducted in exemplary school districts which, among other things, identified what effective school leaders needed to know and be able to do to be regarded as successful. This marked the beginning of trait theory applied to school leadership, and also the culmination of the first scientific management foray into school-district management. Many of the common ideas and folklore surrounding the superintendency that persist today are directly traceable to those influential early professors of educational administration. Many, themselves, served at one time or another as a superintendent of a large school district.

In 1989, Sass, while located at Northern Illinois University, completed a study of the priorities that professors of educational administration accorded to the essential performance areas and competencies previously examined by Sclafani, Drzonek, and Collier. Sass's sample included all of the professors of educational administration appearing in Lilley's List of Educational Administration Programs in the United States (1987/88 list). A total of 169 institutions were identified and 1149 professors received a modified instrument derived from Sclafani's prototype. Changes were made to reflect the different sample type of members involved in this study. Professors were asked to prioritize the eight performance goals/areas and the fifty-two skills in much the same manner that Sclafani had required of her superintendents. The number of professors returning completed questionnaires amounted to 702. Some instruments had to be discarded because of retirement or individuals moving from one university to another.

Sass's data showed nearly a third of the professors had been a superintendent at some time during their career. Most, however, had been out of the public schools sector for between ten and fifteen years. The single largest age group for professors was between 60 and 65 followed by 55 to 60. Clearly, the respondents constituted a senior group; only 29 per cent of the group was younger than 50 years of age. Full professors made up 61 per cent of the sample.

The professors, like the samples of superintendents discussed earlier, perceived the climate performance goal to be the most important to superintendent success, with the performance goal of curriculum delivery and development another major factor. The performance goal of managing finances was ranked sixth. Seventh and eighth performance goal rankings were building strong local, state and national support for education and conducting/utilizing research for problem solving and program planning. When means were tested, there was no significant difference with respect to the performance goal rankings based on the demographic characteristics of superintendents.

With respect to skills, there was some discrepancy between the practicing superintendent groups and the professors. The professor group uniformly found the most important skills in rank order to be (i) human relations; (ii) organizational development; (iii) leadership skills; and (iv) interpersonal communication skills. The two least important, but most telling skills, were using descriptive and inferential statistics and computer skills in order to manage the attainment of educational goals.

Sass also requested that professors in each of the 169 previously identified educational administration programs forward a copy of their graduate catalog, describing the programs being offered in course outlines and to include documented entry requirements. Sixty institutions complied with the request, and, after tabulating the rankings based on the perceived importance of the performance areas and skills, the researcher attempted to relate references contained in course descriptions to those performance goal areas and skills prioritized as being essential by the superintendency. Thus, for example, was the highest ranked performance area of 'climate' actually represented in required coursework? Is it being ranked highly by practitioners? What about the most essential skill of 'human relations'?

While this type of enquiry was secondary to the main investigation, it had a most telling outcome. In general, the course descriptions did *not* match the rankings of the professors. For instance, coursework in building school climate and gaining competency in human relations skills was not to be found in the catalogs at all, and organizational development and interpersonal communication skills appeared occasionally in school/community relations classes. A caveat is in order, since it is very difficult to ascertain what really goes on in a course only by reading a catalog description. This has to be kept in mind when reviewing the evidence and drawing tentative conclusions. It does, however, align with conventional wisdom.

The importance of Sass's study for enhancing our understanding is found in the conceptual picture derived from the professors' rankings. These rankings provide a copybook view approximating the suburban, white, affluent (metropolitan) superintendency, 'captured' by other studies also reviewed in this chapter. Further, Sass's study reinforces previous findings that not one but several superintendencies exist, the needs of which are dissimilar in nature and the skills and competencies needed to be effective. Flexible training programs should ideally be organized to accommodate these differences. To continue to think of the superintendency as the singular monolithic entity portrayed in textbooks and entrenched in the mythology of the profession is quite erroneous, even dysfunctional, for meeting the needs of the new breed of superintendents, professors and policy makers now and the future.

*Thomas E. Glass*

## Conclusion

In reviewing a selected body of research in this chapter centered around the *who* and *what* of the superintendency, there are no claims made for detailed breadth of coverage from the corpus of research available. All the studies addressed, however, are pioneering in their nature and scope and help to bridge the gap between what was a considerably under-researched field until only a few years ago, to one stimulated by the close public scrutiny in which a vigorous and highly focussed research effort is now discernible. It was not long ago that all we knew about the superintendency was that there were approximately 15,000 superintendents, most of whom were male, who were collectively operating a budget of some $50m on behalf of school boards across the USA. The studies presented in this chapter help us to gain a partial picture of the superintendency and its modus operandi, albeit painted from a broad palette. The studies described can be regarded as 'first generation' and, as such, they have laid the groundwork for more detailed investigations on specific skills, competencies and future-oriented effectiveness.

To conclude, the 1992 AASA Ten Year Study also sampled 1734 superintendents to prioritize the eight performance goals utilized by Sclafani, Drzonek, Sass and Burnham. The profile that emerged from this study paralleled that reported by Sclafani in her mid-1980s study of a national sample. One can therefore, with some assurance, conclude that the priorities for effective practice described in this chapter are valid and reliable indicators of what superintendents should be able to do in the performance of their jobs in a variety of settings and contexts.

*Chapter 3*

# Point and Counterpoint: What is in the Context of What Might Be?

*Thomas E. Glass*

The American public school superintendency has moved through three distinct phases of growth and development during the past 100 years or so. It is on the brink of a fourth phase that has just begun. Traditionally, over changed and changing circumstances, the district superintendent has been held ultimately responsible for the success of the public schools. Even though teachers, principals and school board members greatly outnumber superintendents, the bottom line responsibility for influencing and managing the quality of education rests on superintendents' shoulders.

The size and complexity of school districts vary greatly along with the role and responsibility of the superintendent. The past decade has witnessed exhortations from the public for increases in school achievement, stemming from various national commissions and reports, each claiming that American students are not 'keeping up with the rest of the world'. Accompanying a set of higher public expectations have been numerous federal and state mandates, loss of control to state legislatures, restrictions by the courts and a lesser share of the public tax dollars directed toward education. Superintendents, whether located in very small rural districts, or those encompassing large urban slums, feel exposed to the pressure for social change. This is fueled by advancing technology and exacerbated by frequent and sometimes conflicting sets of demands from parents, communities, private sector groups, and government instrumentalities requiring mediation by the district's chief executive. In order to meet the desires of various publics, superintendents have been cast rather reluctantly into roles where they must be 'all things to all people', including being effective instructional leaders, efficient business executives and persuasive public relations experts capable of integrating their communities within the school districts. Many observers both in and outside of the profession regard the contemporary role(s) of the superintendent as being extremely difficult if not impossible to fulfill in all respects, given the need to reconcile a number of often conflicting demands such as increased student scores, pruned budgets and so on.

Just who *are* the school superintendents? What do they do? What are they trained to do? How well do they perform their assigned tasks? These are some aspects of the superintendency that are the focus of attention in this chapter. It is also pertinent to ask at this point whether substantial changes to the screening, selection and professional development of school system executives are also needed in order to meet the challenges of the twenty-first century and beyond. These issues are dealt with in more detail in Chapters 5 and 8.

It is a necessary precondition that, for an organization to lead effectively, it must have a pool of potential leaders upon which to draw. Beyond this requirement the organization must fit the most suitable leader into its system to manage its evolving climate, to meet present needs and give direction to vision-oriented futures. An effective executive, therefore, must be able to conceptualize the direction in which the organization is going and be able to lead and/or direct large groups of employees harmoniously toward the realization of shared goals. A similar logic applies to leading and guiding schools, parents, citizens and students in moving them toward the achievement of selected organizational and educational goals. How well can today's school superintendents perform this vital role? Does an adequate pool of qualified superintendents exist from which school districts can draw their leadership talent? These two vital questions need to be contemplated and addressed by American educational policy makers as they deliberate, in some cases remote from the harsh realities of current school reorganization.

It is not likely that America's schools can restructure, reorganize and revitalize the educational process in the absence of clear executive leadership given by the superintendency. For this reason alone the current and potential role of the superintendency and its future prospects is of more than passing concern to the education profession. Until recently a general lack of cumulative research findings about the nature of the superintendency, its demographics and composition, served to inhibit personnel planning. There is a pressing need for data such as these to guide and inform decision-making in a climate of educational reform. This limitation is compounded by the absence of established national professional standards based on an explicit knowledge base against which competencies might be monitored and developed. Some states have initiated multiple choice tests which must be passed by candidates in order to acquire supervision credentials, as well as providing evidence of relevant experience and other educational prerequisites. These are usually catered for by the completion of a National Council for the Accreditation of Teacher Education (NCATE) approved formal preparation program. Only in recent years, however, has there been concerted efforts to validate goals, competencies and skills associated with relevant job behaviors required for success as a superintendent — witness this book.

Preparation programs for superintendents have been thoroughly castigated in several recent reports seeking to engender reform. The report of the National Policy Board for Educational Administration (NPBEA, 1989) was especially noteworthy in this regard. This body noted that preparation programs for administrators were generally well known by the public more for their deficiencies than for their strengths. In brief, many contemporary reports addressing the training and preparation of superintendents and other school administrators tend to assert that programs are frequently haphazard and unregulated. For the most part they are regarded as being ineffectual in producing the type of executive our schools and school systems require and have a right to expect. The job performance of superintendents is also appraised in reform documents but few, if any, reports advance remedies for the seeming ineffective leadership that is claimed to exist.

In order to gain further insights into the role of the superintendent, a useful study might be to systematically profile men and women who currently hold the senior executive position using interpretive frames of reference. By this means an alternative process perspective can be obtained based on an examination of the role itself and its demands on professional knowledge, skills and behaviors. A certain ambivalence exists concerning this point because the role itself is perceived to operate differentially at the school district level *vis-à-vis* the community. Tensions that exist around the role stereotype also need to be explained and accounted for, and ambiguities resolved if an agenda for future role development is to be pursued validly and with confidence. In an ideal sense, with demographics, role description and preparation requirements comprehensively researched and reported, a viable futures-oriented model of school executive leadership, in our view, is likely to have the best chance of being put to good effect.

There are nearly 16,000 school districts within the United States. The size of each varies, ranging from a single building with 100 students to districts the size of Los Angeles containing half a million students. To complicate the picture further, school districts are situated across a range of diverse geographical locations. Districts in Arizona may have sixty mile bus routes one way from school to home, for example, while others may have 100,000 students to be transported within a four mile radius.

Similarly, the nature of school finances that considerably influence the superintendent's role can also vary widely. Districts such as East St. Louis, Illinois, which currently has only $6000 assessed evaluation per student, exists in the same state where other districts have $400,000 assessed evaluation per student. In summary, school district wealth, demographics, and environment vary widely in the United States and have to be taken into account by a combination of local, state and federal decision makers, sometimes acting singly and sometimes in concert in order to formulate policy. The uncoordinated result is that policies sometimes appear to be framed and enacted with a blatant disregard for the unique and diverse nature of the populations of school districts that collectively comprise the American public education system. A profile of the cadre of superintendents who lead the nation's schools and school districts is presented in the following section of this chapter.

### A Demographic Profile of the Superintendency

*Gender*

Contemporary data on superintendents indicate that at least 96 per cent are male. The number of women superintendents has increased in recent years, but not significantly when compared with the total pool of superintendents (approximately 15,000). There is little variation across the number of women superintendents appearing in different age categories. Some criticisms have been levied by lay people that the superintendency is an 'old boys' club' composed almost exclusively of males. The public school superintendency is easily the most male dominated of any of the 'executive professions' and is recorded as such by the U.S. Census Bureau (Glass, 1992).

## Race

By far, the majority of superintendents are white, Anglo-Saxon males. Blacks are appearing in greater numbers but they still comprise less than 1 per cent of the national pool of superintendents. The same is true of Hispanics. By the year 2010, approximately 35 to 40 per cent of the school population will be composed of ethnic minorities, largely clustered in urban areas, where a black or Hispanic superintendent might be in charge of a district containing 200,000 of these students. Black and Hispanic superintendents do not constitute a large proportion of the total pool, but their influence on American schooling is nowadays more evident as they increasingly become the CEOs of large urban school districts. Approximately two-thirds of the latter already feature superintendents with ethnic minority origins. Nationwide, however, especially in states where there are a large number of minority students residing in school districts outside of urban areas, the need for a substantial and immediate increase in superintendents with minority backgrounds is acute.

## Age Composition

A number of studies of superintendents indicate the 'typical' one to be about 50 years of age. From this it can be inferred they each have about 25 to 28 years of experience in public education (*ibid.*). Examining this statistic further, not many have held employment in areas other than education since they first entered the public schools as kindergarten or first grade pupils. It is noteworthy that few professions exist making it possible for individuals to spend most of their student and professional lives in the same institution, and/or line of business.

Some studies, conducted in Illinois and Michigan (Glass, 1990; Angus, 1987) report that about 80 to 90 per cent of superintendents declare they will avail themselves of the opportunity for early retirement provisions that exist in a majority of states. If this should eventuate, approximately 50 per cent of the nation's superintendents may change employment or leave the education service within the next five years or so although the realization of this projection in practice is rather improbable. Realistically, it is more likely that about a third of the superintendent corps will retire or move on to other types of employment in the non-school sector in the near future.

Most state early retirement plans for teachers make this option fairly attractive to those individuals who have contributed to their programs for over thirty-five years. A superintendent who entered the system aged 22 could retire on almost maximum benefit at the age of 57. Experience suggests that chief school executive officers at 57 years of age do find other job opportunities in most parts of the country. Increasing numbers of individuals in this age bracket are retiring from the superintendency and moving on to other ventures such as small business management enterprises or managing civic programs and teaching in higher education.

One age variable only infrequently discussed in the literature is the effect of tenure. A study on the career patterns of superintendents (Burnham, 1989) reviewed in Chapter 2 found a national sample to have been out of classroom teaching for more than twenty years. The average number of years spent as a classroom teacher was about five before moving into the principalship or some other quasi-administrative role (Glass, 1992).

### Marital Status

All the studies examined as background to this chapter found the American public school superintendent to be a model professional especially in representing public norms and expectations such as belonging to a nuclear family, being a stalwart community member and so on. The studies showed that at least 95 per cent of superintendents are married (Cunningham and Hentges, 1982; Glass, 1992). It is probable that school boards select superintendents, at least partially, on the family image they are likely to project to the community. In many cities and towns the school superintendent must fulfill the societal expectations of being a role model par excellence for others to emulate, as well as a major player in upholding public morals and community values. It may be because of these public expectations that very few superintendents are single or divorced. One study (Ortiz, 1982) reported that approximately 42 per cent of superintendents in the sample were married to other educators — usually teachers.

### Political Preference

Superintendents are often described as the school districts 'educational politicians'. This label is usually attributed to them in a different sense than it is to state, local or national politicians, where in this case, party affiliation and politicking become important areas of involvement. Superintendents in most surveys have been shown to be moderates in the public sphere (Glass, 1992). This is true regardless of whether they are registered Democrats or Republicans. Teachers on the other hand have been found to be more liberal in outlook when compared with superintendents. This assertion is substantiated by the overtly political platform adopted by the American Federation of Teachers (AFT) and National Education Association (NEA) and it contrasts with the far more cautious postures of the American Association of School Administrators (AASA) and the National School Boards Association (NSBA). For the most part, superintendents are restricted from being active in partisan politics either by district policy or custom, and few play a visible role in either the Democratic or Republican party.

Superintendents do, in their sometimes ambiguous role, 'play politics' with a small 'p' in many states, but do so conventionally from the understanding that they are upholding the interests of their school districts. Lobby days, meetings with legislators and groups supporting funds for education on a local or state-wide basis, are often part and parcel of the routine working day of a superintendent. They become very political when, for example, advocating the passage of levy elections and bond issues. Thus superintendents are obliged to be apolitical in some ways and expected to be politically active in others. The latter occurs when working to promote the interests of their school districts and occasionally when representing the broader community in educational matters. Paradoxically the superintendency is popularly conceived as being above politics but the opposite is the reality for most executives (Blumberg, 1985). The degree of political involvement varies from state-to-state and district-to-district. In most states, policy-makers and politicians, including board members, understand the negative consequences of intruding partisan politics into public education and usually efforts are made in good faith to keep politics out of schools. This is not uniform, however, in some states occuring to a much lesser extent than others. On occasion, a periodic and conscious effort is made by elected officials to undermine this ideal in order to make the schools overtly political. As a case in point, Illinois has more governmental instrumentalities than any other state, as well as more elected officials and attendant political patronage. If it is allowed to continue beyond a certain point, it creates a climate and context susceptible to manipulation for political ends.

### Family of Origin Characteristics

As role models superintendents provide examples of upward social mobility made possible through their educational attainments. Data from the AASA Ten Year Studies, conducted over sixty years, show that superintendents far outstrip their parents in education and in generating family income. Very few, i.e., less than 15 per cent, parents of superintendents acquired a college education (Cunningham and Hentges, 1982; Glass, 1992). This is a surprisingly low figure given that a substantial number were identified as having been active in parent-teacher organizations. They place a high intrinsic value on education. It might reasonably be expected that many superintendents would themselves be the children of teachers, but this in fact is not the case.

Evidence suggests that a sizable majority of superintendents come from blue collar backgrounds and have acquired an education as a means of achieving upward social mobility (Glass, 1992). Considering their average age is 50, most superintendents' parents are from the 'depression' era and comparatively few higher education opportunities existed for this cohort during the 1930s. Today, however, the parenting group is probably an affluent blue collar class (Glass, 1992).

### Community Background

Superintendents are small town people. Few were born and raised in large urban areas. It is likely that their values and lifestyles are embedded in 'mainstream America' and they would bring these to their executive positions in the city or the suburbs. It is commonplace knowledge that the number of rural districts in the United States far exceeds those found in the cities. This is of great importance when considering the professional profiles needed by future generations of superintendents who will probably function in a rapidly developing service economy mainly situated in large suburban areas. Trends suggest that large urban, minority-populated school districts will continue to grow well into the twenty-first century, headed by a relatively small number of superintendents drawn from minority backgrounds. The number of rural and small town school districts are likely to decline further in most states due to their consolidation and rationalization of elementary and secondary programs in order to have access to higher levels of technology in the curriculum. The superintendency will need to be responsive to this development resulting from the changing composition and structure of our school systems already underway. For future generations of superintendents, it is likely that more men and women taking on the role will come from middle class backgrounds, with more of the parenting group college educated and residing in metropolitan areas.

*Salaries and Remuneration*

The general career pattern of nearly every superintendent today can be summarized as a progression through a series of appointments of increasing responsibility, starting from classroom teacher, and moving to building administrator, central office administrator and eventually superintendent. This is achieved usually some ten years after first becoming an administrator. As the career progression of the prospective superintendent advances, his/her salary also increases commensurate with increasing responsibility and experience (as does the number of work days per year). When informal meetings of superintendents occur, experience shows that a great deal of time is often spent discussing personal contracts mainly in terms of salary and fringe benefits. In states where superintendents have been able to negotiate fatter contracts with their boards, they acquire more prestige with peers. This is especially so if their district is not a wealthy one or if it is quite large as measured by the number of students contained within it.

In 1987, the National Center for Educational Information (NCEI) found that a majority of superintendents (51 per cent) responding to one of their surveys, enjoyed salaries exceeding $50,000 per contract year. Usually the fringe benefit package for superintendents includes a district contribution to social security, retirement, insurance, annuity and perhaps even a leased car. A few miles away from Chicago, in very small and affluent districts with no more than 1000 students, superintendents are earning in the neighborhood of $100,000–130,000.

The NCEI Report also indicated that 78 per cent of superintendents' households consisted of two-income families. Extrapolating from this statistic, an average superintendent earning $50,000, and a spouse earning $25,000 would have an annual income sufficient to locate them in the upper middle class on a combined income statistic. In comparison with teacher salaries, those of superintendents are closer to the packages of other major comparable professional groups. The salaries of superintendents do not derive from a state regulated salary schedule. Rather, they are determined through individual negotiation with a school board and are usually framed for a two or three-year fixed term.

There is little doubt that many educational administrators have become administrators not because they particularly value holding the position of principal, assistant superintendent, or superintendent, but simply because they wanted a better salary in order to support their families and to enjoy a high standard of living. Whether salary is regarded as the major motivation for career advancement or not, it has to be included as a dominant factor, along with professional advancement, desire for authority, desire for job satisfaction, upward social mobility and influence/social standing in the community being sought by the majority of aspirants. Unfortunately the ranks of the teaching profession from whence most superintendents originate does not contain specific provisions for career advancement and commensurate financial rewards. The payoff for good teaching is to be retained in the classroom *ad infinitum,* or else given a job with higher salary and more status as an administrator. The result tends to be that good teachers are invariably rewarded by being removed from teaching at an early age even though they may gain most of their professional satisfaction from their classroom interactions with students and have little desire to administrate.

While the superintendency represents the top level of the hierarchy of school appointments, it is somewhat unfortunate that aspiring to the superintendency has acquired the public reputation of being a 'dead end'. One reason advanced to explain it is that few school boards are likely to hire a former superintendent as a principal, teacher or central office administrator should he/she subsequently wish to return to the classroom or to building level administration.

To recap, the profile presented of the American superintendent today is one of a stereotypically middle-class white male, originating from a blue-collar working class family background. 'He' typically spends about eight to ten years as a teacher, and an additional eight to ten years as an administrator before becoming a superintendent of schools. He/she is also tenured in his/her position for, on average, about five to six years. In addition, he/she comes from a small town or rural area, has at least a masters degree and is also likely to hold the equivalent of an educational specialist degree qualifying him/her for certification as a superintendent. He/she is a moderate in his/her political views, is married, and, as an 'ideal type', represents the very finest example of the American middle-class to taxpayers and the community at large.

Whether the criticism leveled at the American public school superintendent, characterizing him or her as a member of a homogeneous group displaying these characteristics, is valid depends on the platform one adopts with respect to local control of schools. School board members elected by the local community are responsible for selecting superintendents for their districts in the first instance. The impression acquired by the general public is that boards appear to hire on the basis of personality in preference to demonstrated competencies, track record and previous experience. If this should prove to be the case, school boards will access the same pool of personality types from which to make their appointments. This can be inferred because former teachers undertake the same types of graduate programs in educational administration taught by former administrators with comparable administrative experiences and backgrounds and validated by the 'home' state that perpetuates the recycling syndrome of a closed-system. There is little chance for school board members to select superintendents who have *not* essentially had the same type of background and professional experiences compared with their predecessors. Some variability in personality traits and leadership styles may occur, but, for the most part, the 'men' who fill the superintendency appear to be more alike in personal characteristics and life histories than they are different (Feistritzer, 1988).

Whether this uniformity bodes well for the future of the American superintendency is a moot point and an important matter upon which to ponder by those who screen, select, prepare and develop school system executives. The further question emerging from this phenomenon is, if American schools are to be substantially restructured to meet the challenges of the twenty-first century, will these be met through the leadership of a cadre of predominantly white male superintendents sharing convergent experiences in their preparation and development? Or will school boards, working in unison with state departments of education, develop new certification standards that will encourage districts to hire more 'executive leader types' as distinct from those educational managers who are likely to have been marinated in institutional life over the last thirty or forty years? The nature and form of executive leadership for the public schools is an issue not yet widely addressed by reformers and policy makers, but evidently needing some priority attention (Chapter 1).

It is a theme of this book that many educators who currently populate the nation's schools can improve their leadership potential through access to superior initial training programs at the university. This can be complemented through self-improvement on an individualized professional development basis for those already working in the field (as is made clear in Chapters 7 and 9). The National Policy Board for Education Administration leads public and professional opinion in this area by proposing that increased efforts on the part of states and professional associations be given absolute priority in the initial press for the identification of talent and for improved professional preparation standards — the latter to take the form of a national board examination. If reform proposals such as these were to be taken up, whether they would have sufficient impact to markedly change the demographics and essential characteristics of the superintendency previously described is an interesting question. Part of the answer to it rests in the basic composition of the current teacher corps. If the internal characteristics of the teaching corps change for whatever reason, then it will reflect on the superintendency too, despite externally induced regulatory changes that might also occur in the wider social environment.

What are the basic operating requirements of the superintendency in terms of competencies, skills, and behaviors required on a day-to-day basis? What do superintendents actually do? What are they trained and professionally prepared to do? These are questions relevant to the examination of not only superintendents but virtually any profession involving people holding high public office and public trust. Research on the superintendency is still patchy with a tendency for studies to focus on the simple compilation of descriptive and largely unconnected model characteristics of the superintendent. Others, though limited in number and scope, detail interpretively what specific groups of superintendents actually do during the course of a working day: the decisions they make and with whom they routinely come into contact in the conduct of their duties. This research confirms the place of the superintendent as a significant other in the life of the school district and as the primary architect of the schools' mission, interpreting and implementing this mission in conjunction with teaching staff, parents and the community. Metaphorically speaking, the superintendent is the thread that holds together the patchwork quilt of the school district, the constituent schools and their communities.

A major feature of the literature on the superintendency is that it is substantially normative as reflected in the title of this chapter. A number of investigators report on what superintendents should be (traits); others describe qualitatively how superintendents spend their time. Few scholars examine in depth the role and associated skills and competencies necessary to realize in practice those routinely held effective behaviors that have been identified by research. To the serious reader, it is apparent that until recently the superintendency had largely been ignored by those scholars familiar with basic role theory and sociological methodologies that might be applied profitably in the study of roles and role behavior in this area.

One scholar noted for his development of the superintendent's role is Daniel Griffiths. He has posited several stages that describe and account for the historical development of the superintendency. Griffiths advances the notion that the superintendency has passed through three very distinct phases (1966a). The first was when the superintendent was expected to be a 'headteacher' also responsible for instruction. This period encompassed the beginning of the American common school and continued to the beginning of the scientific management period directly preceding World War 1. The second period witnessed the superintendent become an efficient business person who removed daily control of the schools from their lay boards. Decision-making at this point was subjected to pressures for increasing efficiency and containing costs. The metaphor of a factory production line aptly captures this approach to management. The third phase — still evident today — is one in which the superintendent is a 'professional administrator' who is expected to exemplify many of the contemporary views of professionalism. Today, superintendents are, among other things, prepared professionally to implement management theories. They can be compared broadly with 'executive leaders' having similar functions to those in the corporate worlds of business and industry — but with one major difference. The success of a CEO in the corporate sector is measured by the extent to which profits are maximized to the benefit of shareholders. In education, however, it is measured by the extent to which an executive can equitably allocate scarce resources within say 1 per cent of budget in the pursuit and realization of publicly articulated educational goals. The main distinction between the earlier 'how to do it' vocationalism and the present 'executive professionalism' is on the executive's ability to form a vision of a preferred state for the organization, and from this mediate the mission of the institution to society, directing the organization harmoniously to the achievement of its goals in the process.

Given this scenario, what type of person is best suited for the contemporary superintendency? What types of prior experiences and training are needed to fulfill the role and meet the expectations of a society that is itself undergoing rapid social change? Scholars are now beginning to sense that a redirected research focus should emphasize what superintendents *do*, rather than who they are. The 'trait' theory of leadership, long thought to be of relevance to the field of educational administration, has largely been discredited by researchers such as Stodgdill, Katz, and Nottingham (Hoy and Miskel, 1991). It has been replaced with a view of the superintendent's effectiveness located in the dynamic interaction of three sets of skills: technical, conceptual, and human. Technical skills are those utilizing a specific process, procedure, or technique; conceptual skills allow the superintendent to envisage the 'whole' of the organization and its relationship to its parts; and human skills, perhaps the most important of the three, are those used to shape the behaviors of members of the organization.

Most writers emphasize that well-developed human skills are the most crucial in contributing to the effectiveness of an organization, since they are adjuncts to communication crisis management and staff motivation. Griffiths conceptualized the superintendency as comprising three primary components: the job, the person and the social setting. He then applied Katz's conceptual framework to the 'job' of superintendent within an organizational and societal context (Griffiths, 1966b).

Griffiths, and others such as Goldhammer and Farquhar (Cunningham, 1982) redefined the role of the superintendent in more specific terms using descriptors such as 'developer', 'communicator', and 'motivator'.

This schema was never framed at the level of specific competencies and Griffiths considered them to be too narrow for the broad role requirements of the superintendency. This view has been shared by a number of researchers, most of whom have attempted to ground the profession in theories of educational administration largely derived from the social sciences. This was a predictable reaction to the earlier thinking of those who, in the previous century, employed 'administrative truisms' that are still to be found in many current textbooks on educational administration. Typically, such texts tend to focus on the minutiae of virtually every specific task needing to be accomplished in the school district, providing a 'cook book' approach to the practice of educational administration. The 'theory' approach was designed to assist superintendents in their understanding of the nature of the school system. But in spite of it being well intentioned, this approach has not been particularly helpful in assisting executives to develop strategies, to solve specific problems and to meet particular needs (Glass, 1987).

In our era we have now recognized that the role of the superintendent is temporal in time and space and that it is broadly-based, necessitating the application of a multiplicity of technical and conceptual skills for the maintenance of system and community well-being. Thus, an extensive skills repertoire is needed in order to deal effectively with the complex demands of problem finding and problem resolution in the most efficacious way.

With respect to which personality types and individual strengths might be appropriate to fulfilling the role effectively in different contexts, research to date does not have much to offer. There are few studies in this area dating from 'trait theory' to the present. Research, however, investigating the interaction of aptitude or best fit between person and position in a given context is still an important area of need for present and future research.

Superintendents, like other role incumbents in administrative positions in education, have rarely been subject to assessment either prior to, or after, hiring. As a rule, both superintendent and principal positions are basically 'self-selective' in that individuals independently decide whether they desire to enter the profession, and if they do, they then go about acquiring the necessary training and education to qualify for a state credential. The National Policy Board for Education Administration in its 1989 report, highlights the lack of controls in preparation and certification programs employed to screen out those who are unsuited to the profession. This undesirable situation has developed because of a lack of clearly articulated professional standards, low or infrequent use of developed assessment systems, lack of much needed reliable and valid instrumentation and the generally poor coordination of improvement efforts within the corpus of the superintendency and professoriate. Like teaching, the superintendency tends to be viewed by an informed public as only 'half a legitimate profession'. This conception may have inhibited the rigorous application of screening and selection methods on the scale required to have any noticeable impact on restructuring, reinvigorating and renewing the superintendency as it exists today. Any agenda for deep seated reform is likely to need a comprehensive data base for informed decision-making regarding 'what is', as well as a shared vision of future societal expectations and requirements concerning 'what should be'. These provide the cutting edge regarding what it is to be effective as a superintendent in a quite different social and educational environment to that of the present. Having addressed the 'what is' component, the remainder of this chapter is devoted to some issues related to the future needs of the superintendency in the light of present realities.

## *Through the Looking Glass*

In 1922 the National Education Association's Department of Superintendents published a series of three yearbooks. The first focused on the superintendency itself. The second and third explored the notion of a contemporary curriculum for schools. As the twenty-first century draws near, it appears that, to a certain extent, views regarding the nature and status of the superintendency have undergone something of a full circle. There is a concern abroad today about the efficacy of the day-to-day role of the superintendent in meeting public expectations, and the adequacy of preparation programs for those intending to withstand the rigors of the role. As mentioned previously in this chapter, superintendents are already leaving for greener pastures and retiring in large numbers. At the same time, authorities are pointing out that many aspects of the job are becoming dysfunctional thus providing a crisis mentality toward finding ways of retrieving the situation.

Looking backward to the 1920s the superintendency was embryonic in both its form and function compared with its developed complexity today. There were many struggles, then as now, between boards and superintendents regarding how the schools should, and would, be managed. Many prominent superintendents advocated and implemented the scientific management principles proposed by Franklin Bobbit as a way to create order and efficiency, and necessary to create the infrastructure for expanding school districts. They also advocated a 'business oriented' type of school board. This philosophy, it was thought, would lead to a better articulation with existing theories of scientific management for school administration. Late twentieth century forces are similarly pressuring superintendents to be more accountable in such areas as the expenditure of school funds, management efficiency, curriculum regulation and improving the outcomes of schooling. In the private sector, large corporations are beginning to form coalitions with school districts to help them become more efficient through the application of business management practices to school administration. This movement recurred in the 1960s, when management science underwent a period of development featuring management by objectives (MBO), and performance-based appraisal and program planning and budgeting (PPBS) in the drive for increased productivity and efficiency.

In the educational climate of today, superintendents and districts are being literally bombarded by lobbyists representing parents and other interest groups pressuring them to raise the achievement level of their children. Selected aspects of national reports are used in the print and electronic media to support claims that students cannot spell, compete with the Japanese in mathematics, locate the major European nations on a globe and identify nutritious foods to eat in accordance with a healthy lifestyle. In the mind of the public, schools are not the places they once were — or should be now. In short, public interest groups want school children to produce improved scores on some test or indicator of achievement in order to be satisfied that the system is working and they are getting value for each tax dollar spent on public education. Societal pressures for more accountability pervade every level of education and are manifested everyday in most every district through requiring the schools to become more cost efficient and academically productive. This phenomenon lies at the heart of the current wave of school reform and system restructuring.

Naive and possibly ill-considered as school reform proposals may be, they still create a management dilemma for the superintendent and school board charged with their review and implementation. How to react in order to placate those pressure groups yelling the loudest, and to 'beat the system' of norm-referenced achievement testing being used in the public arena as an index of success (or lack of it) on the part of students, schools, and school districts, has become part of the routine for those in positions of responsibility. Superintendents in the late twentieth century are thus caught in the double play of making schools more cost-efficient (spend less money) and at the same time making them more academically productive (get better test scores). The two aims are clearly at odds with each other. Attempts to achieve both aims concurrently have the potential to increase management conflicts even further, and to compound the pressures under which superintendents and principals must work daily. How are we to select and train school executives to reconcile the two sometimes opposing forces of cost-efficiency and academic productivity? This is a real dilemma. Real school improvement simply does not come cheaply.

### The Selection of Future School Executives

It was previously mentioned in this chapter that career progression in school administration at the principal and superintendent levels tends to be 'self-selective'. A common pattern is one where individuals, with aspirations to become principals or superintendents, seek graduate studies programs terminating in state certification; undertake the courses; serve an on-the-job internship; pass the requisite examinations and are thence certified and eligible to seek an appointment. As the National Policy Board for Education Administration points out, efforts on the part of states and institutions of higher education to be proactive in searching for and recruiting individuals who have the potential to become outstanding school executives are limited. Entry requirements for admission to preparation programs in higher education are minimal and do not as a rule include any type of formal assessment other than prior grades in college work, a score on the Graduate Record Examination (GRE) and letters of reference from individuals self-selected by the applicant. Seldom are assessment instruments used that might enable institutions formally to appraise an applicant's aptitudes, professional skills and knowledge, and basic personality profile before admittance to their programs. In the absence of formal assessment batteries, the selection of future superintendents and principals is based almost exclusively on verbal, quantitative and past grade point average criteria. In addition, few educational administration programs have well developed recruiting procedures explicitly designed to identify successful principals who might make successful school executives, in the professional opinion of significant others.

Why have educational administration programs been so tardy or so resistive to change in the use of formalized assessment procedures and structured recruiting initiatives? Certainly *some* programs in *some* institutions have engaged in both assessment and recruiting in a systematic way, but the majority have not. This may be attributed partly to the fact that many departments of leadership/educational administration are very small with fewer than five faculty members (i.e., the majority in the nation). In these situations the time and money required to conduct assessment activities is not easy and is further inhibited in those universities or colleges dominated by a traditional organization model oriented to past academic experience rather than toward the pursuit of professionally relevant qualifications of high quality. Many colleges of education in the United States appear to have an identity crisis as to whether they are professional schools in the broad sense or narrowly defined academic enclaves. Stereotypically, professors of education seeking advancement spend a great portion of their time as an academic in the narrow sense rather than attending to the professional role they have to fulfill as well. In actual terms this is reflected in conducting research and writing refereed journal articles — conventionally accepted in academia as the way to gain tenure, be promoted or otherwise become recognized for one's contribution to scholarship. In marked contrast some professors are more oriented toward professional training and practical fieldwork. They thus place themselves at a career disadvantage within the professoriate. Pressures in the professoriate to maintain the status quo, combined with a lack of resources, direct the attention of professors of educational administration toward their own academic performance rather than valuing a professional and field experience orientation, although the two points of view are not necessarily mutually exclusive. The AASA Ten Year Study of 1992 indicates that the credibility level of professors of education, as judged by practicing superintendents, has fallen substantially since the 1982 Ten Year study (Glass, 1992). This could be an omen that professors might care to note when planning programs and their own career directions.

Generalizing broadly, the colleges of education are neither provided with adequate resources nor predisposed to prepare educational administrators outside of existing organizational structures and protocols. Seldom are funds outlayed and resources applied to furthering extensive practicums and internships for students. Rarely are neophytes placed in supportive job-related environments where sophisticated management training can occur, and too many college programs tend to be characterized by traditional forms of academic instruction for management professionals.

The American Association of School Administrators, through the National School Executive Development Center and its six pilot centers (see Chapter 10), is working to identify the specific competencies and characteristics of successful school executives. As the knowledge base is verified, the associated competencies will be incorporated into a series of assessment instruments targeting potential school system executives. While this represents an advance in thinking, given the inherent difficulties in 'capturing' complex multidimensional behaviors, instruments currently being developed in areas such as instructional leadership and general management are likely to be limited in scope. It is unrealistic, therefore, given our present state of knowledge, to expect that the needed instrumentation will be all encompassing in work scope or anything other than modest in claims for predictive validity with respect to field based performance. Developmental work conducted to date is, nevertheless, realizing prototypes that have the potential to provide decision-makers with useful data to guide and inform the operation of educational administration programs. At a personal level, the work is providing administrators with a clear idea as to how they personally stand with respect to those skills and competencies needed for school leadership, as well as assessing their aptitudes across a range of activities related to success in the role. The advances made thus far are expected to be widely disseminated in order that they may make a significant impact on the quality of school administration programs in colleges of education (Harris *et al.*, 1992; Carter *et al.*, 1991).

There is also a pressing need to inform and counsel women and members of ethnic minorities aspiring to the superintendency to undertake specific programs of educational administration. Few educational administration programs at the post-principal level of training have any sizable representation of minorities and women. Within the national talent pool, lack of funding for graduate student support and paid internships in school districts are important factors tending to reduce the numbers of women and minorities potentially available for selection. Reduction in the talent pool also occurs through an apparent lack of motivation on the part of principals and other district office administrators to seek entry to the superintendency. This is because they regard it as a role that places too much stress on themselves and their families. Even when the pressures can be withstood, longevity of employment tenure is still not assured. The volatile nature of the environment in which the superintendency is embedded does not attract talented principals and district office administrators to seek the office.

For the administrator not overly concerned with some of the more negative aspects of the superintendent's environment, a problem that arises is where to go to acquire the best training and professional preparation for the role. Another is how to gain the first senior executive position after graduation. Most aspirants, acting rationally, question themselves as to what areas of training and initial preparation they think they are most in need of, and in what program(s) these can best be accommodated. Frequently their actions are conditioned by what is locally available and that will not require the individual to interrupt his/her employment. Another consideration is what is minimally required by the state for certification.

The National Policy Board reports that an overwhelming majority of educational administration graduate students are engaged in study as part-time students while also working full time in demanding teaching and administrative positions. Very few spend any full-time residence in institutions of higher education, and even fewer spend a year or so in an integrated practicum/internship setting in a local district. The inevitable inference to be drawn from this is that the majority of school executives in this country have been trained in part-time, 'hit or miss' types of graduate programs. If this is so, it is questionable whether they have actually been properly trained at all or simply schooled in ways which academics consider to be appropriate to the intellectual study of school administration. The bottom line appears to be the prohibitive cost to be borne both by the individual and the higher education institution. For personal reasons older students, understandably, do not seem willing to forego a year or two of regular salary, experiencing residential dislocation in order to spend time on campus, and then later undergo a formally supervised apprenticeship with a mentor, which the better programs require. The institutions of higher education on their part are loathe to acknowledge the necessity of making graduate fellowships or other forms of financial aid available to prospective applicants. Ultimately the focus of responsibility lies with the institutions to attract good candidates. On the face of it, higher education institutions are remarkably short-sighted and unwittingly abetted by state education agencies in not supporting promising mature-age candidates. As a rule, both colleges and agencies are also lacking in developing state certification codes requiring clinical and outcome-oriented models of preparation for potential senior executives.

We acknowledge that educational administration programs in some high quality institutions do as good a job as can reasonably be expected, within existing resource constraints, to provide an academic background and a technical preparation (curriculum, finance, and management) for their graduate students. Even in such cases it is likely that students will be minimally exposed to the areas contributing the most to executive leadership — namely, climate building, interpersonal relationships, conflict resolution and planning. Many institutions demonstrably fall short in providing much needed on-the-job training and experience from which (among other things) school boards might ascertain if a newly trained graduate should be afforded the opportunity to take on an executive leadership role in their district(s).

### The Prognosis for Educational Administration Programs

In spite of the increasing rhetoric surrounding public schooling in the mass media and in forums espousing reform, the combined political will driving a 'critical mass' needed to create radical and deep seated structural changes is not yet in evidence. Even if sufficient financial resources were to be made comprehensively available in the near future, it is unlikely there would be a corresponding increase in the cadre of professors and trainers prepared to offer a radically different approach to professional selection, training and development.

To reiterate, what is needed are programs that are more field centered than is currently the norm and that include some of the recent recommendations for reform spelled out by the National Policy Board and the University Council of Educational Administration (UCEA). These bodies have called for the application of more stringent admission criteria, an adequate core of professionally oriented faculty specialists and the provision of experiential and more meaningful, needs-based internships. Currently, faculty salaries for professors of educational administration in most institutions are so low that practitioners with good academic qualifications must take salary cuts, sometimes in the order of 50 per cent, in order to take up appointments. Faculties, in turn, are not materially resourced to provide specialized equipment, classroom facilities, travel budgets and practicum arrangements needed to meet a revised code and standards. Thus, to be an educational administration professor at the present time is, for many, a frustrating experience especially if she/he serves in institutions providing for only the bare essentials supporting the academic aspects of a preparation program.

In the case of retired superintendents who would like to become professors, institutions conventionally tend to avoid appointing them due to an anticipated lack of appropriate academic values toward educational administration theory and practice. Attracting experienced professionals is imperative for the recognition of individual merit as well as for enhancing the public status of a college of education operating within a traditional higher education milieu. Even a cursory scan of the vacancy notices for professorships in educational administration in *The Chronicle* repeatedly shows openings available for assistant professors at the lower end of the salary scale. This invariably precludes experienced school executive leaders from applying for a position, and this appointment policy makes the job attractive only to younger, less experienced individuals seeking a professorship in higher education. A deficit of vacancy notices for full professors and clinical professors highlights, by default, the agenda of colleges of education in according a low priority to the sort of staffing profile needed to operate an exemplary training program. It is an indictment of the situation that, at a recent national meeting, one prominent professor of educational administration admitted to a large gathering of his peers, that, after thirty years, he found it next to impossible to be both an academic professor and a professional educator within the single confines of his own institution.

In the light of this commentary, the outlook for colleges of education in attracting high quality professors of educational administration seems rather dismal unless there is a clear change in direction. The profession does need young, relatively inexperienced academics with advanced theoretical knowledge in areas such as policy processes, organizational theory, and research. It cannot be overemphasized, however, that the vital core of any good training program, and its final test of worthiness, is in developing testing and validating those skills and competencies needed for job effectiveness and their outcomes when applied to field settings. 'Knowing that' and 'knowing how' are sometimes very different. In the execution of leadership it is particularly germane to develop both aspects together. The leader might know everything that is worth knowing about human motivation, for example, but whether he or she can engender this in others, through the intelligent application of a number of managerial competencies initially learned at college then practiced and refined in the crucible of experience, can only be validated in the field. 'The proof of the pudding is in the eating'. The life chances of children and the careers of subordinate staff depend ultimately on the quality of the senior educational leader. Society has a vital interest in the quality of this leadership too. Quality is satisfied when public confidence in the achievement of successful school outcomes is high.

For maximum effect a more comprehensive role for the training and preparation of school executives needs to be undertaken by the school districts themselves in the form of internships, practicums and mentoring programs coupled with regular in-service (Milstein *et al.*, 1991). On reflection it is unrealistic to expect this to become a practical reality. Most districts have fewer than 3000 students and consequently insufficient administrators available to exercise this preference — assuming the notion was a tenable one in the first place. Similarly, 'lighthouse' school districts, in which the environment for excellent leadership training and mentoring exists, are not numerous enough nor networked sufficiently well to provide coordinated field-based programs. Another initiative, leadership academies, is now in place in many states but the availability of the academies' services are not well developed to the point where they can make a significant overall impact on the profession. Whether states will evolve these academies further in order to perform a majority of the tasks necessary for the preparation of school system executives is speculative. At present, most boards rely on the institutions of higher education to provide coursework at pre- and in-service levels but this may change. If the demand for significant reform of education programs continues to escalate, the certification role of institutions of higher education may be removed altogether in some states and vested in alternative modes of learning. A noteworthy example is an alternative model using professional associations and coalitions currently evolving in California and Oregon.

*What Should be Done?*

The history of public education over the course of the past half century indicates that if a word or slogan is used long enough by enough people then, by common usage, it becomes regarded as a 'truth'. In the 1960s the buzz word was 'quality' and in the 1970s it was 'accountability'. The 1980s referent was 'restructure' or alternatively 'reform', while in the 1990s it seems that the banner is 'choice'. Through the process of repetitive discussion of issues in journals and at different educational forums, sufficient 'energy' for the cause is generated to create the right environment for the implementation of initiatives representing the embodiment of the fad word or slogan. The groundswell for change in this sort of instance may occur without any comprehensive system planning and in the absence of adequate funding and resource provision. Demonstrably, reforms that have occurred in this fashion, without much proper planning and support, have frequently resulted in disenchantment and disillusionment on the part of their initiators. The vacuum created via disillusionment and failure then opens the way for the next new fad. When it recurs once again, to be taken up piecemeal from its surface features, nothing really seems to change very much and things go on below the surface much as they did before the fad came on the scene.

Tyack and Cuban (Tyack and Hansot, 1982; Cuban, 1988) have between them developed a thesis putting the ritual and the traditional lock of school systems into a historical model. If their explanation is valid and the model is perpetuated, it accounts for forces likely to mitigate against attempts to achieve deep-seated changes concerning the manner in which children learn, teachers teach and administrators lead more effectively. It appears unavoidable to escape the notion that American society does not seem to be ready to divert significant amounts of new money and more human resources to the schools in order to effect changes of the order required now and in the foreseeable future. 'Realists', conditioned by past experiences, comment that infusions of new money into schools for reform purposes will simply result in additional failure, claiming that current funding levels are adequate to the task (Sarason, 1991). The only thing really required, according to this view, is a radical change in teacher and administrator behavior. Critics of urban school systems, as in the case of Chicago, assert that the reason for the almost total collapse of the schools can be laid at the feet of the educational bureaucracy, rather than admit to other sources of failure located in dysfunctional families, squalid school environments, parents without jobs, inadequate health care, and oppressed teachers who are themselves victims of the system. No! The failure of schools, as in the ghettos of Chicago and New York, must ultimately rest upon the shoulders of the central office administration, not because there is inequitable financing directed from the state legislature or the absence of meaningful support from the private sector (Glass, 1990). Unfortunately, the situation in Chicago, translated on a national scale, seemingly epitomizes public attitudes toward education today. The impression given nationally is that no one is to blame for the failure of the schools and their clients, especially those children seriously at risk, other than the educators and bureaucrats. This type of societal indictment is short-sighted, blatantly incorrect and potentially destructive in a country that desperately needs to make social and economic adjustments, among other things, to remain competitive in world markets. The ills of society, however, have to be cured by society itself acting at all levels in a concerted way. Unless entrenched attitudes on the part of political, corporate and academic elites in this country become more enlightened, it will not really matter how dedicated and proficient school executives and other professionals are. They will continue to work under handicaps that prevent their organizations from reaching even a modicum of their potential in realizing the vision of a better society (Giroux, 1992).

To summarize the thrust of this chapter, true and deep-seated reform, requiring the restructuring of American schools, will not occur as a consequence of current or future fads manifesting themselves under slogans proclaiming 'choice' or 'site-based management'. What is needed first is that society at large must come to consensus about what the nature and role of schools will be, nationally and at the local level. The historical concept of local community control is no longer tenable if we are serious about deep-seated planned change. The child who goes to school in Minnesota has at least a 50 per cent chance of living and working in some other state during the course of an adult life. In a period of increased mobility, for one district and one state to control the educational content of instruction in isolation from others is neither practical nor sensible when considering the long term 'common good'.

Second, the preparation of educational leaders should follow the establishment of a national consensus regarding the aims of education since these people will shoulder the major responsibility for leading the nation's schools toward desired goals. Individuals who undertake this mission must be carefully selected, trained and of the caliber to confront the tasks that lie ahead. They must be prepared to engender a predictable transformative and surely-guided development of school organizations that educate all children for a productive life, an entitlement that will be of benefit to themselves and to the society in which they will live as adults. At the present time, it is difficult to be optimistic regarding America's will to furnish the means or to allocate the resources needed to create a national system of schools. We would argue that these need to be decentralized in some respects to meet local community needs, but centralized on a state and national basis in other ways in accordance with common and democratically agreed priorities.

A worthwhile precursor to the development of America's schools for the next century would be to institute a dramatic reform of the professional preparation of the next generation of leaders who will head up our schools and school systems. It is imperative that leaders be prepared now to lead the schools in directions that individual states and the nation as a whole can mutually agree upon for the 1990s and beyond.

Education as an investment, not an expense, means outlook is needed. It takes many years to adequately prepare an executive, and it is costly in terms of both the financial expenditure involved and the energy expended to provide learning opportunities for the neophyte superintendent to gain relevant experience in the practice and refinement of his/her newly-acquired skills. The great plus to be gained in doing this well is that, in the process, value is added to scarce human resources while also allowing for less tangible gains to accrue to individuals of high caliber as they are assisted toward professional maturity. The time and the context is right for the rebirth of school executive leadership preparation and training programs. This should become a priority item on the public policy agenda leading each of the states to help signpost the educational future and with it the future prosperity and well being of all Americans.

# Chapter 4

# Exemplary Superintendents: Do They Fit the Model?

*Thomas E. Glass*

The earlier chapters of this book have attended to reviewing selected studies of the superintendency and cognate areas with implications for policy and practice. In this chapter the focus is narrowed further to review some contemporary work regarding superintendents who have been identified as *exemplary*. While this group receives attention in this chapter, the reader will no doubt effect comparisons with superintendents in effective districts examined in Chapter 1, and with profiles of the national and effective groups of superintendents appraised in Chapter 2.

Even though America is heavily urbanized, the pattern of public education is still predominantly small town. About three-quarters of the nation's school districts are populated by one or two central office administrator types (Glass, 1992). Who are the superintendents serving in this broad spectrum of districts, large and small, rich and poor, rural and urban? What personal characteristics and district variables differentiate them in terms of the quality of their performance? In brief, which ones are exemplary in the position, and what type of selection procedures and preparation programs are likely to provide the public education system with future exemplary types?

The data on which this chapter is based come from the results of a nationwide survey of superintendents identified as exemplary by their peers and significant others in the field of education (Stott, 1991). It is complemented by data drawn from the most recent Ten Year Study of the American superintendency that is conducted in each decade by the American Association of School Administrators (Glass, 1992). Stott administered the instrument utilized in the AASA Ten Year Study to a group of superintendents designated exemplary on the basis of nationwide competitions sponsored annually by the National School Boards Association (NSBA) and the American Association of School Administrators (AASA). An important question to be addressed later relates to the validity of the selection protocol involved, i.e., whether the 'exemplary' superintendents identified by AASA and NSBA do in fact operate as 'executive leaders' or whether they are in effect managers maintaining the operation of schools through micro-management techniques.

In retrospect, the position of 'city schools superintendent' had already existed for about 75 years, when, in 1916, Ellwood P. Cubberly first wrote that the qualities of leadership of successful superintendents were such that, 'he must learn to lead by reason of his larger knowledge and his contagious enthusiasm, rather than to drive by reason of his superior power' (Cubberly, 1922, p. 138). This assertion, however, needs to be evaluated in the light of other conclusions such as those of Thomas and Moran (1992) concerning the power of the superintendent in the Progressive Period.

Even though Cubberly's remarks are now nearly 75 years old, they seem to be very much up to date for they closely parallel current writers who advocate 'executive leadership' as the *sine qua non* of the superintendency and principalship.

Further, Cubberly seems to endorse the current concept of strategic planning, saying that a superintendent should, '. . . out of his larger knowledge, see clearly what are the attainable goals of the school system, and how best and how fast to attempt to reach them. From his larger knowledge, too, he must frequently reach up out of the routine of school supervision and executive duties into the higher levels of educational statesmanship' (Cubberly, 1922, p. 138). While Cubberly's dictums seem quite contemporary, his vision of how a superintendent should act in carrying out 'his' duties would be considered managerial today, but were probably regarded as being very executive in orientation in 1916.

With the benefit of hindsight, the superintendency, in the early days, was undoubtedly managerial. Even though the 'grandfathers' of the profession, such as Cubberly, Strayer, Mort and even Barnard wrote textbooks that were compendiums of 'best practices', a serious reader would note the writers' preference for leaders exhibiting a wide vision. Also preferred was an ability to recognize leadership as a pervasive influence on all the groups involved in the school, and of possessing a vision as to the direction the school should be moving as well as ideas on how to get there (Glass, 1987).

## Identifying Exemplary Groups of Superintendents

After searching the literature on the superintendency, only two national groups of exemplary superintendents could be found. The first group of 290 superintendents was identified from the recipients of NSBA's 'Top 100' educators, first initiated on an annual basis in 1984, selected by *Executive Educator* magazine. A second exemplary group of 125 superintendents was drawn from those who represented their states in AASA's 'Superintendent of the Year' award that began in 1988.

## Descriptions of the Exemplary Superintendents

What characterized those superintendents commonly regarded as outstanding or exemplary? What was different about them compared with 'the norm'? What did they do that was qualitatively different from the way other superintendents went about their business? These and related questions about what distinguished them as being exemplary suggested the need for a descriptive survey in order to provide some answers.

A suitable instrument previously used in the just completed Ten Year Study (Glass, 1992) was already available. This instrument elicited superintendent information concerning demographics, leadership characteristics, relations with school boards, preparation and training, feelings of stress and fulfillment in the job,

Table 4.1:   Comparisons of exemplary superintendents and the AASA national sample

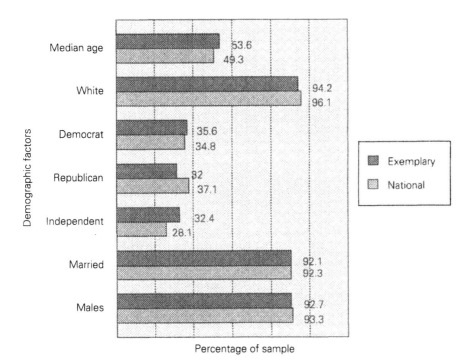

career paths, and programming of their districts. If the exemplary group completed the same instrument then further comparison with the AASA sample would
most likely reveal differences and similarities between the two groups on the same
variables. Notwithstanding, the AASA instrument contained 110 validated questions that comprehensively delineated the characteristics of the exemplary groups.
Stott surveyed a sample of 400 superintendents identified as 'exemplary'.

Some 2500 superintendents out of a population of 15,500 had been sampled
previously in the AASA survey and only a handful of the 410 exemplary superintendents had been drawn in the AASA sample. A number of superintendents in
the exemplary group had retired or moved into the private sector and several had
gone to institutions of higher education. Of the exemplary group, 291 returned
completed instruments representing a return rate of 70 per cent. The survey team
was well satisfied with both the overall representativeness and proportional strati-
fication of the sample as shown in Table 4.1 (Stott, 1991).

There were six evident differences between the exemplary group of superintendents and the national sample. In general, the exemplary superintendents fit
more into the conceptual model of the executive leader (chief executive officer)
rather than that of a middle level manager (*ibid.*).

The criteria used for nomination by both AASA and NSBA are derived
predominantly by reference to reputational sources. Individuals are nominated
using mechanisms such as notices in the *Executive Educator* and the *American School
Board Journal*. Subsequently state and national selection committees judge the initial

*Table 4.2:   Types of districts of exemplary superintendents*

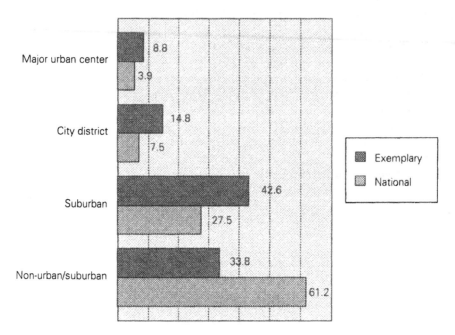

worth of the information received on nominees. Additional comments and data are then sought that are also evaluated and upon which the finalists are selected. The selection protocols, though purposeful, have no claims to being scientific but this does not necessarily invalidate them in practical terms.

It should be remembered that the purpose of the study was not to identify and validate those criteria that identify and can be used to evaluate effective or exemplary superintendents, but rather to focus on differences between two groups of superintendents selected within the constraints and practicalities of the sampling design that had to be adopted. Following from this, the conclusions should be regarded cautiously in the absence of further research in this area. They do, however, correspond with experience and the conventional wisdom of the profession.

### Exemplary Superintendents are More Urban

The exemplary group was distinctly more urbanized than the national group of superintendents. Over a third (37.8 per cent of the group) grew up in the suburbs or large cities, while 72 per cent of the national group had been raised in very small towns or rural areas. The exemplary superintendents served in large suburban districts more frequently than those in the national group. Only one member of the exemplary group of superintendents actually served in a small rural district (*ibid.*).

The statistics shown in Table 4.2 are predictable, since the typical suburban school district is wealthier and better supplied with administrative support than either the very small or extremely small districts. The latter typically have more homogeneous populations and this tends to result in low levels of conflict in districts where superintendents are afforded the opportunity to develop quality programs untroubled by the need to mediate between the various conflicts of religious, political, racial and/or socioeconomic groups, or having to overcome the deleterious effects of inadequate school or parental resources.

The suburban districts evidently do attract high quality superintendents. In the Northern Illinois area, for example, it is not unusual to have 150 applicants for superintendent positions in the affluent bedroom communities and many superintendents in this locality enjoy good salary packages in keeping with their role. School boards in the suburbs have an opportunity to pick the very best of applicants and this type of school district is well represented in the sample. Also, due to the availability of fiscal and other community resources, superintendents can develop highly visible programs that will draw attention favorably to themselves proving their abilities and thus enhancing their career prospects.

The presence of a disproportionate number of exemplary superintendents in suburban contexts is an important finding in Stott's study. On the face of it, it seems as if the resources and community profiles to be found in suburban districts are magnets for exemplary superintendents, but this requires further validation through more research.

The exemplary superintendents tend to be a bit older than the national group, and also more liberal and Democratic in their political party preferences. The average age is 53.6 years while that of the national group was found to be 49.3 years.

### Career Paths

The career paths of the exemplary superintendents (Table 4.3) were markedly different from those of the national group. The exemplary superintendents were far more likely to spend a few years in central office positions before acquiring appointments as superintendents. In contrast, the national group progressed from the principalship to the superintendency on a more regular basis. In accounting for this, it is likely to be the most common career path of superintendents in smaller districts simply because there are very few central office positions in small districts.

This is an important difference between the groups, however, due to the ever increasing complexity of school finance, budgeting, personnel, curriculum, special programs and facility maintenance. The exemplary superintendents were more likely to have had an opportunity to gain knowledge and experience in many of these areas before becoming a superintendent, whereas the superintendents in small districts most often learned on the job since the principalship does not as a rule provide much preparation in these areas. Additionally, many of the exemplary superintendents in their earlier position(s) as central office administrators, had the day-to-day opportunity to observe their superintendent in action. There is evidence to show that a majority of the exemplary superintendents spent most of their careers in larger, not smaller, districts before becoming superintendents. The exemplary superintendents indicated they had received the assistance of a mentor far more often than those in the national group (Stott, 1991; Glass, 1992).

*Table 4.3: Career patterns to the superintendency*

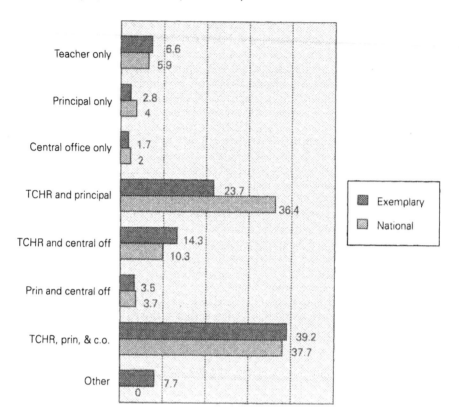

## Career as a Teacher and Administrator

Sixty-three per cent of the exemplary superintendents indicated they had been a classroom teacher five or less years. Forty-six per cent of the national group had taught for five or less years. Fully 68.5 per cent of the exemplary group obtained their first administrative position between the ages of 25–30. The mobility of the exemplary group was also a bit higher than the national group. About 36 per cent of the national group 'rose from the ranks' in their districts to become superintendent, while only 25 per cent of the exemplary group were hired from inside. Fewer than 40 per cent of the exemplary group had held only one superintendency while 50 per cent of the national group had only served in one superintendency (Stott, 1991).

Some other career path differences apparent in the data were that the exemplary group obtained their superintendency positions in districts more often where boards had utilized the services of a professional search firm (see Chapter 5 for more detail on this). This conclusion may appear to be inconsequential until it is realized that most of the professional search firms are staffed by former and retired superintendents. They examine very closely the credentials, experience and past performance of candidates before referring them to their client boards for

*Table 4.4:   Board reasons for hiring*

|                              | Exemplary | National |
|------------------------------|-----------|----------|
| Personal characteristics     | 29.1      | 38.5     |
| Change agent for district    | 29.8      | 27.4     |
| Maintain status quo          | 1.4       | 2.1      |
| Instructional leader         | 30.5      | 22.3     |
| Perform a specific task      | 1.8       | 1.8      |
| No particular reason         | 7.4       | 7.9      |

interviewing. This process seeks to identify superintendents with not only the best preparation for the job but also track record.

### Superintendents Explain Why Their Board Hired Them

When the superintendents were asked to identify the key reason their boards hired them (Table 4.4), the exemplary group stated the primary reason for their hiring was for their abilities in the area of instructional leadership. The national group indicated the primary reason their boards hired them was because of personal qualities. It is likely that on the one hand the exemplary group perceive themselves as being more like highly trained professionals hired to provide instructional leadership. On the other, it is possible that the national group perceive themselves to be 'educational generalists', hired to ensure that all of the basic functions of a school district are accomplished smoothly.

There is some research, supported by the 1992 AASA Ten Year Study, to suggest that board members generally hire superintendents in the first instance for personal reasons and fire them again for personal rather than professional reasons (Grady and Bryant, 1991). Thus, whether superintendents consider themselves to be superb technicians, managers or leaders, it appears that personal characteristics and the right 'chemistry' are most important in board/superintendent relations.

Another difference was that the exemplary group was far more active in participating in state and national professional organizations. This could be a contributory factor to their nomination as outstanding in the first place. Nevertheless, they first had to obtain the position in a district that had the resources to assist them in becoming visible within their state. Since most of the professional organizations that superintendents participate in (such as AASA, AASA state affiliates, ASCD, and NSBA) provide extensive professional development opportunities, it is most likely that the exemplary group receive continuing additional training commensurate with their positions. This feature is not as commonly occurring in the national group. Professional development opportunities emphasized in recent years include (i) strategic planning; (ii) curriculum auditing; (iii) site based management; and (iv) goal-based learning outcomes and instructional leadership.

The exemplary group also felt more personal fulfillment in their jobs (Table 4.5) than did those in the national group, and especially superintendents from very small districts. Additionally, the exemplary group exhibited lower stress levels (Table 4.6).

From Stott's data it can be inferred that the exemplary group of superintendents were more fulfilled and felt less stress than their contemporaries. This is understandable given the suburban nature of their school districts as previously

*Table 4.5: Amount of fulfillment in superintendency*

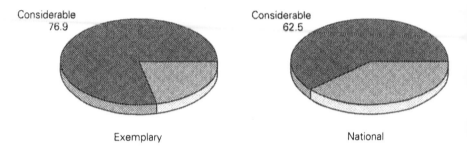

Considerable
76.9

Considerable
62.5

Exemplary

National

*Table 4.6: Amount of stress in superintendency*

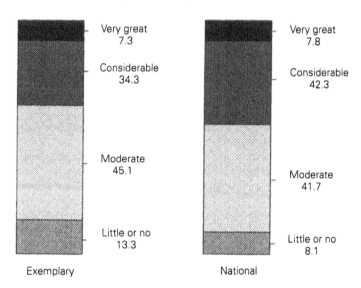

Very great
7.3

Considerable
34.3

Moderate
45.1

Little or no
13.3

Very great
7.8

Considerable
42.3

Moderate
41.7

Little or no
8.1

Exemplary

National

described. Also, a number of the board members in suburban districts are likely to be individuals with management training themselves and have the sort of perspective that empathizes with the superintendent as an executive leader rather than a micro-manager.

### Position Tenure

In recent years there have been frequent stories in the media concerning the dismissals of superintendents heading up the large urban districts. There is evidence to show that in the very largest urban districts tenure for a superintendent lasts for about two-and-a-half years (Rist, 1991). In the popular consciousness, many gain the impression that the superintendency is a quick turnover position. While there is an element of truth in this, data on the exemplary and national groups show a length of tenure comparable with that normally expected in a private sector

*Table 4.7: Mean length of tenure of superintendents*

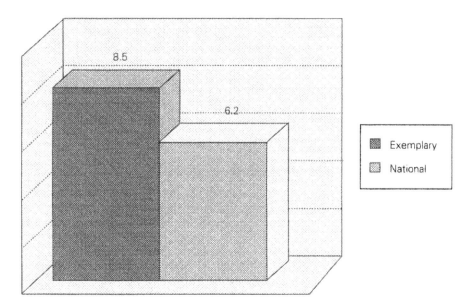

executive leadership position. There was, however, evidence to show some insta-
bility in the exemplary group moving from one job to another. Thirty-nine per
cent of these superintendents had held only one superintendency, while an additional 30 per cent were occupying their second superintendency (Stott, 1991). The
national group was more mobile than the exemplary group, although nationally
the mean length of tenure was 6.2 years (Table 4.7) (Glass, 1992). Both groups of
superintendents typically located in one state, but when it occurred, the national
group tended to move out of state more often.

### On the Job Performance and Conditions

The factor that the exemplary group of superintendents found interfered with
their performance most was the trivial and insignificant demands placed on them.
The national group indicated that the most serious problem inhibiting their job
performance was lack of adequate finances. The exemplary group included well-
planned and well-organized leaders who were likely to resent efforts to make
them spend time non-productively. Also, the exemplary leaders are situated in
districts that have adequate finances to meet most needs. A self-perceived and serious
issue facing the districts headed up by members of both groups was that of inadequate financing. The second most serious problem for both groups was assessment and testing. It appears that the nationwide drive for achievement-score
productivity is creating some further problems for districts and their superintendents. With the popular notion that 'the buck stops here', pressures for the
reform of school districts from parents, politicians and others has placed a heavy
burden on the shoulders of superintendents under the rubric of accountability
(increased production). Many superintendents, including the ones in the exemplary

group, were concerned about increasing student performance outcomes in their districts. The amount of testing now occurring in American school districts is believed to be unacceptable when counted in school hours and school days given over to it. When students only spend 17 per cent of their time in school, and when much of it is taken up with testing rather than teaching, then accountability pressures work against, rather than for, the processes of teaching and learning (Finn, 1991).

Superintendents in both the national and exemplary groups evidently did not regard superintendent/board conflicts as a serious problem. When they do occur, and especially if they're based on some personal altercation affecting family members (boards or superintendents), conflict seems to easily lead to firing (Grady and Bryant, 1991).

### School Boards and the Superintendents

The exemplary superintendents actively sought to involve more citizen participation in the work of schools: they emphasized strategic planning, and frequently shared the setting of board meeting agenda and the initiation of policy with board members. Further, they felt their board members to be better qualified for their work. This suggests that exemplary superintendents were more interested in sharing responsibilities in partnership with board members than did their contemporaries. Also, remembering the exemplary group work in the larger districts, the necessity of forming central office teams probably extends more readily into symbiotic relationships with board members.

Working with many groups of citizens, parents and staff who display adversarial stances is one of the most difficult public challenges facing superintendents. Most likely the type of superintendent who is successful in coping with potentially conflict-laden situations is one who feels comfortable when working in a team approach to problem solving and secure enough to delegate responsibility when and as necessary. The survey data indicated that members of the exemplary group seemed more amenable to share and delegate than did those comprising the national group.

### Professional Preparation and Standards

Over three-quarters (78 per cent) of the exemplary superintendents had an earned doctoral degree (Table 4.8). Forty-four per cent of the national group had doctorates. Almost all of the doctoral degrees for both groups were in educational administration. This clearly indicated that the level of formal preparation on this indicator was much higher for the exemplary group. Vacancies in larger and better financed districts often require that applicants have an earned doctorate making the degree almost a minimum prerequisite to being appointed. This trend is likely to increase in the next decade for the most desirable positions in which there are in excess of 100 applicants for a single vacancy.

As noted elsewhere in this book, interest groups have strongly criticized the worthiness of preparation programs for educational administrators offered by the institutions of higher education (Clark, 1989). They have been labeled 'Mickey Mouse' (Finn and Peterson, 1985). Not only are some academics and opinion leaders critical of the programs, significant numbers of superintendents, especially in the exemplary group, reported a dissatisfaction with them too (Table 4.9).

*Table 4.8: Superintendent education levels*

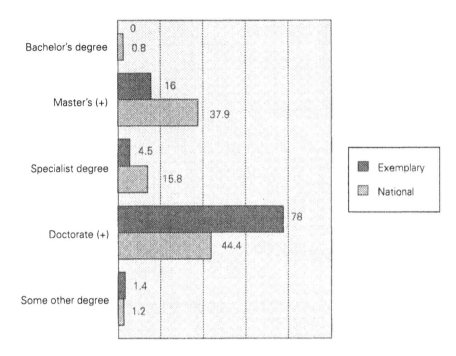

Over half (50.2 per cent) of the exemplary groups rated graduate programs in educational administration as being 'fair'. This contrasted with the national group which was not so critical of the programs, or of the professors of educational administration. However, responses to the two questionnaire items that asked superintendents to rate both graduate programs in educational administration, and the credibility of professors of educational administration, were revealing. Levels of support for both programs and professors have diminished since the 1982 AASA Ten Year Study (Cunningham and Hentges, 1982).

### Some District Characteristics

In the exemplary group, district characteristics were markedly different, especially with districts of under 3000 enrollments, from those headed up by superintendents in the national group. A noted management and leadership authority, W. Edwards Deming, advocates that for schools to be truly reformed, the initial steps of developing community support and understanding, establishing school business partnerships, and managing schools as adult learning centers must be accomplished (Rhodes, 1990). The survey data (Table 4.10) show that the exemplary group of superintendents are working in districts where there are school/business partnerships, where there is significant efforts toward community involvement and where there is a strong emphasis on instructional leadership. Similar programs also occurred in many other districts, but not as often as in the districts of those superintendents featured in the exemplary group (Stott, 1991).

Table 4.9: *How superintendents evaluate graduate programs*

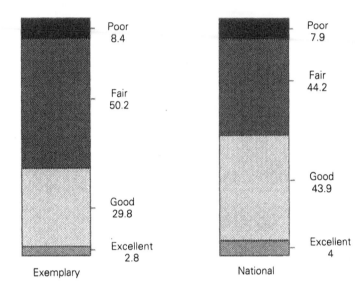

Exemplary / National

Poor 8.4, Fair 50.2, Good 29.8, Excellent 2.8 (Exemplary)

Poor 7.9, Fair 44.2, Good 43.9, Excellent 4 (National)

## How Are the Exemplary Superintendents Different and Are They Effective?

In profiling those characteristics that distinguished a sample of nationally identified exemplary superintendents from a national sample of superintendents, the following important differences are summarized from the survey data:

(i)    Exemplary superintendents were more frequently employed in larger suburban districts and received higher salaries;

(ii)   More of the exemplary superintendents held a doctoral degree in educational administration. They also belonged and participated in professional organizations more regularly than other superintendents;

(iii)  The exemplary group appeared to be much more interested in instructional leadership than the norm;

(iv)   More frequently they serve a number of years in a central office position before acquiring a superintendency;

(v)    They were hired more often through a professional search group, and also enjoyed a relationship with a mentor;

(vi)   They tended to emphasize community involvement in their districts as well as placing more emphasis on strategies such as teaming;

(vii)  Generally they exhibit a better fit with the literature definition of 'chief executive'.

## The Twenty-first Century Superintendent

If the superintendency is going to have a viable future, a number of factors will have to change in the very near future. The manner in which superintendents self-select into the profession will have to be addressed (see Chapter 3). The

*Table 4.10: Special programs in nation's school districts*

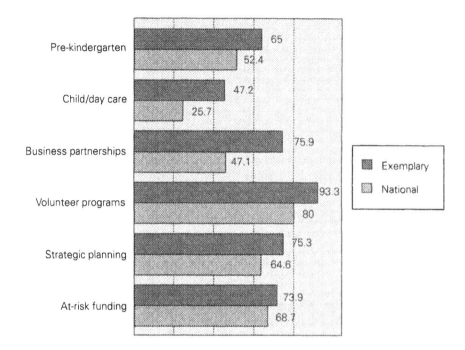

establishment of professional standards tied to performance criteria along with diagnostic instruments needed to assist potential superintendents in assuring their professional development programs are both appropriate and needed (Hoyle, 1989a). Today's preparation of superintendents is largely fragmented, uncoordinated, ineffective and not reality based (Finn and Petersen, 1985; Clark, 1989). It is becoming evident that the superintendent of the twenty-first century will have to be a very well prepared and multi-faceted leader, technician and bureaucrat.

The type of individual willing, able and suited to taking up the heavy and conflict-laden burden of the superintendency in the twenty-first century is yet to be resolved. With up to 50 per cent of the present cadre of superintendents leaving in the next five years their heir designates should now be undergoing preparation. Is this in fact the case? The answer is both yes and no. There are many principals and central office administrators attending an educational administration course or two at a nearby institution of higher education in order, at least, to satisfy state certification requirements for the superintendency credential. Their districts may also periodically send them to 'workshops' for a day or so here and there. There are no 'teaching hospitals' for future superintendents. As discussed in Chapter 3, there are very few field-based and closely supervised internships/residencies. To become an executive leader of a school district one currently needs only to 'pass' campus courses in educational administration, research methods, foundations, curriculum and perhaps educational psychology. Then, generally, complete a semester-long internship without release time and answer perhaps 100 modest questions in a state exam. Superintendents are simply not being prepared in a systematic and rigorous manner, reflected in a literature replete with comments that the superintendency has generally been the bailiwick of the 'good ole boys'.

It is a matter of some concern that the level of criticism has increased since the 1982 AASA Ten Year Study. Superintendents are evidently not terribly happy with current educational administration programs. This strengthens the case for massive reform of preparation programs, perhaps along the lines of the one described as a case study in Chapter 8, as well as for remedying inadequacies in state certification schemes.

## Conclusion

Anthropologists have reported that cultures in which they have actually done field work were vastly different from that portrayed in the literature they reviewed before going into the field (Sarason, 1990). The same logic can be applied to acquiring experiences of the reality of life in schools and school districts. The contrasts between textbook explanation and field reality are very pronounced. Since insider experience constitutes the operational reality for executives then the locus of advanced superintendency preparation needs to be conducted in field settings much like medicine, anthropology, dentistry, psychology and sociology. This ideal is far from that currently realized for most executives newly appointed to the superintendency. The sort of program advocated and exemplified in this book remains substantially an impracticality until new funding is made available to sponsor large numbers of suitable candidates.

Thought also needs to be given to the type of person to be prepared for the superintendency. School administrators have never been portrayed as 'risk takers' (Konnert and Gardner, 1987). Elements of the literature pejoratively record them as not being intellectual or high academic achievers. Some writers regard the majority not as executive leaders but rather as routine managers (Rhodes, 1990). As portrayed in Chapters 2 and 3, the common profile is that they substantially consist of middle-aged Anglo men, coming from working-class backgrounds and usually represented as the epitome of the middle class. Is this pattern of 'sameness' to be perpetuated into the twenty-first century where superintendents and other administrators appear as stereotypes in their professional characteristics, some of which are already redundant for future needs (Feistritzer, 1988)?

Who are these future superintendents likely to be? How are they going to be selected? These are key questions ultimately impacting the quality and effectiveness of the superintendency — the leading inspiration for our schools now and in the future. These 'input' considerations are just as important to social development as the content and context of the next generation of formal preparation programs. In the end, the quality is likely to be a function of the amount of fiscal and human resources expended by the federal government, state education agencies and school districts, as well as the quality of the candidates themselves.

## Acknowledgment

The author would like to thank Jim Stott for providing the tables used in this chapter. The data are derived from both his study and the AASA Ten Year Study.

# Chapter 5

# Superintendent Selection and Success

*Shirley M. Hord and Nolan Estes*

The selection of a superintendent can easily be considered the most important decision that the board, and by extrapolation the community, will make regarding the quality of education offered in a given school district. Thus, it is rather curious that there is a widespread lack of written policy and explicitly stated procedures in place to guide the selection of superintendents and other school administrators (Miklos, 1988). Pringle (1989) points out that school board superintendent selection decisions have 'a great impact on communities, districts, school personnel as a whole, and individuals' (p. 6). Since board members are responsible for providing for the district's future, *vis-à-vis* the effective schooling of its young people, it is incumbent on the board to make sound decisions regarding who will direct the schools in their mission. Such district guidance is highly complex and takes many forms involving 'personnel matters, taxation, construction programs, and maintaining control over a sophisticated financial enterprise' (*ibid.*, p. 13). Thus, it is evident that the selection of the district's top school executive is no small matter, and is not to be addressed lightly.

In order, then, to gain some clarity about the selection of superintendents, this chapter explores the published research literature as well as some recent studies in the field. It also reports the experiences of consultants engaged in the search for superintendents in order to shed further light on superintendent selection processes and their consequences for those (preparing and) hiring superintendents, as well as for superintendents themselves. The chapter concludes with some considerations and implications related to the conduct of searches for superintendent selection.

## What Research Tells Us

In the research base on the superintendency there are examples of studies that focus on the board's expectations of superintendents they hire, and on selection factors that appear to be given some detailed attention.

### Role Expectations

In studying school board requirements for the superintendents' position, Chand (1983) found that 35 per cent of the districts studied — a sample of small,

medium, large; urban, suburban, or rural; and located in any state of the nation
— required that the candidate be skilled in management and administrative skills
and/or have leadership skills and experience. As indicated by the boards' advertisements for the position, the tasks required of prospective superintendent candidates: a focus on curriculum 10.3 per cent; school finance 10.3 per cent;
community, staff, board, public relations 8.7 per cent; collective bargaining 3.8
per cent; bilingual/cross-cultural education 2.9 per cent; planning 1.6 per cent;
ability to delegate 1.6 per cent; school loans 1.1 per cent; and others receiving less
than 1 per cent mention *(ibid.)*. Salley (1979–80), however, was of the opinion
that boards placed more value on a candidate's actual personal qualities rather than
on the skills the superintendent should bring to the job.

Identifying the professional competencies and skills required of superintendents was the motivation for one study conducted on both board members and
superintendents in South Dakota (Haugland, 1987). Although certain role requirements for the superintendent as perceived by board members and superintendents were remarkably alike, some differences in perceptions were also
discovered. School board members and superintendents ranked superintendent
competencies as follows *(ibid.*, p. 41):

| **School Board Members** | **Superintendents** |
|---|---|
| personnel management | superintendent/board relations |
| school finance | personnel management |
| curriculum development | public relations |
| accomplishing board's goals | school finance |
| superintendent/board relations | accomplishing board's goals |
| public relations | curriculum development |
| policy formulation | policy formulation |
| school construction | school construction |
| collective negotiations | collective negotiations |

Board members considered personnel management to be a high priority predictor variable for success in their school systems, wanting the 'superintendent to
be the educational leader of the school while handling the district's finances in a
professional manner' *(ibid.*, p. 42). The superintendent perspective, on the other
hand, reflected that most concern occurred over board relations.

When the data from the Haugland study were analyzed on the variable of
district enrollment size, additional findings were reported. Board members in
small districts were more concerned about school finance while board members
in medium and large districts considered personnel management as being the most
important for success. Superintendents in small and medium size districts ranked
personnel management first; superintendents in large districts rated superintend-
ent/board relations as the highest priority.

A study of superintendents and other district level executives' perceptions of
their instructional leadership role was conducted by Hord (1991). The components of this role most frequently identified as most important by the study
respondents were instructional planning and organizing for instruction. Staffing,
human resource development, and evaluation collectively were ranked in the lower
third of seventeen tasks. The executives most frequently selected planning and

organizing for instruction as best descriptors of their capabilities. In summary, there was a clear convergence between tasks deemed most important by district executives and those identified most frequently as capabilities.

Other observers and interested parties have also expressed opinions about the superintendent's role. Tucker (1988) concludes that for the past two decades manual work has been declining and knowledge work has been increasing. As a consequence, he challenged school boards and superintendents to change their management procedures in order to incorporate shared decision-making rather than managing by telling staff what to do. Responsiveness to this challenge, Tucker stated, is prevalent in American corporations today and is a basic premise underpinning the restructuring of schools.

Looking ahead to superintendents' roles for the twenty-first century, Estes (1988) speculated about possibilities for change in both school system organization and in the executive leader's role. In so doing, he cited organizational changes: successful schools will become decentralized units; principals and teachers will work collegially to meet challenges; goal setting, personnel selection, allocation of resources and staff development will move from central office to the school. Estes suggested further that superintendents will require 'professional skill in exercising influence over these administrative components: the principal, the work structure, the school culture, technology and student outcomes' (p. 28). Estes' views of new roles are already being realized in practice.

*Selection Factors*

While personal attributes including 'judgment, personality, character, open mindedness, physical and mental health, poise, intelligence, sense of humor, voice, and cultural background' have been deemed important in administrator selection (Miklos, 1988, p. 54), studies of superintendent selection have identified other factors. Criteria viewed as relevant and related to the position of superintendent have been functionally oriented: understanding how the school board operates, and how the board and superintendent relate; management of the budget and financial resources; and developing relationships with parent and community groups (Powell, 1984; Robertson, 1984). While these factors appear rudely simplistic, Miklos (1988) notes that administrative work is perceived as being multidimensional in its nature and scope, requiring that multiple selection criteria should be employed for the selection of superintendents.

Women and minority group members perceive barriers that place limits on their inclusion in selection pools (Martin, 1981), and a study by Frasher and Frasher (1980) led these researchers to conclude that gender operated to women's disadvantage in superintendent screening and selection. On a broad scale, political factors, such as the selection committee's conservative or liberal attitudes, may influence the final decision to select (Morris, 1980). And the cultural context of the district may also be a strong factor in selection (more on this in the next section).

Career patterns have been studied (see Chapter 2) and Gaertner (1980) identified two upwardly mobile paths to entering the superintendency. One path to the top executive position came by way of the secondary principal position that was fed in turn by the assistant secondary principal position preceded by secondary curriculum supervision and assistant elementary principal positions. A similar route has been identified by Burnham (1989). The second path was such that secondary curriculum supervisory positions led to administrator of instruction, to assistant superintendent, then to superintendent. The position of assistant super-intendent was likely to be used by incumbents as an assessment position and for gaining entry to the superintendency. Cunningham and Hentges (1982) reported that during the period of 1971–82, the percentage of individuals moving to the superintendency through the teacher/principal route decreased, while those moving from teacher/principal/central office increased.

Other factors such as academic qualifications may enhance selection desirability. Holding higher degrees or doctorates, seems an important secondary factor for the superintendent position (Fuqua, 1983) and the specific doctoral program may be an important aspect. Age is another consideration, in that the earlier that career goals are defined and an administrator career initiated, the faster the likely rate of upward mobility, and the greater the probability of obtaining a superintendency in a large district (Craig, 1982). Career planning then seems to correlate with attaining the superintendent position, as do other internal factors such as career aspirations. Johnson (1979) reported that twice as many men as women aspired to be superintendents, and certainly more than that percentage of superintendents on the job are men (see also Chapter 2). Farmer's (1983) study of female principals indicated that most of this sample identified their position of principal as their ultimate occupational goal. However, females with greater intentions and readiness to seek the superintendency seemed to position themselves in the right place at the right time.

While planning, aspirations, and positioning enhanced opportunities for selection, chance factors such as an unsolicited job offer seemed to be important to women aspiring to become superintendents (Jackson, 1981). Support and sponsorship from the 'good ole boys' was seen as important to male aspirants (Fuqua, 1983) and its absence was seen by women as a negative factor for advancement (Pacheco, 1982). Advancement may also be tied to the type and size of an individual's first teaching and administrative appointments, thus logically those who wish to be superintendents of large districts should gain initial employment and administrative experience in such districts (Craig, 1982).

In concluding this brief sketch of the research literature related to advancement and selection to the superintendency position, Miklos' (1988) assessment of the literature is shared. He stated that few areas of research on the processes of administrator selection and careers have been explored intensively. Most of the research has been carried out in doctoral programs and reported in dissertations. Although these make a valuable contribution, dissertations tend to contribute to the knowledge base in an *ad hoc* way. They do not necessarily contribute systematically to the coherent development of an established body of research in a given area. Such a goal may only be reached through 'professional research', Miklos has suggested, although in our view this is a moot point.

Miklos also commented on the research methodologies used. A number of studies have been interpretative, employing small samples of incumbents in particular administrative positions with distinctive characteristics, thus limiting the generalizability of results in a positivistic sense. Notwithstanding, Miklos recommends (i) 'descriptive surveys of wider populations and in-depth case studies,' and (ii) qualitative naturalistic studies that would 'penetrate the depths of how these processes are actually experienced by people' (p. 69). A modest qualitative study, not intended in the first instance to study selection, provided the data for the next section.

## Recent Voices from the Field

A series of small related studies (Curcio, 1992; Hall and Difford, 1992; Hord, 1992) investigated the vulnerability of the school district CEO. Interest in the vulnerability issue was stimulated by multiple reports of current vacancies in the superintendency across the nation in rural as well as urban districts (Blackledge, 1992; Hall and Difford, 1992). The Hord study focussed particularly on the possible relationship between superintendent preparation, success or lack of it on the job, and a tendency toward a premature departure from the position. Believing that observations of the superintendent's role and analysis of its condition by widely knowledgeable, broadly experienced, and politically astute individuals would contribute meaningfully to understanding the phenomenon of interest, twelve persons were selected for the characteristics identified above for the study (Hord, 1992). Eight had been in the superintendency. The superintendency-experienced respondents had been successful chief executives; most had also experienced troubled terms in the office. Seven had or were in the process of exiting the superintendency. Five of the subjects had moved from district executive administration to superintendent preparation and/or continuing development, at higher education or other centers serving the development of leadership. Two of the subjects were women; ten were men. All were Anglo. All had been nominated as reputationally 'savvy' about educational leadership and the superintendency; all have records of publishing and presentations at recognized national and international conferences. They were viewed as knowing and, to a great degree, having experienced the triumphs and traumas of superintending.

Superintendent preparation, as revealed by these informants, was a non-issue; success or non-success and subsequent exiting appeared to be related to 'proper' selection of individuals for the particular superintendency or district. A summary of the findings follows.

### *Vision of the Role*

The subjects of the study volunteered that individuals are drawn to the superintendency because there are ego needs of the individual that the superintendent leadership position fulfills; they think they will be able 'to change the face of the world in one district' through their spirit of reform. However, the siren song of potential superintendents is not unadorned egomania, they said, but altruism and an appeal to the part of the ego that needs to serve the organization, making a contribution to the profession. There is the opportunity to make an impact, to make a difference, and this is exciting to persons contemplating the superintendency. They really want to be where 'the action is . . . there's no place in America that has more action than the superintendency'. Another part of the ego involvement, respondents seemed to agree, is based on ambition and self-efficacy, and seeing oneself as a leader among others.

## Preparation for the Job

The respondents reported that the superintendent is a person who is constantly seeking and searching out new talent, and developing the capacities of others, as well as themselves. According to all informants, there is very little useful pre-service preparation as it is currently conducted for the superintendent's job. Most of the education 'for the job is on the job'. The most important aspect of superintendent development, then, does not come from coursework. 'They have been socialized through the job more than formally educated to be successful today as superintendents'. It's experience, and 'from my point of view, they need to go up through the ranks, through the steps and not miss any step so they don't get blind-sided'. Those steps should include building work (school), and central office — some central office staff work in addition to line work because line officials don't have an appreciation of staff work.

Those who become better prepared for the superintendency are those who have had administrative and leadership experiences at lower levels and have reflected on those experiences, so 'that they learn from their own experience'. Reflecting requires time and introspection, and frequently, someone to stimulate or guide such introspection. The consistently clear assessment among the respondents, including those who are currently engaged in superintendent preparation, is that universities' certification programs are not preparing people for the real job. The issues raised by this assessment have been addressed in Chapter 3. Superintendents must learn to do the job while they're doing it, thus, they must be or become self-directed learners in order to become more successful.

### Superintendent Success

Evidence of a superintendent's success is receiving a consistent majority vote from the board at each board meeting, consistently from one meeting to the next. In addition, if the board extends the executive's contract and he or she keeps the job, that too spells success. Some might feel successful, however, if they 'didn't keep their job . . . if they are doing things they know are right and the board presents lots of opposition . . . and they resign . . . they don't consider that they have not been successful'.

Some respondents asserted that board approval, implying success, in one place might be different from elsewhere. Board approval and success, for example, might be measured differently in large urban centers than in smaller suburban areas. Another way of differentiating success was offered by one respondent who identified a three-fold typology of board's preferences for and expectations of the superintendent: expectations for a *maintainer* (if things go along smoothly, this person is successful); expectations for a *developer* (if new programs lead to higher scores, this person is successful); and expectations for a *change agent* (if changes get made, success is at hand). From the foregoing, a good match between board preferences and superintendent capabilities logically increases the executive's potential for success, and at some point is likely to be a function of the selection criteria and processes employed.

Respondents expressed a healthy respect for the latent power of the board. Nearly every person reported troubling incidents with particular board members that, for the most part, had resulted in the premature departure of the super-intendent — frequently this occurrence was based on the superintendent's own analysis of the situation and his/her decision to leave.

Tenure is the likely casualty when the board and superintendent hold different expectations for the requirements of the role. If the superintendent tries to by-pass the system to do what he or she thinks 'is right' despite the board's wishes, trouble usually follows in its train. Some new superintendents have been 'quite surprised when they have assumed the initiative and actually tried to run the schools'. They find out what that can really mean in personal terms if they are not in harmony with the board. Expanding on these concerns, respondents spoke to the lack of clearly defined boundaries between board policy-making (the 'appropriate' role of the board) and the board's interest in the daily micro-management of the district (the superintendent's domain).

Boards that tend to regard themselves as representatives of the 'school or-ganization to the community' rather than as representatives of the 'community to the board' make it possible to plan strategically what needs to be done to identify and address district priorities. Board members should, as one very seasoned respondent reported, be strategic leaders focussing on tomorrow, next month, next year, and many don't 'have a clue about what being a strategic leader means'. And that makes it a risky business for the superintendent to attempt to act strategically which is what superintendents must do by planning now for five to ten years into the future. The superintendent will get 'his head handed to him' figuratively speaking, if he/she is evidently out of step with the board.

Is selection 'good' for forever and what are superintendents' expectations about being selected? Many go into the big cities 'with a missionary mentality, into an impossible job, to see how long they can survive and how many kids they can help. They know they will not win the war, but they might win some battles — and the salary and perks are nothing to sneeze at'. No matter what size the district, most go in 'knowing it's not forever'.

### Superintendent Failure

One explanation offered by informants for the failure of some superintendents to remain securely in position is a 'matter of the values of equity, excellence, and efficiency' that society expects its institutions to support. Communities must be concerned about all three since they are not mutually exclusive. 'We expect our schools and leaders to advocate all three'. But board members are typically elected to school boards on the basis of one of those three and they select superintendents on that same basis, so informants suggested.

When a member takes his/her place on a school board, he/she is either pushing excellence, equity, or efficiency, and most of their behavior can be referenced back to that. The superintendent has to try and understand where members are coming from and help them to be successful in realizing their agenda so the superintendent in turn can be successful in achieving the district's agenda. If the superintendent identifies with an agenda that is seemingly at odds with the board's, then it manifests as a problem. When the superintendent's platform gets out of harmony with the values expressed by the majority of board members, then it is clearly time to move on. On the other hand, it is known for some superintendents to move the board into alignment with their views and to accept a new agenda.

It's not that a superintendent comes in and sells his or her program; it's that a superintendent comes in and leads board members through a process of developing a vision and helps them to commit to it in a shared way. When asked, one respondent affirmed that 'probably 20 per cent of the superintendent incumbents can be successful with this kind of model'.

A practicing superintendent respondent considered there was a deeper underlying factor causing some of these problems, namely changes in the make-up of the district. As a community becomes more multicultural, and less homogeneous, community standards (or values, as suggested earlier) become more diffuse, or come into conflict with each other. This makes it difficult to respond to community issues and concerns from the point of view of the majority, while also democratically protecting minority rights and ensuring their views are represented. The superintendent gets out of sync with some segment of the community, makes a decision that upsets some of the community, and this sub-group decides it needs someone else. 'It's not usually that you really made some big bad mistake; you just made a dumb political mistake. You made that mistake because you're not able to read all the ins and outs of the community; you don't have enough time to study it'. This respondent suggested that for superintendents in large districts, they need a sociologist or a political analyst on board to help read and provide feedback on all of the politics concerning what's going on.

In short, it appears that a superintendent will not be successful in a district where selection has not forseen and taken into account the coping mechanisms needed to interact successfully with a board with whom he/she is at odds, or deal effectively with the pressures, tensions and challenges of a rapidly changing society and its attendant value systems.

The Hord study reported that the selection of appropriate individuals to fit particular districts was a primary factor in a superintendent's success or lack of success. Success was defined as completing a contract while maintaining harmonious relationships with the board and community. It is becoming increasingly self-evident that changing district demographics drive an increasing cultural diversity in many communities and sensitive responses are required from the superintendent. Thus, contextual and sociological factors have become important selection factors, as we shall see in the next section when initiating and conducting a search and selection procedure for a superintendent.

## Screening or Searching and Selecting

In terms of economic growth and social development, as well as educational improvement, the most important decision a board can make in representing the community is in the selection of a school superintendent. Burnett (1988) reported that the higher the board's satisfaction with the selection process, the higher the satisfaction with the performance of the person selected. According to a nationally recognized consultant, there appear to be two well-represented procedures that culminate in superintendent selection: one is a screening process; the other is a search for appropriate candidates.

In the screening process, the job position with its background requirements of candidates for relevant training experience and needed attributes is advertised in newspapers and professional journals. Individuals submit their applications, and, from this pool, the board, and perhaps an expanded committee of community representatives, selects several persons to attend for interviews. Based on the interviews, a final selection is made and a new superintendent is appointed.

The search strategy is more comprehensive but highly focussed and is thus more complex. It may be conducted by a consulting firm or by a school board or citizens' committee. Given the idea of looking (searching) broadly for candidates, the search is more likely to be contracted out by the board to a professional consultant(s). An initial procedure is to agree on the definition of the sequence of steps to be taken with an accompanying timeline.

### First Step

A first step in the search process is to identify the characteristics of the superintendent that the board and community value and most want. Consultants, meeting with board members as well as those representatives of the district's professional and local community groups designated by the board, assemble a formalized position description and statement of qualifications for prospective candidates. This document serves as the basis for the subsequent development of brochures and advertisements to be used in the search, as well as providing a set of criteria for screening and interviewing applicants.

At open meetings with groups mentioned above, frequently at night for maximum attendance of members, answers to several questions are sought. Typically, these are:

(i)     What are the strengths of the district?
(ii)    What are the areas that need to and can be improved?
(iii)   What are the personal and professional characteristics that are desirable in your superintendent?
(iv)    From (i), (ii), and (iii), what are you willing to pay for an executive of the kind and caliber you want?

Two general themes emerged out of a consulting group's recent experience, when working with business, industry, the board and other community members. First was that the new superintendent, when appointed, be able to maintain the existing standards of excellence in the district evidenced by its high number of merit scholar winners, SAT scores, etc. This expectation is with respect to an affluent district containing a lot of corporate international headquarters; however, the district has a 51 per cent black student population and also the highest dropout rate in the state. Thus, the second theme to emerge from the discussion and meetings between board, community and consultants was the need for a superintendent who could provide for more equity and advance the achievement levels of the large minority population in the schools.

In short, without compromising the top performance levels, this district required:

(i)     an instructional leader with a demonstrated ability to improve student achievement;
(ii)    a good manager, familiar with strategic planning, who, on appointment would develop a five-year plan with a vision for the district, and

who would know how to back it up and move the district forward step by step toward the achievement of the plan and the realization of the vision; and

(iii)  a good community relations person who would build bridges and establish harmonious relationships between very diverse elements within the community.

In contrast to the three areas identified above, another district requiring a national search had a singular issue for a superintendent in mind: instructional excellence. The district did not want a superintendent with a conspicuous high profile in the community or going to a lot of meetings; they wanted their superintendent to be on site making sure that the number of merit scholars would continue to increase. This second example comprises a small, very affluent district, with some diversity and 21 per cent minority population, but here the minority is middle class. The superintendent doesn't have to be out pulling people together; they're already 'of a like mind' that instruction and college prep is the ticket.

### Second Step

Here the consultant engaged to conduct the search places advertisements and listings of the vacancy in general media and professional bulletins and journals. Following this he/she aggressively seeks out and contacts qualified candidates encouraging them to apply for the position. Because all those individuals who meet the search criteria are not likely to be looking for a job, in a nationwide search the search consultant or team will actively seek and identify persons who match the skills and attributes of interest, and then lobby them to apply for the position.

### Third Step

During this screening and evaluation stage, the search team reviews applicants' profiles, looking at credentials and checking references. Attention is focussed on securing matches between what the district wants and what the applicants can provide. In the search experience cited above, for example, where the district was looking for a combination of instructional leader, strategic planner, manager and community relations-oriented person, a superintendent in a nearby state was interested in the job. He is an instructional leader and expert planner, but his human and community relations skills are somewhat short. The search team concluded that his style and manner in dealing with community members would not be well received by the board and community. The search team therefore considered another candidate who knows instruction well, is a strategic planner, and knows how to involve the community. Although he is caring, concerned, and compassionate, he has not worked with a large minority population. He has not had the prior sorts of experience that would allow him to demonstrate his ability to turn a 51 per cent low achieving minority district around. Consequently, the board would have been taking a risk if they hired him even though he has the three qualities they desire.

*Fourth Step*

After screening is completed, the search team reports to the board in confidence with a list of recommended candidates and the reasons for its recommendations. The keys to making recommendations are first, finding out what the board and community want, and second, thoroughly investigating the background and personality of prospective candidates in order to ascertain if there is a good candidate/ board match. The extent to which the search team identifies and understands the explicit and more subtly implied factors required by the board of their superintendent, the higher the likelihood of a good match and hence superintendent success.

*Finally*

The search team assists the board in interviewing candidates through its recommendation of interview procedures, preparation of questions for board member use in interviews, and making scheduling and other arrangements that become necessary. On occasion, the team may also advise the board on how to make a productive visit to gain further insights from the home communities of short-listed candidates.

Since no candidate 'walks on water' and everybody 'has warts', the team works with the board in considering compromise positions. If there is more than one vacancy at the executive level (for example, that of assistant superintendent), then a solution might be to develop a cooperative approach to the superintendency, where a team of several persons is hired to represent all of the district's requirements.

While there are a number of variations, the steps described above parallel those advised by the American Association of School Administrators (1979 and 1983). Boards of education were found by Burnett (1988) to be most satisfied when preliminary planning was done, and when interview data were supplemented with additional information in the selection process. These activities appeared to be more often used by districts employing a search team.

### Considerations, Questions, Implications

In this chapter some exploratory research on superintendent selection and related issues has been examined. Studies identified the functions of the superintendency in different contexts as important considerations when selecting superintendents. Other variables that appear to impact selection are gender, academic qualifications, age, career planning and aspirations. Career patterns leading to selection as a superintendent were reported. The selection committee's political persuasion, the community's cultural context and support of 'the good ole boys' were additional variables identified in the literature.

The second section of the chapter focussed on findings from a recent study inquiring into the phenomenon of superintendents exiting their districts and/or the superintendency, with relevance to superintendent selection. It further confirms some of the research reviewed in Chapters 2 and 3. While this study revealed

that superintendents viewed themselves as change agents, they found little preparation for their job in formalized course work. Study, reflection and self-analysis
on the job appear to be the tour de force to the superintendency. A major stress
of the job revolved around superintendent/board relationships and the congruence
or lack of common views and expectations of the job as perceived by the board
and its superintendent. Thus, selection of a superintendent who is a strong fit with
board and community preferences was a clear message from this study.

Finally, in the third section, an illustrative example of the recent experience
of a search team's efforts to enhance and facilitate superintendent selection was
presented to add further perspectives to the infrequently documented process of
selecting superintendents. Five steps were identified in the search and selection
process. Again, the message of selection was, make certain that the executive and
board/community are a good match in terms of the superintendent's competencies and the community's needs and expectations.

From the preceding discussions, several questions come to mind. Clearly, an
urgent theme emerging from this chapter is the critical need to match potential
superintendent's strengths with district expectations. To identify transient district
needs, one practicing superintendent suggested the use of a sociologist, or perhaps
a political scientist, to continuously monitor the district's social environment in
order to 'keep a finger on the pulse' to detect and report changes in demographics,
cultural beliefs and values so that appropriate responses and actions might be taken
by the superintendent and the board. As alluded to previously, in preparing a
search for a district's selection of superintendent, a search team meets with and
interviews a wide array of professional and community members to identify their
beliefs and values concerning what the district educational system and its chief
executive should be about.

It would appear that each of the two approaches described at the start of this
chapter for identifying community values as well as candidates whose value sets
match them, is based on observation, interviews, inference, checking hypotheses
and reaching some reasonably defensible conclusions. In a quest for precision in
the selection process, are there rigorous means for adding objective data to decision-
making? Are there instruments that can be used? One idea with some merit is the
use of the six domains of performance identified as crucial to effective leadership
at the executive's level, and which provide the framework for the DECAS described
in detail in Chapter 6. The over-arching domains include:

Domain 1   General education
Domain 2   Instructional leadership
Domain 3   Administrative leadership
Domain 4   Human relations
Domain 5   Personal capabilities
Domain 6   Multicultural perspectives

If these domains represent five competency areas plus general education of
a particular flavor, and have been carefully identified and empirically verified as
areas significant to developing the leadership capacities of superintendents, then,
ideally, superintendents should be developed in and able to demonstrate degrees
of competence across all these areas. In practice, this is not a realistic expectation
since the complexity of the role and the social situations in which it is undertaken

are so complex and varied that it becomes impossible for an individual to be completely knowledgeable and competent in all of its facets over the whole of a career span. Further, some districts will have differential needs for superintendents to exhibit strengths in some areas more so than in others. Because of the temporal nature of the superintendency in time and place, certain contexts will demand particular competencies at a given time. If instrumentation is devised, based on the six leadership domains for superintendents, and used objectively to identify particular superintendent strengths and competencies allied to district needs, then the probability of making the match is likely to be more successful than currently appears to be the case.

A second notion that has not emerged as a theme to date, nor been mentioned so far in this discussion on selection, is what the individual executive superintendent, him/herself, values and wants professionally from an appointment. The focus of this text has been on a community's preferences and how meeting community priorities will enhance a successful superintendency from the board's point of view. What about the candidates? They, in turn, must take cognizance of community wishes and whether they match with their own values and self-perceived strengths. They must also consider how they want to administer a district in the light of their own educational philosophy and ideals. Is the match good from a candidate's point of view as well? Could the six domains and/or the three categories of values (efficiency, equity, excellence, previously mentioned in the second part of this chapter) be used for further self-analysis and decision-making for the initial job application and subsequent job acceptance?

The foregoing considerations are compensatory ways of thinking, assuming the community knows its values in a broad sense at least and what it currently wants and/or expects. It doesn't speak to what the community *should* be thinking about and aspiring to for children's and young people's education for today, tomorrow and in the future. What is really needed is a visionary to crystallize a variety of views and suggest alternative futures. Are there ways to select individuals capable of envisioning, who are able to articulate and communicate to the community tomorrow's needs and how the education system can work to produce the outcomes needed? Across *all* contexts this universal requirement should be a factor for selection — to be visionary.

Understandably, the community will select someone to meet their immediate needs and interests, to help improve on what they do now; but it is incumbent on the superintendent to take efforts in a measured, patient, practical way to make the community open and receptive to ideas and to help it think about its future and the future schooling needs of its children. With cultural sensitivity, the superintendent enables the community to become aware of what exists right now and also what it could or might become. The superintendent is selected as someone who can introduce new ideas and intervene on behalf of the community as the community's own teacher — one of the three roles of superintendents eloquently articulated by Cuban (1985).

For futures-oriented scenario building, Cuban's three roles help to describe and account for the tensions between the manager-superintendent who 'keeps fires out' while meeting the community's needs; the politician-superintendent who 'puts out the fires that inevitably erupt' while keeping himself at the job; and the teacher-superintendent who 'starts fires' by visioning and preparing the community to meet future needs. This visionary firebrand tells the community, this is what you will need and want. Put your faith in me as we change for a better future.

The search committee may find this three-role model useful as they formulate search and selection protocols for a new executive leader. Such a leader is likely to view the world and the district as in a state of flux. Heraclitus advised us many years ago: the district will be in a state of *becoming*; its status will always be an approximation of what it can ultimately become, but to which it never actually arrives in the drive for self improvement. Such a leader takes the community's 'fixed targets' or immediate needs, and moves the system to an 'ends in view' mindset linked to a vision of some ideal state of the future or alternative futures. The leader then assists the district in collective decision-making, leading to decisions that move boards and their communities to realizing a future that is not too far removed from what was envisaged.

Quite a task for the search and selection process.

Chapter 6

# Diagnosis, Self-prescription and Treatment

*David S.G. Carter and Ben M. Harris*

Assessment center methods have demonstrated, over four decades, that they are powerful tools for providing scientifically based, validated data for making outcome-oriented personnel decisions. Tensions exist, however, between the use of conventional assessment center methods for the purposes of selection, screening and induction of candidates as distinct from diagnosis for professional growth.

It has become increasingly obvious, as methods and procedures have been refined, that in spite of the benefits to be gained from their use, there is a high cost to pay for the power embedded in the methods. This becomes evident in the protracted labor-intensive procedures that are applied to complete an assessment of a candidate. The severity of constraints appears to be causing personnel managers in business and industry to think again about the cost effectiveness of assessment centers *per se* as they exist in their current form and operation.

Starting with a consideration of present conceptual difficulties and tensions regarding the assessment of school system executives using assessment center methods, this chapter appraises selected assessment models. Tensions between the concurrent use of data for summative and formative personnel decisions are then explored. We subsequently provide an alternative approach to assessment using highly focussed techniques to gain specific performance data for action planning that is described and illustrated in some detail. The chapter concludes with a number of considerations concerning assessment and its relation to planning for professional growth that occurs within the framework of a specific model, namely, the Diagnostic Executive Competency Assessment System — DECAS. Further considerations of professional development planning and the utilization of learning models to put plans into effect, extending on ideas introduced in this chapter are considered further in Chapter 7.

### Identifying Leaderly Behaviors

Current theory and research in educational administration focuses primarily on the interaction of leader traits or styles with situational variables and their effects on performance in field settings. This effort to date has not been particularly fruitful in discovering what type of leader fits what type of situation. Further, the emphasis has been on 'building level' leadership. With respect to the district superintendent, specifically what the leadership role is, and what desirable personality traits, technical skills and professional competencies are needed within the context of a set of situational variables, is not definitively known, in spite of elaborate claims by commercial purveyors of instruments, programs and modules.

In a cognate area, industrial psychologists have, over a number of years, conceptualized the study of leadership within more interpersonal and system-oriented paradigms (McCleary and Ogawa, 1985). A body of research findings is now available for the guidance and information of staff developers, findings that also appear to have some promising applications to educational administration. Studies in industrial psychology, in contrast to those in education, have stressed the executive levels of leadership and tended to deal with broadly generic styles and functions.

Recent research sponsored by the University of Texas, under the auspices of the American Association of School Administrators (AASA), and assisted by funds provided by the Meadows Foundation, has made significant progress toward defining the skills and competencies superintendents require in order to be effective in their districts. Initial recourse to the relevant literature in the formative phases of this project proved to be inconclusive. Consequently, a nationwide survey of superintendents was undertaken in a series of preliminary exploratory studies (Sclafani, 1987; Collier, 1987; Burnham, 1989) and summarized in Chapter 2. Investigations were initiated to ascertain if there were generic skills and/or performance areas clearly associated with effective educational leadership in the superintendency. Outcomes from this research did identify skills and performance areas but these were not found to be generally transferable across different contexts. Sclafani (1987) reported that, on the basis of some key demographic variables including school district location, size and community characteristics, superintendents with quite different skill repertoires and competencies, specialized local knowledge, and who possibly possessed unique personality traits as well, were apparently effective in exercising different arrays of leadership behaviors. Hoyle *et al.* (1985) reported a common set of broadly-defined behaviors related to leadership, which seem to enable success in most administrative roles, but also determined that there are specific skills in evidence peculiar to the various types of superintendencies that exist. Early studies, however, utilized such a broadly defined mixture of skills, knowledge domains and general competencies that many of their findings, while self-evident, have limited utility for other researchers and staff developers.

From these and related findings, the difficulties inherent in importance as well as complexity in developing an operational diagnostic assessment model of use to senior executives is readily apparent. Difficulties are especially acute when the model is required to cater for ongoing professional development in an open ended way over the course of an executive's career. Burnham (1989) reports that 'exemplary' superintendents move into their positions over short spans of time with only limited experience in teaching and school administration. AASA's Executive Committee has launched a major effort, the National Executive Development Center, on the assumption that the need for continuing professional development implies a diagnostic assessment process with highly individualized opportunities for on-the-job development of new competencies (AASA, 1989). The National

Policy Board (1989) simultaneously proposes much more elaborate pre-service preparation programs with substantial implications for clearly defined and diagnosed assessment processes.


### Assessment Models

A considerable body of knowledge now exists regarding the nature and leadership roles of school principals. Since they provide a large portion of the talent pool for the selection and preparation of superintendents and other school executives there seems to be an appealing logic, if professional leadership development is considered to be a continuous process, for linking and coordinating parallel programs across the principalship and the superintendency (see Chapter 1). It remains problematic, however, given some fundamental differences in the extra role requirements of superintendents, *vis-à-vis* principals; the special contributions of supervisory experience in school districts (Burnham, 1989; Little, 1980); and the particular requirements and opportunities available to superintendents for their ongoing professional development.

From a program integration point of view an appropriate assessment model tends toward the well-known 'industrial assessment' center approach embodied in the National Association of Secondary School Principals' (NASSP) Assessment Centers (see also Chapter 7). Such an assessment center typically employs a set of standardized procedures, involving multiple activities undertaken by potential or practicing administrators, to evaluate their performance in validated skills areas. The assessment activities conventionally include at least one simulation among other things incorporating decision-making skills. A manpower intensive process of observing, scoring, judging and interpreting assessed performance leads as a rule to summative decisions.

NASSP centers assess across twelve skill dimensions, claimed to be necessary for success as a principal (McCleary and Ogawa, 1985; Hersey, 1989). The purpose of the assessment process is primarily for the screening and induction of principals. Special problems occur, discussed later in this chapter, when data such as these are also used formatively for diagnosis in a professional development mode.

The relationship of Hoyle's Task Areas and the NASSP skills with respect to the NEDC's Leadership Domains are shown in Figure 6.1.

Wendel and Sybouts (1988), drawing on the experience gained with assessment centers by business and industry, government and the military in the post-Second World War period, conclude that assessment centers using the form and *modus operandi* of the NASSP approach possess great potential for improving the way administrative applicants are screened. They are, however, more cautious in advocating this particular approach for diagnostic purposes, noting:

> The assessment method has also been used for diagnostic purposes . . .
> If participants (sic undergoing diagnosis) were found to be weak in a dimension, some form of developmental recommendation could then be suggested. While this use of the method has been employed, there is not yet sufficient experience or data collected to determine the degree of effectiveness of assessment center methods as diagnostic tools. (*ibid.*)

*Figure 6.1: Relationship of Hoayle's task areas, NASSP skills and NEDC leadership domains*

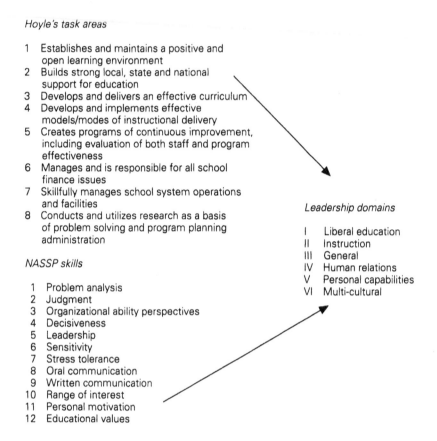

*Hoyle's task areas*

1 Establishes and maintains a positive and
  open learning environment
2 Builds strong local, state and national
  support for education
3 Develops and delivers an effective curriculum
4 Develops and implements effective
  models/modes of instructional delivery
5 Creates programs of continuous improvement,
  including evaluation of both staff and program
  effectiveness
6 Manages and is responsible for all school
  finance issues
7 Skillfully manages school system operations
  and facilities
8 Conducts and utilizes research as a basis
  of problem solving and program planning
  administration

*NASSP skills*

1 Problem analysis
2 Judgment
3 Organizational ability perspectives
4 Decisiveness
5 Leadership
6 Sensitivity
7 Stress tolerance
8 Oral communication
9 Written communication
10 Range of interest
11 Personal motivation
12 Educational values

*Leadership domains*

I    Liberal education
II   Instruction
III  General
IV   Human relations
V    Personal capabilities
VI   Multi-cultural

The assessment center process developed by Bolton (1988) and his co-workers at the University of Washington has more diagnostic design features and may in the end prove to be more effective overall.

AASA has opted for a professional development approach, using formative assessment procedures in accordance with the mission statement of its newly formed and still evolving National Executive Development Center (see Chapter 10). This is summarized as follows:

The mission of the AASA National Executive Development Center (NEDC) is to provide a process for guiding the professional development of school executives. The mission is achieved through programs and activities that will assist participants to:

* become aware of their personal and professional knowledge, attributes and skills;
* develop personal time-sequenced professional development plans;

* pursue personal and professional standards of excellence and improve working relationships;
* establish self-directed support networks for mentoring, coaching and peer counselling;
* select institutes and seminars through NASE, NEDC, and other resources to further assist their continuing development. (AASA, 1989)

The model proposed is designed to assess leadership behaviors and associated knowledge, skills and competencies of school system executives related directly to the performance areas of the superintendency. Assessment is assumed to be conducted for the purpose of structuring professional development plans for guiding the ongoing professional growth of senior school system executives. The diagnostic process is illustrated in Figure 6.2. In an effort to operationalize and test notions about diagnostic assessment as promoted by AASA's National Executive Development Center Advisory Committee, a set of performance domains were outlined and an operational model formulated.

The AASA's National Executive Development Center system draws heavily on the research of Hoyle *et al.* (1985), Harris (1986), Sclafani (1987), and Bolton (1988); as well as previous studies by Evans, Palmer and Harris (1975) and Bailey (1985); and focussing on the supervisory performances of central office personnel. Additionally, the general literature in the fields of administration, leadership and supervision of instruction was scrutinized for the identification of domains of performance and tasks that appear crucial to effective leadership at the executive's level. The design and instrumentation of the diagnostic assessment system is based upon the creation of a taxonomy of identified tasks and competencies and derived from a set of leadership goals referenced to successful school leaders — including superintendents (AASA, 1982, pp. 1–5).

The set of fundamental tasks and competencies referred to above is categorized into performance domains, defined as task areas, and further specified behaviorally as tasks, sub-tasks and competencies. This scheme has been translated into the necessary instrumentation to support the operational testing, since 1987, of the Diagnostic Executive Competency Assessment System (DECAS) using a battery of diagnostic techniques within a completely formative self-actualizing framework and philosophy. The actual diagnostic process requires approximately ten hours and operates using a workshop format accommodating from fifteen to fifty executives.

As a prelude to discussing the Texas interpretation of AASA's preferred approach to executive assessment, represented in its National Executive Development Center, some considerations regarding the use of assessment data for formative and summative decision-making are discussed in the next section.

### Summative Versus Formative Assessment Center Decision-making

Latent psychological and practical problems quickly surface when an assessment process employs the same criteria and data forms for making both formative and summative decisions. The mode of response and reactive behavior of the individual is likely to be altered as a function of his/her perceived use of the data by

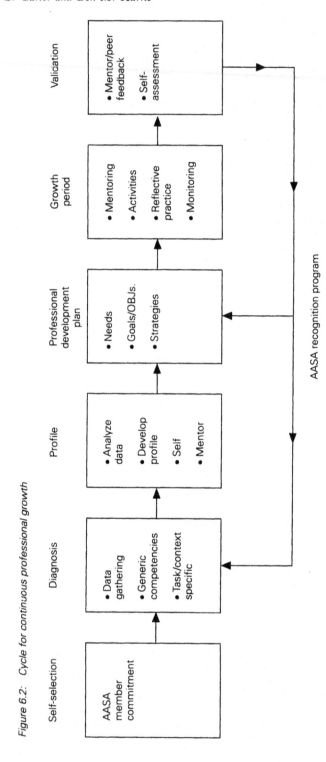

Figure 6.2: Cycle for continuous professional growth

decision-makers. Consequently atypical behavior will contaminate data derived initially for formative/diagnostic purposes, when the same data may also be used summatively, albeit at a later date — say three years hence when a contract comes up for renewal. Time is considered to be an insulator in this context with individual psychological concerns being reduced, it is argued, when the summative use of performance data is projected to a relatively remote point in the future. The uncertainty of the time frame, however, may well be a further complicating factor.

When only very specific and fragmentary facets of a total repertoire of skills and knowledge are being assessed, the anxiety regarding possible summative uses is diminished. By contrast, assessments utilized for dual purposes tend to be broad-gauge and hence more immediately threatening. The assessee's degree of concern is likely to intensify with increasing proximity between the use of his/her personal data at the time of its collection, and its deferred summative utilization. When summative uses are clearly intended, assessors making independent and objective observations and judgments are required. Self-estimates or negotiated decisions, while possible, are of limited value in most settings. Yet for enhancing professional executive performance, with its enormous scope and complexity, reliance on self-estimates is not only desirable, it is essential. Concern for objectivity continues to be important in the form of a better introspective analysis.

The foregoing argument assumes of course that the threats to an effective diagnostic assessment process are overwhelming unless the summative uses of the data are clearly foresworn and made abundantly clear (Harris, 1986).

At a practical level, highly specific diagnostic data, which inherently only represents a small and highly focussed sample of behavior within a total performance, is unlikely to be of much use to decision-makers for the type of global decisions required for selection, induction, screening or the promotion of candidates. This necessarily reduces the utility of such data in isolation for making dichotomous personnel decisions, unless *a very comprehensive and highly specific* diagnosis has occurred. The latter is usually unavailable within the assessment center approach in its conventionally accepted forms.

Obverse considerations also apply. The more general and global evaluation data required for making summative personnel decisions, positive as well as negative (i.e., being perceived as advantageous or disadvantageous by individuals and/or the organization), are similarly inadequate due to their inherent, broadly based nature and comprehensive scope. This restricts their utility for formative purposes because of a lack of focussed diagnostic power.

Because of the tension existing between the collection and use of data for joint formative and summative purposes, and the underlying assumptions explicated above, the project team at the University of Texas at Austin developed the DECAS diagnostic procedure primarily for use by senior school system executives within the superordinate AASA Executive Assessment Center framework. It employs assessment center methods and procedures to generate diagnostic data for the purpose of executive professional development over a career span of indeterminate length. The development of a diagnostic profile in a specific area of knowledge, skills and competencies using personally derived multiple data sets, becomes the precursor to developing a personal growth and action plan. Assessment is conducted primarily through executives completing a procedure before, within and following a diagnostic workshop. The procedure can be iterated as needed by executives across self-selected leadership domains according to individuals' present and future professional development needs and aspirations.

### The DECAS Rationale

The AASA philosophy and approach has been refined, and a comprehensive system, incorporating diagnosis and professional development planning, has been developed and validated.

After describing the form and function of this system, the remainder of the chapter will address certain characteristics of the diagnostic instruments that have been developed, their individual and collective purposes, and their integration into a diagnostic workshop employing an assessment center approach for formative, as distinct from summative, purposes.

The DECAS is based upon a diagnostic design with associated instrumentation, which, unlike the more generally recognized assessment center approaches utilized for selection, screening and promotion, is *not* designed for making summative personnel decisions. The latter use would be anathema to the nature and purpose of the DECAS. This is an important point of departure for the DECAS when compared with other assessment center approaches — for example, that of the NASSP (Hersey, 1982).

Design of the comprehensive system incorporates survey and diagnostic instruments together with techniques of self-analysis, utilizing simulations to stimulate rigorous introspection. These are integrated and sequenced so that the executive moves from an initial broadly-based composite profile of his/her task capabilities through a number of hierarchical levels of increasing specificity over the course of a ten-hour diagnostic workshop. During this process, increasing precision — together with a narrowing of scope and sharpening of focus upon specific tasks, sub-tasks and competencies within a self-selected task area — occurs (Figure 6.3).

### Performance Criteria Utilized in Instrumentation

All instruments utilized beyond the pre-diagnostic survey phase of the workshop are based on task areas within a particular leadership domain, circumscribed by a set of performance criteria, framed in behavioral terms as specific competencies. An illustration of this is presented below for the Instructional Leadership domain (see also Appendix):

DOMAIN 2: INSTRUCTIONAL LEADERSHIP

TASK AREA 2: STAFFING FOR INSTRUCTION

**Task 2.2.1**          The executive maintains adequate staffing levels while anticipating future changes in staffing needs

**Sub-Task 2.2.1.1**   **Monitors to maintain staff adequacy**
     2.2.1.1.1 Analyzes staffing patterns to determine the *status quo* regarding class size, qualifications, and mis-assignments.

*Figure 6.3: Sharpening the focus from domains to competencies*

**Domains**

1　Liberal Education.
**2　Instructional Leadership.**
3　General Administration Leadership.
4　Interpersonal Leadership.
5　Personal Capabilities.
6　Multi-cultural Perspectives.

**Tasks**

2.5.1　Structures and applies a unified policy framework.
2.5.2　Develops a formative personnel evaluation system.
2.5.3　Directs a summative evaluation system for personnel.
**2.5.4　Coordinates a system of evaluation of instructional programs.**
2.5.5　Studies information from evaluation reports to identity priorities.

**Task areas**

2.1　Instructional Planning.
2.2　Staffing for Instruction.
2.3　Organizing for Instruction.
2.4　Human Resource Development.
**2.5　Evaluating Instruction.**

**Sub tasks**

2.5.4.1　Develops a comprehensive plan.
2.5.4.2　Provides for economical and feasible procedures, instruments, and sources.
**2.5.4.3　Coordinates systematic gathering, analyzing and using data.**
2.5.4.4　Arranges for dissemination, review, and follow-up actions.
2.5.4.5　Analyzes and interprets data.

**Competencies**

2.5.4.3.1　Demonstrates through comparisons of evaluation data whether students are reaching expected levels of accomplishments.
2.5.4.3.2　Designs a testing program that regularly assesses student progress with instruments that provide input for program evaluation.
2.5.4.3.3　Documents the strengths and weaknesses of programs through a strategically designed evaluation process.
2.5.4.3.4　Insures through the evaluation process that all program resource materials and textbooks are ethical, legal, non-discriminatory, and educationally sound.

2.2.1.1.2 Analyzes staffing patterns to project anticipated retirements, leavers and non-renewals.

2.2.1.1.3 Confers with administrator and instructional specialists regarding shortages and other discrepancies.

**Sub-Task 2.2.1.2 Assesses needs for staffing changes**

2.2.1.2.1 Reviews proposals for additions and changes in staffing patterns.

2.2.1.2.2 Determines special staffing needs for new instructional programs.

2.2.1.2.3 Recommends goals for meeting needs for minority and special teachers in scarce supply.

2.2.1.2.4 Projects staffing requirements for long-range planning.

Reduction of a domain to a set of performance criteria, using a task-based approach is accomplished initially by reference to the specific literature for a given task area. Usually the literature does not help in a direct sense with respect to illustrating processes such as staffing, for example, but advice on what to do, such as manpower planning, selecting staff, screening and the like, is abundant. Establishing construct validity is achieved by subjecting selected criteria, like those above, to the scrutiny of experts using a reputational sampling method and also accessing the professional wisdom of practitioners. Well over 100 senior executives — superintendents, assistants and directors — have participated in DECAS workshops and report that the performance criteria 'make sense' to them under operational conditions. In fact, instruments derived from these performance criteria are being systematically validated in use by securing reports of both the importance of criteria and estimates of practitioner capability from peers and individuals themselves.

### Instrumentation

Four different instruments are utilized in the DECAS based on the performance criteria being explicated in several domains. The survey phase of the system may use the devices such as Educational Administrator Effectiveness Profile (EAEP) instrument (AASA, 1984 and 1988) as an optional introduction to self-appraisal. The survey process is given some substantial focus, however, when an executive assessee makes a domain selection, and completes a Task Analysis Inventory (TAI) for that single selected domain. The task inventory is a forced-choice instrument and is completed as a self-report and also by selected peers or colleagues. The analysis of the data generated is profiled to reflect patterns of perceived capability in certain task areas. The formal workshop allows for a review of individual task profiles and the selection of a single task area for further diagnostic analysis.

Three instruments are employed for focussed data gathering:

(i) *The Competency Analysis Inventory* (CAI) is a forced-choice instrument containing all competency statements within a single task area. Executive assessees complete these individually and analyze their own self-report data.

(ii) *The Task Quizzes* (TQs) are tests of knowledge in a multiple-choice format. A single quiz is designed for each task within a task area.

Executive assessees complete as many quizzes as they wish or have time for during the workshop. Once the instrument is completed, self-scoring takes place so that almost immediately feedback is available to workshop participants.

(iii)  *The Competency Self-estimate* (CSE) instrument is a simple device calling for overall estimates of capacity to perform each sub-task within a single task area. These self-estimates are repeated only after being utilized in the diagnostic analysis process.

## Simulations

Simulations and leaderless discussion are strategically placed between the individually conducted paper and pencil diagnostic activities. Their location is shown in the workshop flow chart presented as Figure 6.4. The social simulations are not intended to assist directly in assessing each executive's performance, since their diagnostic power is limited. They do have a motivational value within the workshop setting, however, in assisting participants to become reflective about their own position in the context of shared meanings with activities such as school district in-basket, problem-solving and a simulated school board meeting. Out of a common scenario in a real time setting, problem-solving and decision alternatives are slanted toward the application of knowledge and rehearsal of skills within a self-selected area at the task and sub-task level.

Executives are organized into groups of five to seven people who have chosen to undertake their diagnosis within the same task area. They therefore share common frames and interests as they complete the simulated activities and discuss their reasoning behind the decisions they have effected under 'safe' conditions. The simulations' unique contribution to the value of the workshop lie in their stimulating participants to make critical assessments of their own capabilities as they compare and contrast their percepts with those of colleagues.

The simulations, in-basket, discussion, and role-playing draw upon accumulated personal experience, i.e., the tacit knowledge referred to earlier, for the purpose of self-analysis and introspection at the task and sub-task level. They also demand sharing with others, through the medium of leaderless discussion, certain proposed actions drawing consciously on executives' tacit knowledge. Each proposed course of action is evaluated with the benefit of hindsight, and in the light of decision alternatives proposed by peers within the small group setting.

## Operation of the Diagnostic Workshop

Central to the construction of an executive's diagnostic profile, within a self-selected domain, is the assessment workshop. Diagnoses of executive knowledge, skills and competencies are derived from self-estimates, tests of knowledge, forced-choice analyses and simulations, each of which has been referred to earlier. Analyses of diagnostic data utilize special techniques to specify accomplishment and needs for professional development at the sub-task level. These techniques are described later in the chapter.

Reference to figure 6.4 illustrates the flow of events in order to accomplish

Figure 6.4: Diagnostic steps for growth planning

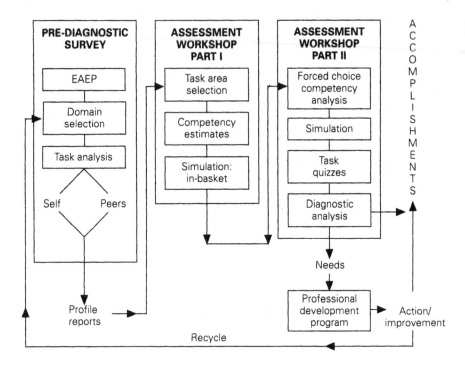

a diagnosis as a precursor to growth planning. In the developmental phase of the project this procedure frequently, though not necessarily, commenced with the use of the Educational Administrator Effectiveness Profile (EAEP) with each executive selecting one domain for detailed treatment later in the workshop. Domain selection is followed by completion of the appropriate task inventory by the executive as well as selected peers in advance of workshop participation. For this to occur instruments requiring completion are distributed and returned by mail in the weeks prior to the advent of a scheduled workshop.

On arrival at a workshop site a 'profile report' is presented to each executive, summarizing the computer analysis of the task inventories previously submitted. Competency self-estimates are completed on-site by executives, and an in-basket exercise is conducted in small groups. The competency analysis inventory is subsequently written up resulting in a forced-choice profile.

A second workshop simulation then occurs that incorporates role play and leaderless discussion of issues, concerns and interactions. The scenario is a school board meeting alluded to above, in which agenda items are related to the selected task area. As previously indicated, participants are grouped according to the task area in which they have chosen to work.

Toward the end of the workshop, quizzes are administered that are precisely focussed on the self-selected task area to illuminate the knowledge base of the executive. Each quiz tests knowledge related to a single task. Hence, there are seven quizzes in the Staffing for Instruction task area, for example. Again, executives exercise free choice; they select the task of most interest to them and may complete only one quiz or as many as are preferred and time allows. Clearly, the more quizzes that are completed the more comprehensive the diagnosis that eventuates. All quizzes are self-scored for privacy and to provide immediate feedback to individuals.

Analysis is conducted by visual inspection of three data sets that have been generated by individuals undergoing the diagnostic process at this point. These are fully discussed in the next section.

### Diagnostic Analysis Process

In concert, the quizzes, together with the competency self-estimates and competency profile data, provide three different databases derived from different instruments using different methods and presenting different perspectives on the competencies and perceived capabilities of individuals to function at the task and sub-task levels. The databases retain their separate identities but are consolidated into a personal, composite and clinical profile facilitating visual inspection by individual workshop participants. Neither database in itself is likely to be completely diagnostically valid, but each one presents a separate perspective on the same phenomena (i.e., knowledge, skills and competencies) that is presumed to possess its own unique character imbued with *some* validity. These data differ from the 'usual' ratings such as opinion polls especially where the perspective may be unknown or not made abundantly clear.

A search for congruence between data sets ensues in order to extract meaning from patterns occurring within them. The analysis is done individually and personally by each executive with certain guidelines provided and embodied in the material itself. Ultimately the executive arrives at databased decisions concerning personal areas of strength and needs for professional development. It is the latter, however, that logically assume priority for the production of a Professional Development Program plan (PDP) following from the diagnosis.

### Congruence Analysis

This is a multivariate analysis technique first developed by Evans, Palmer and Harris (1975) and simplified for use in teacher assessment by Harris and Hill (1982). It is based on the notion that, with complex human performance, no single variable is in itself a good predictor of a multiple array of behaviors constituting the more complex performance *per se*. Virtually any truly important aspect of performance by school executives is an exceedingly complex synthesis of knowledge and skill(s).

The underlying assumption of congruence analysis is that if one can obtain three or four independent estimates of a larger holistic performance, in which the individual performance estimates themselves differ from each other according to their *source, method and/or substance*, then their congruence can be the basis for inferring validity. Given that each data set has some validity with strong agreement or congruence between at least two data sets, and preferably all of them, validity can be inferred with sufficient import to complete a diagnosis.

97

David S.G. Carter and Ben M. Harris

Figure 6.5: An illustration of the search principle

| Competence analysis inventory (CAI) | Competence self estimate (CSE) | Task quiz (TQ) | Diagnoses |
|---|---|---|---|
| H | H | H | = A |
| L | L | L | = N |
| H | M | L | = NK |
| L | L | H | = NT |
| M | M | M | = NR |
| L | H | L | = U |

Legend:

A = Accomplishments
N = Need for Improvement
NT = Training Need
NK = Knowledge Need
NR = Refinement
U = Uncertainty
H = High
M = Medium
L = Low

Through cognitive processing of the data, and the search for congruent patterns within it using performance estimate guidelines and designators provided in the workshop material, the executive completes a personal diagnosis of accomplishments and areas of need. A hypothetical set of data is provided in figure 6.5 to illustrate the search principle.

With reference to Figure 6.5 the two most self-evident diagnoses that can be derived are represented by data sets high-high-high and low-low-low. These highly congruent patterns suggest 'accomplishments' and 'needs' respectively, but many patterns reflect little or no congruence. There are twenty-seven possible patterns and many combinations offer no logical basis for inferring any diagnosis except 'uncertainty' (Harris, 1986). There are, however, a variety of patterns that might logically be utilized diagnostically. For instance, a 'high' estimate on knowledge combined with 'low' estimates on the other two instruments focussing on skills and their applications on-the-job, can be inferred as a 'need for training' diagnosis.

## Professional Development Program Planning

The concluding activities in the DECAS workshop use the completed self-diagnosis as the basis for initiating a Professional Development Plan (PDP). Executives are guided through a review of their diagnostic data in which prioritized decisions are made by them, together with the identification of human and material resources needed to support a PDP. To be achievable it has to be based on a realizable time frame of target accomplishment dates. A suitable supportive infrastructure has still to be developed at the state and national level, but a start has been made with the further development of AASA's National Executive Development Center using a consortium of six pilot sites spread geographically around the nation. Each site is responsible for developing a particular domain of leadership behavior based on the task analysis approach delineated earlier in the chapter, with the exception of the General Education Domain (which is qualitatively different). The responsibility of each pilot site for developing a specific leadership domain within AASA's over-arching NEDC framework is described in Chapter 10 (q.v.).

### For the Future

Materials have still to be developed to widen the choice of task areas available to executives for self-diagnosis. So far, in Texas, two task areas in the Instructional Leadership Domain, and one in the Human Relations Domain have been completed and validated. This is a priority area for further development and validation of new *materials* although the workshop *procedures* appear to have stabilized. The next phase of the research involves the application of new information technologies to make the system widely accessible, irrespective of location and context. Research is also needed to test and validate different forms of follow-up training using coaching and mentoring, independent self-study, and peer group support networks involving high technology applications where appropriate. Alternative approaches here are considered further in the next chapter.

It is expected that the outcome of this work will contribute significantly to the improvement of public education, the intrinsic satisfaction of school executives and the enhancement of the profession.

*Chapter 7*

# Assessment-based Models for Learning and Growth

*Judith G. Loredo, Ben M. Harris, and*
*David S.G. Carter*

For a number of years AASA has been working toward developing a process for guiding the professional development of school executives, making it both portable and accessible to executives in the field via a decentralized network of centers, and subsumed under the direction of a National Executive Development Center. The Diagnostic Executive Competency Analysis System (DECAS), described formally in the last chapter, is a response to the need expressed by AASA for a professional guidance system with focussed diagnostic power, upon which a systematic approach to action planning with realistic growth targets for individual executives could be based. In the previous chapter the emphasis was mainly on the diagnostic aspects of the system — together with its rationale.

In this chapter we shall consider further the 'output' side of this particular approach to professional guidance and development and how it might be applied in practice. This aspect is necessarily speculative because a much needed infrastructure to support current initiatives is still emerging. A further problem allied to the portability criterion lies in the application of new information technology to appropriate models of learning and growth and making these accessible through a network of sites that are themselves still evolving and not yet stable. Progress has been made, however, and it is the purpose of this chapter to capture the essence of this by indicating a range of possibilities from which selections can be made.

It would be a mistake to think that AASA's concerns lay exclusively with the field-based executive when the organization, like UCEA, has a vital interest in the selection and initial preparation of school system level executives too. It has been stated very clearly there is a need to radically restructure the selection and pre-service preparation programs for administrator training (Wendel and Sybouts, 1988), using more inductively-based learning approaches but also needing to base programs on sound and justifiable theoretical principles. The issues these considerations raise are comprehensively treated in Chapter 8.

However, it seemed appropriate to outline a curriculum process model for professional learning and growth, conceptualized out of the work of the Meadows Project Team at the University of Texas at Austin. This appeared to have a certain currency for those being formally prepared to enter the profession of educational administration, as well as those who prepare them to undertake leadership roles at a senior level. The model proposed is generic in nature and can also underpin the theoretical bases of in-service professional activities intended to guide the further development of leadership competencies with already established practitioners.

After a consideration of assessment center approaches and their modification to align with AASA's philosophy, the chapter will attend to some specific learning models with implications for use in an evolving NEDC network of sites. There is no reason why the approaches described cannot be applied within a continuous change curriculum model covering both pre- and in-service levels of administrator development, and it is with this that the chapter concludes.

### Assessment Center Methods

The origin of the assessment center concept is accredited to German psychologists in the 1930s who used it to select military officers. It was reinterpreted in the USA and used for similar purposes by the Office of Strategic Services during World War 2. The concept spread to business and industry and consequently the growth of assessment centers has mushroomed in applications to this area of endeavor. The use of assessment centers in education is a relative latecomer to the scene. Most readers would be familiar with the National Association of Secondary School Principals Assessment Centers (Hersey, 1982 and 1989) that commenced operation in 1975.

The methods used have become progressively more sophisticated and refined, but the conventional *modus operandi* is to administer standardized sets of procedures and activities in order to evaluate individuals for selection, placement and promotion. These appear to have been successful in providing reasonably accurate information on three important aspects of leader behavior, namely motivation, communication skills and personality factors (Walker, 1989).

A common approach is to use simulations like leaderless group activities, stress exercises and in-basket tasks as described in the preceding chapter. Participants are observed by a team of trained observers, usually on a ratio of one observer to two or sometimes three subjects, making it a very labor intensive enterprise. The defining characteristics of an assessment center, minimally, are:

(a) the use of multiple assessment techniques, at least one of which is a simulation, must be employed;
(b) specifically trained multiple assessors must be used, with collective judgments made based on pooled information across assessors and techniques;
(c) an overall evaluation of behavior must be made by the assessors removed in time from observation of the behavior;
(d) assessors agree on the evaluation of the dimensions and any overall evaluation that is made.

In the National Association of Secondary School Principals Assessment Center there are twelve behavior dimensions. They are: problem analysis, judgment, organizational ability, decisiveness, leadership, sensitivity, stress tolerance, oral communication, written communication, range of interest, personal motivation and educational values. Criterion measures used as indicators of competence in these areas include the following examples:

**Judgment** — skill in identifying educational needs and setting priorities; ability to reach logical conclusions and make high quality decisions based on available information; ability to critically evaluate written communication.

**Sensitivity** — ability to perceive the needs, concerns and personal problems of others; skill in resolving conflicts; tact in dealing with persons from different backgrounds, ability to deal effectively with people from different backgrounds; ability to deal effectively with people concerning emotional issues; knowing what information to communicate and to whom.

**Leadership** — ability to get others involved in solving problems; ability to recognize when a group requires direction, to effectively interact with a group and to guide them to accomplish a task.

What do we know about assessment centers? According to Bray (1989) we know that overall assessment center performance is strongly related to job performance. We have also come to a better understanding concerning the relationships of dimensions to overall performance and assessment exercises to dimensions. This makes it possible to select or design exercises appropriate to the dimensions we wish to evaluate.

A large repertoire of assessment exercises is available including not only variations on the traditional in-baskets and leaderless group discussions but completely new designs as well. Some of the latter include oral fact finding, simulated appraisal interviews, evaluations of fictitious subordinates after viewing videotapes of their job behavior, planning and scheduling, and so on. Creativity has been given full scope in tailoring assessment to specific purposes.

Nowadays it is possible to train assessors much more efficiently than hitherto. This capability has been provided by the advent of cheap and easy videotaping. It has allowed those being trained to see the same behavior that expert assessors have viewed, and to compare their reports and ratings with good models.

On the output side we have learned repeatedly that organizations adapt much more readily than one might have thought possible to the application of assessment center methods and techniques in personnel matters. Assessment center methods no doubt will continue to be refined and to evolve into a process that will itself reflect still further improvements and refinements in the method, its results, and its applications.

If the assessment center method becomes more widely used in educational settings and acknowledged as an accepted approach to assisting in the selection of administrators, its influence will possibly expand to other related areas across the whole domain of school administration. Assessment center 'content' will undoubtedly be incorporated into administrator preparation programs and instructional methodology will, at least in some instances, parallel and complement that which is reflected in assessment center approaches. Placement services and certification of administrators are other cognate areas that may ultimately be influenced by assessment center methods.

The NEDC approach to assessment, however, is quite different from that of NASSP's assessment centers in both its philosophy and method of operation. First, NEDC, unlike the NASSP assessment center, is not in the business of screening and selecting individuals for administrative positions. The National Executive Development Center is designed primarily for school system administrators with substantial experience who wish to increase their personal self-awareness, develop attributes, increase their professional knowledge and enhance and refine their skills. The emphasis of the NEDC is on professional growth stemming from a preliminary diagnosis of executives' strengths and weaknesses, and, from this, developing personalized professional development plans. While drawing its inspiration from traditional assessment center techniques, DECAS, for example, is ideologically well removed from the summative ideology and externally applied frames of the former. This becomes apparent in the formative use made of the personnel data obtained for self-energized and ongoing senior executive development, deemed to take place in an open-ended system in which the individual generates and maintains absolute control over his/her data and its subsequent use as a guide for action.

Personal development growth plans are self-directed in contrast to other-directed staff development activities which seem to be characteristic of many contemporary programs. In other words, initial engagement with the process and subsequent participation is based on an individual's personal commitment, not on another person's or group's nomination of a prospective 'client'. Individuals set their own pace of learning with time-sequenced activities, integrated with benchmarks, to help them fulfill the obligations of their PDPs in meeting the personal goals they have established for themselves.

By this means NEDC facilitates the pursuit of personal and professional standards of excellence through (a) self-directed support networks of mentor, coaches and peer counsellors, and, (b) activities and resources made available through a variety of delivery systems and referenced to individual needs. Examples of the latter include providing novel modes of access to institutes and seminars provided by NASE, NEDC, universities and colleges, and professional organizations. The means of delivery is considered further later in the chapter.

### Professional Development Program Planning

The purpose of diagnostic assessment is to assist executives to identify those skills and competencies they consider require further development or refinement. The approach adopted by the NEDC operates on the premise that leadership behavior for instructional excellence can be resolved into discrete components enabling an accurate and meaningful assessment of strengths and weaknesses to be developed. Thus, stemming from an initial diagnosis a professional growth plan can be formulated around personal goals, consisting of activities and resources focussed explicitly on identified areas of weakness and/or professional needs which the assessee considers are in need of further development. Ultimately, the underlying purpose of this activity is to promote and activate the development of educational leadership in an ongoing and continuous manner, in which assessment, in order to achieve this outcome, clearly has to be formative in both its nature and application.

*Judith G. Loredo, Ben M. Harris, and David S.G. Carter*

Research, as well as experience, indicates that, for the formative processes to be effective, the system for developing executives must have validated diagnostic power. In practical terms this means measuring performance in on-the-job behaviors and in sufficient detail to clearly separate an individual's strengths from his/her professional needs for further development in selected areas. From the acquisition of these baseline data the design and prescription of individualized training programs addressing practitioner needs and aspirations can be meaningfully constructed.

### The Professional Development Program (PDP) Plan

Toward the end of the diagnostic workshop executives use their diagnostic profiles to develop a plan of action, which, when followed, leads to the acquisition or development of new competencies related to previously diagnosed needs. This process, while confirming strengths, encourages the executive to focus on specific tasks and sub-tasks where performance appears to be weak (see the diagnostic workshop procedures described in Chapter 6 for more details on this). Assistance is given to participants in identifying optimal activities for growth opportunities. The planning process also requires the selection of a mentor who will assist the executive in completing the plan, specifying realistic target dates and negotiating time commitments in order to achieve development goals.

### The Process of PDP Planning

As previously mentioned, the purpose of the diagnostic assessment component is to assist participants in identifying skills where professional growth is needed. The system is designed around the premise that leadership for instructional excellence can be specified as discrete behaviors in the first instance, so that an accurate and meaningful profile of one's strengths and needs in a specific area may be developed. Based on the diagnosis, a professional development program can then be developed in which activities and resources are brought to bear to meet professional needs for improvement in the self-selected area.

It should be kept in mind that the entire focus of the operation ultimately is to promote the development and continuous improvement of executive leadership in school systems in a formative way. Further, a growing body of research and experience tells us that in order to be effective in the formative process, systems for developing executives must be able to diagnose their knowledge, skills and competencies validly and with precision. This means measuring performance in terms of actual 'on-the-job' behaviors and in sufficient detail to clearly differentiate strengths from needs. From these baseline data the design and implementation of training programs that meaningfully address the individual needs of executives may then be formulated.

To guide and inform the processes of PDP planning an instrument has been developed at the Texas pilot site for use in the concluding phase of the diagnostic workshop described in Chapter 6.

The planning process follows a sequence as follows:

**Step 1 — Prioritization:** Select several diagnoses, choosing from among diagnosed needs for improvement and assign a priority ranking to each;

**Step 2 — Decision:** Review performance criteria for selected diagnoses at the task, sub-task and competency levels. Choose a single sub-task for further planning;

**Step 3 — Action Record:** List all competencies related to the selected sub-task; describe activities and resources to be employed; and designate dates for completion of each activity;

**Step 4 — Mentoring Arrangements:** Identify a mentor, confer with mentor and reach agreements on meeting and working together.

This four-stage process has been designed specifically for use in the DECAS workshop where it serves to direct executives toward personal decision-making consequent to the diagnosis. The instrument also serves as a record of workshop events.

A critical component of the planning process is the identification of professional development resources that can be made available to executives as they plan and implement their programs for improvement. As an executive proceeds through the system, the process assists him/her to identify specific sub-tasks and competencies that need strengthening. At that point, the system must have the capacity to suggest suitable human and material resources that can be accessed by the executive as an improvement program is developed. This requires a search and retrieval system for identifying materials relating to each competency and a delivery system for making identified resources available to executives as they implement their plans.

In the case of Texas, for example, this is operationalized via the LEAD Center Resources Bank, which is a major resource in its own right as well as a source of information, inspiration and ideas for PDP planning. The Center utilizes a database in which consultants, seminars, presentations, audio-visual materials, software, self-paced modules, books and other professional publications are itemized. The Bank is usable in its present state, but even greater utility can be achieved when each resource is indexed and cross referenced to the competency statements in the DECAS. Retrieval of resources matched to competency statements is of inestimable value to the formulation of the PDP plans. It is anticipated that eventually an executive will be able to access the Bank through remote terminals in order to identify available training resources related to specific competencies that are in turn referenced to diagnosed competencies and ultimately linked to needs for further training and development.

Given the comprehensive nature of the system, developed as materials are matched to the competency statements, it is not unlikely that gaps will occur where resources are simply not available. This implies that a continuing search for needed materials will become a necessary part of the NEDC operations. Education Service Centers could play an important role here. They could be involved not only in the development of training programs but also serve as resource centers for existing materials. ESCs already serve as media centers for school districts in their region. All centers have media collections and distribution systems that have operated since their inception. It is envisaged that the potential of this existing system for NEDC use would be expanded to include resource materials for professional training.

*Judith G. Loredo, Ben M. Harris, and David S.G. Carter*

### Alternative Training Models

Three training models have been postulated by the Texas project team. Field comparisons across the models to ascertain their efficacy should be conducted at a later date, although it seems reasonable to assume that all three are likely to be effective in varying degree for some executives in specific circumstances. Accordingly, perfecting materials and procedures and determining their efficacy and operational limitations become the foci for evaluation of the models' effectiveness, against the criteria of meaningfulness, practicality and affordability as well as efficiency and effectiveness.

The three basic training models developed thus far include:

(i)     The Self-directed Study Model
(ii)    The Directed Study Group Model
(iii)   The Continuous Development Model

Their rationales and basic features are outlined in the following sections.

*Self-directed Study Model*

Professional development needs are raised initially by individual executives working singly when they review and reassess their own professional growth planning needs. This model has the potential to be widely used because of its inherent informality and flexibility. The underlying rationale for its use is that many executives are self-directing, intrinsically motivated and can recognize and articulate their needs without external assistance. Having done this, the assumption is that they are able to organize and facilitate their own learning in significant and unique ways.

The basic features of this model incorporate those minimum requirements and expectations needed to maintain the integrity of this approach to self-development. Individuals are encouraged to initiate a variety of activities selected and sequenced in accordance with their preferred learning style. In NEDC settings, commitment is needed from individual executives to remain actively engaged with this model for a reasonable developmental and growth period of say two years.

The basic structure and organization of this model is loosely defined and is guided by the individual's needs and interests. The executives are empowered to develop their own professional program plans as well as to select and sequence activities in which they need and/or wish to participate. The individual evaluates his/her own progress toward the achievement of professional growth targets and personally determines the need for reassessment.

Suggested professional development program activities could incorporate mentoring, independent research and reading, viewing video tapes, attending conferences and visiting school sites. The model when implemented as intended requires the formal completion of a Professional Development Plan and timely and ready access to training resources on individual demand. It also establishes the means for scheduling, organizing and directing periodic reviews of each executive's progress toward completion of the professional development plan. Over a career span, the executive is encouraged to return to the diagnostic assessment process periodically at will as a part of a continuous process of learning, growth and development.

### The Directed Study Group Model

The derivation of this model at the Texas pilot site is based on experiences gained through working with an ongoing group of thirty superintendents and college professors (CSP Fellows). In this model, after initial individual diagnosis, groups comprising individuals with similar professional development needs are formed. Its distinguishing feature is the formation and maintenance of a small group in which synergistic processes are used to effect learning. It allows for collective decision-making but in ways that are sensitive to and can accommodate the needs of individuals within the group as well as the group as a whole.

Group maintenance is crucial to support ongoing individual development in this model. An important consideration for planners when operationalizing it, is that training activities need to be designed with sufficient breadth to accommodate individual differences while taking maximum advantage of group norms and dynamics. The model allows for a facilitator to be selected, for example, from Education Service Centers, business and industry, and the universities, who would participate in and enhance the activities of a functioning group-oriented approach to professional development.

In the directed study group model the professional development program would be characterized by the following sorts of activities: networking, group discussion, special group activities such as research projects, material development, material evaluation, materials refinement, and monthly scheduled meetings for sharing experiences, review and planning mutually supportive activities.

### The Continuous Professional Development Model

This pattern of organization provides for small group activities, independent self-study and mentoring. Periodic meetings for sharing with individuals is also possible as well as conferencing with project and/or school staff. Evaluation of the professional growth process is accomplished through the use of structured instruments such as questionnaires. Protocols accommodate the selection of one or more scholars/practitioners, individuals from business and industry, to assist individuals and the group with their training and in meeting their needs for leadership development.

This model is something of a hybrid from the other two and features a highly individualized approach to professional development, based in this case on the preliminary DECAS workshop outcomes and guided formally and explicitly by the Professional Development Program plan. The latter is evolved by following the four-stage planning sequence previously listed above. The model uses a broad range of experiential alternatives, selected eclectically and pragmatically, that allow for the formation of groups for some specific training purposes, used in conjunction with separate or individualized activities where and when these are deemed necessary. As in the Self-directed Model, mentoring, coaching and networking are regarded as essential components for its successful operation, but more structure and organization is embedded in the latter approach in order to optimize the effectiveness of sequenced activities in a needs-specific way.

The model in operation is identified by its requirement for diagnosis to be the precursor and *primary focus* for guiding professional development. Here activities organized on a group basis are harmonized with the needs focus of individuals within the group. This implies that group arrangements would have to be sufficiently flexible to facilitate the meeting of precisely defined individual needs as well as sufficiently structured to accommodate the group's aspirations and processes for directed study.

Professional development activities are typified by the use of computer software programs, courseware study materials, audio visual tapes, books, visits to schools, mentoring conferences, projects on-the-job as well as group review, attending workshops or seminars and special workshops tailored to meet individual needs. The list is illustrative rather than comprehensive.

For the systematic development of leadership competencies regardless of location and context, the models previously described, when used discretely or in combination, are likely to have more power and efficacy if they are supported by, and integrated with, new learning technologies. An illustrative sample of these, together with their potential, is addressed in the following section.

### Innovative Learning Technologies

It is now self-evident that a significant shift has occurred in the United States from an industrial-based economy to a technological-based economy in a global information society. As a consequence of this shift now, and in the foreseeable future, one thing is clear — information and the ability to access it is power. Those who can access information, use information, transform information and create information will be distinctly advantaged on all the indices of success that accrue to a complex technological society. Those who cannot create and transform information will be dependent on those who can. The significance of the latent power embodied in accessing and using information in education has been developing at least over the course of the last decade, and the point is now well recognized if not (yet) comprehensively addressed by the public education system.

Under this scenario the kind of leadership needed for the 1990's and beyond, that guides us to the New Learning Society, is currently the subject of intense debate. Among other things receptivity to the notion that virtually anything can be learned for any reason on virtually any topic at any location has to become embedded in the public consciousness. Not only does the new information technology make this assertion possible, but as far as our schools are concerned, advances in technology in conjunction with an associated range of skills needed to manage information, presents us with some quite revolutionary learning imperatives.

An educational response to this situation requires a close examination of the nature of that type of leadership required to meet the challenges presented by new information-rich environments. Stearn (1968) has pointed out that new technologies construct a totally new environment, and that this radically alters the way we use our senses and thus the way we act and react to things. If we accept this premise, then the restructuring that necessarily occurs as a consequence of introducing new technology alters our entire lives, as it is intended to.

In the context of professional development it is necessary to distinguish between that technology specifically designed for use in learning tasks and the use of technology to enhance, manage and at times make learning possible. Both of these conceptions concerning the application of technology to the enhancement of learning and its delivery are germane to operationalizing the NEDC. The use of innovative technology for maintaining communication, monitoring progress and delivering training at the point of need is given special attention in each of the models described in the preceding section. The infrastructure and means for utilizing at least a few technologies such as interactive video for special training purposes is a vital assumption underpinning the use of the models in remote locations. A wide variety of telecommunications systems will necessarily be required in a fully developed NEDC. These have the capacity to be used as tools with which to teach and to provide for communication between adult learners who are widely displaced geographically and possibly isolated too. Experiences gained in the use and evaluation of these systems, by executives, also constitutes an important knowledge base for them since they will have to consider the effective use of related technologies in the schools. Some possibilities for new information technologies and their professional applications are summarized below.

**Computer-based Assessment** — This application utilizes the concept of an assessment center where individuals undergo intensive evaluation of their administrative skills. Computer networks can provide a variety of self-administered exercises in order to ascertain skill levels, provide insights into administrative styles and create databases for monitoring progress based on individualized personal development plans. Although some assessment techniques, for instance in-basket and structured role play, will continue to be used in live settings, it is anticipated that computer-based assessment will become an important if not essential aspect for optimizing time and effort by participants in NEDC processes where they are isolated and/or geographically dispersed.

**Database Access** — It is envisaged that a variety of databases will be accessed using the personal computer as a remote terminal. In addition to existing bibliographic sources, such as ERIC or Psychological Abstracts, participants will be able to query databases such as LEAD Centers' resource banks to locate materials and/or to access the regional service centers for locating, ordering and receiving print and non-print materials.

**Management DataBase** — Once these are established they would rely heavily on computer access for management of assessment data, word processing, personnel and participant files, budget information, travel and meeting schedules, etc. Having remote access to this sort of information from terminals (subject to conventional security procedures) would be needed to operate efficiently.

**Television/Teleconferencing** — Current technology provides for teleconferencing for both small and large conferences utilizing telephone-based conference calls. It would be of particular utility in its application to the Continuous Professional Development Model previously described in this chapter.

A wide variety of video materials are available for use both for communications applications and for skills development activities. Some materials are already available and others will no doubt be created. Possibilities for resource development include locally-produced video tapes of guest speakers and panel discussions, video tapes demonstrating managerial skills and the provision of remote access to national and international conference presentations.

Existing telecast and narrowcast programs (such as those produced by PBS for business executives) have a potential for use by executives in order to gain an understanding of contemporary issues for the purpose of consciousness raising, and alternatively for use as a formal training medium.

**Facsimile Document Exchange** — Each participating executive acquires access to a facsimile machine for the purpose of transmitting and receiving print material. Hard copies can then be used to create document files for rapid dissemination when timely print or graphics materials need to be sent to mentors, significant others or the members of an operating study group.

**Computer-based Document Exchange** — This application enables participating executives to send and receive documents to and from multiple destinations, including print as well as data files.

**Computer-based Instruction** — Utilization of CBI allows participants to retrieve and use software designed to provide new knowledge and information to learners and the acquisition and practice of specific skills as needed. Some of this software might be downloaded for local use while other packages are intended for interactive use with a host computer. It is anticipated that CBI would be augmented with video tape and laser disks for developing the higher order thinking skills of problem finding and problem solving.

**Electronic Mail** — Existing facilities allow for transmission of daily memoranda, letters and other print-based communication by this medium including electronic bulletin boards, and a range of other facilities available on international networks such as Compuserve and Internet.

### *Future Use of Technology*

The practical application of currently available technologies requires some creative thinking about how and where the initial preparation and further development of school system executives might occur. Simply stated, new information technologies must be utilized creatively for maximum success in realizing more individualized approaches to the professional development of administrators. Just as society can no longer entertain the notion of excellence with respect to student teaching and learning using obsolete technology, it can no longer accept inadequate delivery mechanisms for the preparation of those executives tasked with leading the nation's public education systems. In order to meet this requirement, new technologies have to be intelligently applied using appropriate models to both individualized and team learning processes and contexts.

In a fast moving high technology environment, projections will require modification in the light of further advances and increasing sophistication in the application of technology (especially remote access) to executive professional development. Further consideration in this area might include some, any, or all of the following:

**Video Conferencing** — Two-way video conferencing, using digitally coded signals distributed over telephone lines in order to accommodate transactions between four to six distant sites, could be utilized for group instruction.

**Satellite Video Conferences** — Programs developed for national audiences as well as special purpose conferences could be held. Programs may take the form of a traditional presentation followed by question and answer using phone return to regional programs that capitalize on existing interactive systems.

**Computer-based Network** — Using a personal computer with a phone modem link to a computer-based network, participants would be able to extend their knowledge base in much the same way as they do now by attending conferences or holding staff meetings. New digital distribution systems and computer peripherals, such as CD-ROM, magnify the ability of executives to extend the limits of their intellectual capacities.

The conceptualization of executive development within a geographic network of institutions and nationally distributed learning centers, places a heavy reliance on communication and interactive technologies in order to service both individual needs and the coordination of effort in team situations. It is also necessary in order to:

(a) use effective tools to plan, develop, conduct and manage comprehensive executive professional development; and,

(b) help individuals learn about existing and emergent telecommunications/ information processing systems so that current and future leaders may invest wisely in technology to improve the effectiveness of schools and school systems.

## A Process-Oriented Continuous Change Model

The educational response to pressures for reform of administrator programs shows a trend emerging toward more clinical, field-based inductively-oriented approaches. This is much needed and admirable, but in the search for professionally-oriented programs seeking to take advantage of professional wisdom there is a danger that the pendulum may swing too far, rejecting theory altogether and losing some of the better aspects of more traditional approaches to administrator preparation in the press for reform and restructuring. There is an incipient danger here of throwing out the same baby with the bathwater. Miskel (1990), citing Murphy and Hallinger (1987), reports among other things a growing disenchantment with the theory movement and increasing dissatisfaction with the university training model. Before this is allowed to move too far, this is addressed in a number of chapters in this book, since educational administration as an applied field of endeavor *does* have a body of coherent professional knowledge that is a fruitful area of enquiry and research in the university tradition.

In an environment of reform it is important to establish in the public consciousness that educational administration is a profession, and as such, is underpinned by a dynamic and revisionary knowledge base, specialized high order skills and clearly recognizable professional practices and behaviors. The utilization of these occurs ethically in the enactment of leadership responsibilities. No less important to any concept of executive development is the implicit obligation of school system administrators themselves to take some personal responsibility for the upgrading of their profession.

Stemming from these sorts of considerations, in order to unify practice with theory across pre- and in-service levels of professional preparation and

*Figure 7.1: Content spiral*

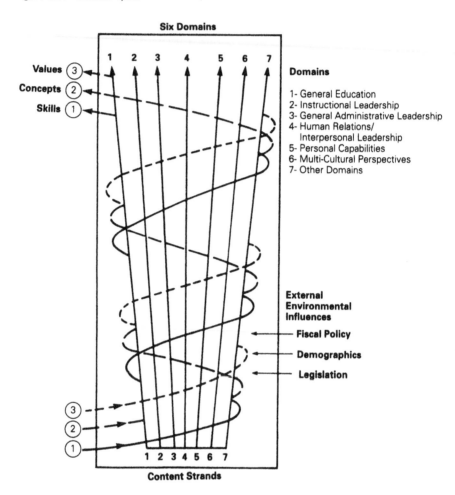

**Six Domains**

**Domains**

1- General Education
2- Instructional Leadership
3- General Administrative Leadership
4- Human Relations/
   Interpersonal Leadership
5- Personal Capabilities
6- Multi-Cultural Perspectives
7- Other Domains

Values ③
Concepts ②
Skills ①

**External
Environmental
Influences**

Fiscal Policy

Demographics

Legislation

**Content Strands**

development, Texas researchers developed a professional curriculum process model for the design of administrator preparation programs and their implementation. Its purpose is to give form and structure to more individualized approaches to developing leadership competencies in conjunction with the professional knowledge base, to legitimize a specialized curriculum in ways capable of withstanding professional scrutiny, and to operationalize the model over the whole of an executive's career span from initial preparation and induction to exit and/or retirement from the profession. The model, in its essential form, is described below. It is based on the notion that professional preparation, learning and development takes place in three dimensions, namely, *content* (professional knowledge), learning *processes* and learning *contexts*. It is also believed that a generic model should allow these to be combined in various ways to meet the individual needs, strengths and weaknesses of those participating in the courses and programs developed from the

*Figure 7.2: Experiential spiral*

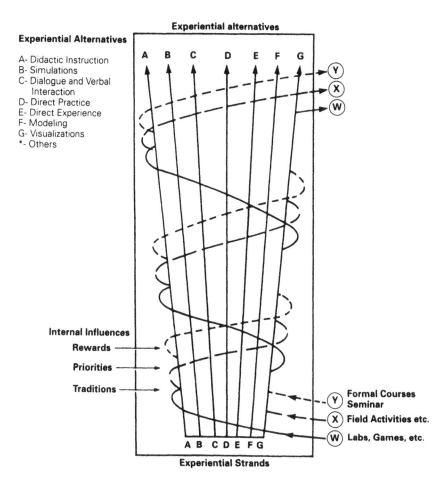

**Experiential alternatives**

**Experiential Alternatives**

A- Didactic Instruction
B- Simulations
C- Dialogue and Verbal
    Interaction
D- Direct Practice
E- Direct Experience
F- Modeling
G- Visualizations
*- Others

**Internal Influences**

**Rewards**

**Priorities**

**Traditions**

Ⓨ **Formal Courses**
   **Seminar**
Ⓧ **Field Activities etc.**
Ⓦ **Labs, Games, etc.**

**Experiential Strands**

Continuous Change Model. (When following the description, frequent reference should be made to Figures 7.1, 7.2 and 7.3).

While claims are made for the model's utility as an in-service device, for the purposes of exposition, the following description relates mainly to pre-service preparation programs. In the first instance the development of a model preparation program for school executives is theoretically conceived in terms of dual spirals presented diagrammatically in Figures 7.1, 7.2 and 7.3 (q.v.).

A *content spiral* (Figure 7.1) is utilized to guide the continuous development of executives with respect to leadership skills and competencies, concepts, understandings, and values. The content strands are subject to change via additions and modifications to the strands, because of the revisionary nature of the professional knowledge base previously alluded to. An *experiential* spiral (Figure 7.2) parallels the content spiral and guides the selection of teaching methods and learning experiences related in turn to content. Six content strands are defined as

*Figure 7.3: Interaction between content and experiential strands*

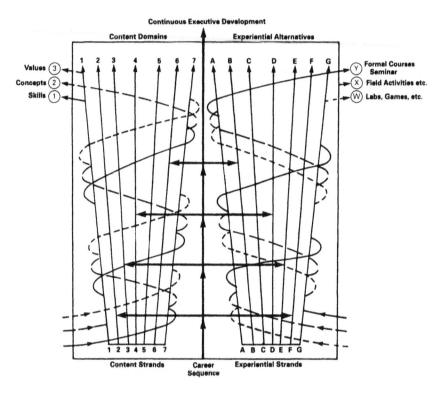

tasks, capabilities, and pervasive issues challenging school leaders at the senior executive level. The appendix presents one example of a completed set of performance descriptors in the instructional leadership domain.

The special challenge presented to professors of educational administration in colleges of education concerned with pre-service preparation, and mentors at the in-service level, is to identify specific skills, competencies, concepts and values of prime importance at various stages of career development for executives in a range of positions across different contexts. A third component in the model recognizes that learning contexts consist of a set of *experiential strands*. The latter are defined as 'distinctive forms of experience structured for effecting learning'. Each strand represents a kind of experience which logically has a special contribution to make in facilitating context-related learning of one type or another.

The conceptual model has to be fully tested to confirm the efficacy of various teaching-learning configurations represented by the spirals, although it has been operationalized in the Cooperative Superintendency Program at the University of Texas at Austin and is described as a case study in Chapter 8. To illustrate the point, a configuration could include vertical problem solving teams, diagnostic assessment of performance capabilities, formal and informal mentoring and technological applications to self-instruction and distance learning. It needs to be kept in mind here that the spirals focus on administrator initial preparation programs linked to and also encompassing a career development sequence of indeterminate length, in which continuous professional development is taken to be desirable and essential to leadership success.

The internal and external forces that inevitably interact with and shape the character of the training programs also influence the executives themselves as they progress in their careers. The model is designed to be responsive to change and infinitely flexible to both accommodate and direct the forces of change. The clear and careful specification of strands of content and experience serve to offer strength, continuity and robustness to the program. Whims, fads, mandates, and political and economic movement may, on occasion, be detrimental to the longer term needs of society. Recognizing this, the Continuous Change Model is designed to allow for the flexible adaptation of context, content and process to changing requirements for leadership. It also filters certain pressures and forces evident in the turbulence of modern educational environments that may be passing phenomena and diversionary, and thus potentially wasteful of energy and resources.

Interactions between the two spirals, shown as double-tipped arrows in figure 7.3 show the dynamic nature of the conceptual model presented here. Interaction between the spirals and internal and external forces is also shown in the figure. Just as the content strands and the experiential strands provide stability in representing enduring factors associated with leadership behavior on the one hand, and adult learning on the other, so, too, the spirals offer flexibility in their mutual interaction with each other and with the needs of individual executives. To translate the model into practice, formally structured graduate seminars can become a vehicle for learning, drawing on one strand for concepts related to power and another for concepts related to communications. These can be focussed quite differently for library research, assignments and individual presentations. It can thus be seen that there is inherent flexibility in the design of the model for a variety of interpretations resulting in different program alternatives, yet maintaining the basic integrity of the overarching design.

A variety of context variables will inevitably set limits, influence changes, and restrict alternatives in the practical operation of administrator preparation programs. The capacity of the model needs to be checked for its ability to accommodate to both externally and internally induced forces of change and its responsiveness to changed and changing circumstances in ways that, while avoiding conformity, maintain continuity and cumulation in learning sequences.

### Conclusion

The theme of this chapter has been on learning for professional development and growth for the purpose of developing leadership competencies. This is conceived to take place at entry to the profession and continues in an ongoing way. For this to be realized on a grand scale, structured learning opportunities have to be made readily accessible to senior executives and presented in a form that takes into account the 'pressure cooker' world of superintendents. The application of new information technologies in conjunction with appropriate learning models referenced to personal contexts and preferred learning styles may assist greatly in this respect. Necessarily they must be quickly brought to bear with increasing power in effecting the ideal of a continuous professional development and guidance system that can be made available to all senior executives in the public education sector.

Effective leadership development is most likely to occur when individual strengths and weaknesses are identified and programs tailored to individual needs in a highly focussed way. Assessment center methods provide one means for conducting diagnoses in powerful ways. This approach requires some modification, however, in order to move diagnoses to internal frames of reference in which self-energized executives, with assistance, generate their own formative data to construct profiles of personal strengths and weaknesses. These data can then be used for personal decision-making for professional growth and action planning. It is a fundamental philosophy underpinning this approach that individual executives maintain confidentiality and control over their own data, reflecting as it does sensitive individual performances in easily identifiable areas of professional knowledge and competence. Further, in linking this philosophy and related theory to practical decision-making in order to develop professional curricula and shorter in-service programs, the last section of this chapter described the Continuous Change Model. This process model is tentative in nature and requires further validation in operation, but it is a first step toward connecting practice with theory as a basis for program development in a justifiable way.

Issues were also raised in this chapter concerning the problematic nature of leadership training and development and enhancing capacities in this area. The argument presented was that this should commence with initial selection, training and induction to the profession. Some of the issues raised in regard to this and the essential characteristics of pre-service preparation programs are taken up at greater length in the next chapter.

*Chapter 8*

# Enter the Neophyte: Preparing Administrators for Leadership Roles

*Judith G. Loredo and David S.G. Carter*

The impending retirement of large numbers of school administrators, who will have to be replaced during the remaining years of this century, focusses attention on selection and recruitment issues and the extra demands this will place on already scarce educational resources. The replacement of experienced superintendents and senior central office executives, together with the significance of their roles for improving standards of excellence in education, provides imperatives for upgrading methods of administrator selection and preparation for leadership roles within the profession.

Important aspects of screening, selection and preparation of neophyte administrators are addressed in this chapter. Also some issues are raised by the fact that 40 per cent of US school administrators are likely to retire by as early as 1995. Finally, the provision of a model illustrative of the type of program that has to evolve to integrate more closely the realm of theory with the realities of practice is described. This exemplar has implications for university field-based professional schools preparation programs and can be adapted to a number of different contexts.

**Imperatives for Change in Graduate Preparation Programs**

In a groundswell of rising public discontent, persistent and strident calls for the reform of administrator preparation abound. In concerns they appear to emanate from higher education institutions, state departments of education, professional associations and governors, as well as private individuals and significant others within the profession of educational administration itself. The pervasiveness of a general dissatisfaction with the status quo is captured in numerous reports, position papers, monographs and public statements, beginning in the late 1970s and culminating in 1983 when *A Nation at Risk* was published (Firestone, 1990). A number of reports appeared in quick succession including, significantly, the report of the National Commission on Excellence in Educational Administration in 1987, and latterly the 1989 report of the National Policy Board for Educational Administration entitled *Improving the Preparation of School Administrators: An Agenda for Reform*. In sum, they point to the fact that inadequacies exist in the ideology and organization of university curricula designed to prepare school system leaders.

Perceived deficiencies have now reached critical proportions if the voices from the community of interest are to be believed. The American Association of Colleges of Teacher Education (AACTE) notes 'Dramatic changes are needed in programs to prepare school administrators if they are to lead their schools and faculties rather than just manage them' (1988).

This theme is echoed by Hoyle (1989a and 1989b) who raises criticisms of preparation programs for school system administrators because the former are frequently fragmented, unfocussed and lacking a carefully sequenced curriculum. Rather than being a clearly articulated systematic program of studies, the preparation process is characterized as a hit or miss agglomeration of courses and institutions, which tend to be selected haphazardly by potential school administrators.

It is claimed that the university ethos is itself part of the problem (Clifford and Guthrie, 1988). Schools of education led by some high status universities, short change practitioners and yet infrequently produce research findings useful for the guidance of policy makers and practitioners. This tends to occur because of the high priority emphasis placed on canons of research and scholarship, using social and behavioral paradigms, subscribed to by elite universities. They provide the model for others seeking higher status to emulate. While the pursuit of knowledge is commendable and in keeping with the fundamental purpose of a university, within professional schools such as education, an overemphasis on high status discipline-based knowledge at the expense of other considerations has generally served to alienate professional executives and their organizations in the public schools from the universities. On the face of it, this is because senior school system executives, whose concerns lie in the field of practice, consider their professional and practical needs are not being met by academe.

The news, however, is not *totally* bad. Practicing administrators do not all subscribe to the views circulated by the critics of university-based administrator preparation programs, although their voices are subdued. A 1987 study by the National Center for Education Information, cited by Hoyle (1989a), noted that '. . . one in four superintendents and principals said that their university preparation was "excellent"; some 50 per cent said that it was "pretty good"; only 1 per cent of the superintendents and 2 per cent of the principals described their preparation as "poor" ' (p. 376). These findings are supported by Cunningham and Hentges (1982), although they also noted that superintendents in their study were critical of some specific courses they had encountered, as well as highlighting deficiencies in the area of field experience they considered important to integrating theory with practice.

Notwithstanding, the fundamental criticism of administrator preparation remains in the discrepancy between what potential administrators learn in formal university-based graduate programs and what they need to function successfully in the field (Griffiths, Stout and Forsyth, 1988). In short, administrators claim they are inadequately prepared for the realities of work in the pressure cooker world of the superintendency. Adding fuel to the fire, professional associations such as the American Association of School Administrators (AASA) and the National Policy Board for Educational Administration (NPBEA), are becoming increasingly articulate and strident in voicing their concerns. Leaders are convinced that practitioners within the profession itself must have an increasing say and a larger role to play in defining standards, as well as contributing to the design and implementation of preparation programs that seek to put the standards into effect.

Under the rubric of educational reform significant others have called for the restructuring of the school as a workplace (National Governor's Association, 1986).

While the discussions in supporting research have focussed primarily on the school site, any adjustments made to teacher and principal roles also have implications for the roles of superintendents and other school system central office staff. For administrator preparation to remain aligned with the redefinition of roles and associated educational restructuring, fundamental changes to administrator preparation assumes something of the importance of a survival imperative. Responsiveness of graduate preparation programs to dynamic educational environments requires continuous evaluation and feedback between the content, context and processes of programs, and changing professional requirements drawn from the world of practice. In reconceptualizing professional work roles, practitioners and scholars alike share a widely-held belief that the time-honored practices for preparing and selecting individuals for these roles in school systems are inadequate (March, 1977; National Commission on Excellence in Education, 1987; Pitner, 1982). The National Commission on Excellence in Educational Administration (Hawley, 1988) has stated that administrator preparation programs should be modelled upon professional, as distinct from academic, schools to include components of theoretical knowledge, applied research and supervised practice in clinical settings. Administrator preparation, ideally, should become a sequenced and mentored path directed toward helping prospective administrators internalize practice/theory relationships, be accomplished in blocks of full-time study, be organized across cohorts to develop collegiality and shared professional values, and be a joint responsibility of the university and the profession. The Commission also argues that cooperation between universities and school agencies is *essential* to develop relevant and meaningful learning experiences, and to select administrators from a talent pool of high quality candidates. Together, these recommendations represent a radical departure from current practices evidenced in the preparation of school administrators located in many graduate schools of educational administration.

The 1987 Report of the Commission proposed five strands around which curricula concerned with administrator preparation should be organized. These are:

(i)  The study of administration
(ii)  The study of the technical core of educational administration and the acquisition of vital skills
(iii)  The application of research findings and methods to problems
(iv)  Supervised practice
(v)  Demonstration of competence

They provide at least one legitimate organizing framework as a starting point for the total restructuring of administrator preparation curricula. The days of 'disjointed incrementalism', i.e., of tinkering around with programs in a piecemeal fashion, is redundant to the needs of present and future school system executives. This theme of what needs to be done is visited again later in the chapter, after speculating further about perceived deficiencies with the current situation as reflected in the contemporary literature and voiced by prominent people.

*Judith G. Loredo and David S.G. Carter*

## The Two Cultures of Theory and Practice: Once More Into . . .

The increased public vocalization of work-related concerns by professional groups and associations, and their willingness to become more involved in debate over matters of controversy surrounding administration preparation and induction, is a relatively recent phenomenon. The public mood for widespread reform is self-evident, is reflected in the bills of many state legislatures and made tangible through the inception of Leadership in Educational Administration Development (LEAD) projects within the states. Their *raison d'être* with federal support has been to initiate and develop creative approaches to the improvement of preparation programs as well as to the ongoing education and further professional development of executives over the whole of their careers.

Closer examination of the public critique levied by professional administrators and academics and driven by community concerns quickly confirms that all is not well. Disagreement occurs, however, over the specific causes for perceived inadequacies, as well as the means for correcting deficiencies and the sort of initiatives required to generally improve the system. Given, at source, the normative nature of the educative enterprise, values conflicts expressed in the public's concern for educational reform (not least in the preparation of potential administrators for leadership roles) are to be expected, and this can be regarded as a healthy sign in the working through of democratic principles.

Within academia itself, divisions about developing an appropriate theoretical focus versus the development of professional skills and competencies also occur. It should be noted that the waters are very muddied around the links between theory and practice in many professional schools, not only in departments of educational administration and educational leadership. In law faculties, for example, a tension exists between educating students *in* the law (which is predominantly an academic function), and preparation for *the practice of law* (which is vocational and professional in its orientation). In this example the academic and professional functions appear to be discrete, but are by no means mutually exclusive at the level of practice. The legal profession itself assumes a major role in the induction and further credentialling of newly qualified lawyers, but there is also considerable internal debate about what the role of the university actually is, and ought to be, concerning the adequate provision of competent lawyers to meet societal needs.

Guthrie and Clifford (1989) regard the ambivalent role played by elite schools of education in research-oriented universities as a significant contributory factor to the current lack lustre situation in educational administrator preparation (see also the report of the National Policy Board for Educational Administration, 1989). It is contended that the coping strategies of select schools of education, in their bid for survival, have been less than successful — even dysfunctional. The strategies that Guthrie and Clifford identify are (i) a search for legitimacy as a social science; (ii) academic intensification; and (iii) interdisciplinary appeasement, and each strategy is appraised below.

*Educational Administration as Social Science*

In the search for scientific legitimacy and access to high status, discipline-based knowledge-elite institutions, it is claimed, seek to employ social scientists as members of faculty. Where appointments have been accompanied by an academic's general lack of experience in the schools and with administration in a school system, a general disaffection with academic performances in educational fields by practitioners has tended to occur. From a university perspective the appointment has resulted in the increased research of scholars rather than practitioners' productivity and the policy, therefore, is regarded as being successful.

From a professional point of view, one of the identifying features of a profession *qua* profession, is a dynamic and revisionary core of knowledge and expertise. Whether this lies in regarding education as a branch of social science and its attendant paradigms, or whether education is a quite distinct and distinctive field of endeavor in its own right remains a moot point between academics and educators.

Unlike medicine, law, engineering and other high status professions, in educational administration there has been little or no attempt to systematically build theory into practice, to generate 'grounded theory' or develop a theory of practice (praxis). Clearly, it is both naive and misguided to try and sustain the argument that abstract disciplined knowledge can be called upon directly to guide practical decisions under operational conditions. In the practice of educational administration it was never intended that substantive knowledge acquired in preparatory courses would 'tell me what to do' in this or that set of circumstances, although the search for recipes underpinned by a technicist rationality is not easily abandoned. The realities and the vagaries of human nature are, however, far too complex for this 'idea' to be realizable (or even tenable) across the board.

For a number of professions, empirical observations form the building blocks of theory which in turn helps to shape practice, to provide the context for practice, and, if authentic, to give meaning to practice. This is its proper and legitimate role in the development and exercise of professional knowledge. There is nothing so practical as a good theory (Dewey, 1929) and there is evidence to show that superintendents and principals believe that research *can* make contributions to the profession of educational administration as evidenced by this book.

### Academic Intensification

Guthrie and Clifford (*ibid.*) also note that an even more widely practiced strategy, related to the search for legitimacy in prestigious departments and schools, is the adoption of a scholarly orientation realized through a theoretical emphasis allied with the employment of abstract empiricism as the main means for advancing the frontiers of knowledge.

The form this elitism takes, as a rule, is the adoption of research and teaching styles of the academic, in contrast to the practice and service-oriented styles of professional clinically-based practitioners. A scholarly orientation tends to be confirmed by way of the PhD degree being seen as the *sine qua non* of academic achievement and research training and accorded higher status over the EdD with its professional orientation. It is noteworthy and reflects professional concerns, that the National Policy Board for Educational Administration (NPBEA) in its proposed 'Agenda for Reform' recommended that the EdD be a prerequisite to national certification and state licensure for full-time administrators who are placed in charge of a school or school system. This stance is clearly counter to the prevailing orthodoxy of academically-oriented departments and schools of education in many universities and colleges. Note though, Murphy and Hallinger (1989) caution that newer inductive approaches to administrator preparation should integrate these with the best of traditional approaches, rather than simply rejecting the latter. They also point to the need to ensure that programs are based on justifiable theoretical bases.

Hoyle (1989a) has come down in favor of the abandonment of the present university-based, research-oriented preparation model that produces PhD degrees altogether. He has advocated the adoption of a professional-studies model that is at the same time more intellectually demanding *and* more practical and would lead eventually to the award of the EdD. According to Hoyle, while the EdD ranks in status with the MD, DDS, and JD, none of these enjoys the same public esteem and prestige as the PhD and this is the very qualification and values set elite schools of education seek in prospective candidates when appointing new staff.

### Interdisciplinary Appeasement

This strategy manifests when schools of education in their search for status and legitimacy become subservient to other disciplines and departments. The form commonly taken is a joint interdisciplinary appointment to the field of education and a discipline area. The justification for this is that such appointments act as bridges between the areas of disciplined knowledge and their application to school settings. In this way they add intellectual substance to the practice of education.

The strategy, however, tends to work against itself because of some inherent problems such as the academic being required to fulfil the norms of two departments, in which the claim to knowledge of each and the attendant reward systems may be quite different. Also, when the appropriate conditions prevail, scholars tend to ally themselves with the parent discipline(s). Frequently it is here that the core identity of the scholar is vested rather than lying in a field of professional knowledge. In this regard Guthrie and Clifford (1989) assert:

> When joint appointments fail, the loss to education may extend beyond
> the personal interests and research energies of faculty members who return
> to the cognate disciplines. The failures of joint appointments can seem to
> certify the low status of education . . . (p. 381)

With the broad sweep of the field now in view it is evident that two cultures have been created with different value sets, reward systems and incompatible perspectives. In the field of practice, effective leadership is acknowledged and rewarded accordingly. Academic recognition, however, is based on achieving excellence in standards of scholarship and research productivity the main indices of which are one's ability to attract research funds and publish in highly regarded research journals. Current tensions then are related to the incompatibility of the two cultures as they try to coexist within the same institution.

While there are common concerns for the preparation of future school system leaders, there appears to be little chance of building a common culture that reconciles the practice-theory dichotomy within existing institutional structures and constraints. The old assumptions upon which the delivery of education was based have already passed us by, and the same can be said for the selection, preparation and induction of our future school system leaders. Simply to maintain the *status quo* is to regress in this situation. Reconciliation of the two cultures is a problem requiring our immediate attention together with the provision of adequate resources in order to put this into effect. In dealing with extant problems, a reconceptualization of administrator preparation is required, that extends well beyond current piecemeal tinkering with graduate administrator preparation programs in order to accommodate them to existing structures and institutional arrangements.

### An Agenda for Reform

With increasing broadly-based recognition and articulation of the philosophical and structural problems of administrator preparation, constructive recommendations are beginning to emerge. The fact that many of these appear to be based on reviews of a fragmented literature, rational analysis and conventional wisdom attests to the extent of the disaffection for the *status quo*; for the pervasiveness of the problems which have been identified; and because of deficits in the available empirical data. A synthesis of the views of scholar-practitioners and recommendations are now addressed.

In its report entitled *School Leadership Preparation, A Preface for Action* (1988), AACTE recommends that programs in educational administration be modelled after 'professional programs' rather than replicate the liberal arts approach to graduate education. Further, that faculty, before appointment, have acquired demonstrable leadership and/or teaching experience in schools. Themes such as these are featured in the recent literature in which a general preference for a professional studies model leaning toward the exemplars of law, medicine and other high status professions is recurrent. Some caution is needed in extrapolating too far. A comprehensive exploration of alternative frameworks is needed within the professional studies conceptual framework. Among other considerations this is in order to avoid premature closure around a 'classical' approach derived from conceptions of an 'ideal' professional preparation seen over the fence to be occurring in other areas. Such a viewpoint is likely to derive from a deficiency model of educational administration compared to the ideal of a profession typified by law or medicine. This perspective is quite different from that of a profession of educational administration developed on its own terms, from its own frames to meet its own needs.

As well as the need to integrate academic study with professional practice, a number of concerns that have been voiced center on the selection and screening of potential administrators; on funding since the scale and pace of reform is likely to be expensive and require the injection of new money in addition to current expenditures; and, as mentioned elsewhere in this book on the derivation of a set of national standards for the profession. There also appears to be a preference for an EdD as the terminal award on completion of an initial graduate qualification, and a rejection of the PhD in education in those programs that attend primarily to the preparation of school leaders. To address these concerns seriously requires a fundamental reorientation to the profession and paradoxically a strengthening rather than a loosening of academic links. As the Holmes Group rightly asserts 'no major occupational undertaking has achieved professional status without an institutional connection to higher education' (Guthrie and Clifford, 1989, p.380). In moving to a more desirable state of affairs it is advocated that the connection to higher education be seen as secondary to the education of practitioners. Faculty members in schools of education *must* also come to understand the culture of schooling if this is to happen.

Thompson (1989) suggests that the education department of major research universities, in particular, should refocus their priorities. Professional education programs for school administrators and teachers, according to him, need to be placed on a par with research efforts and be perceived by scholars as such. Like AACTE Thompson rejects the model of the arts and sciences in which research is elevated to a position of supremacy, and which cannot be allowed to continue to dominate if professional education is to be allowed to flourish in the manner desired by professionals.

Necessarily, the preparation of future leaders should encompass knowledge about, and appreciation of, academic research, including becoming intelligent and critical consumers of the research literature, and appraising its relevance and considered application to the solution of practical problems. Being critical in the sense advocated here means also being able to reject research findings if the methodology is weak, the data inadequate, or the conclusions unwarranted or not supported by the evidence. Developing critical faculties does not require that programs be oriented primarily to the pursuit of academic inquiry. Hoyle (1989a), with his vision regarding the preparation of superintendents for the twenty-first century, also addresses this theme. He recommends that the present university-based, research-oriented, preparation model leading to the award of PhD degrees should be abandoned entirely in favor of a professional studies model that is more intellectually challenging as well as being more practical in its nature and scope. An alternative path needs to be available for research training in which ultimately PhD degrees would be awarded after the completion of programs of study in educational administration that are more specialized and research-oriented than the EdD with an essentially clinical focus.

Hoyle also contends that new partnerships and coalitions among faculty members across related disciplines must be formed. Classes and clinical experiences should be team taught, involving professors of education and educational administration as well as in the social sciences, the humanities and general management, and by leading superintendents who could also serve in a dual role as clinical professors. This combination of expertise and experience could emphasize, as well as exemplify, the development of certain intellectual and academic bases for informed school management.

A relevant professional preparation includes the provision of creative learning situations with a process orientation. Extensive empiricism, including the provision of opportunities for students to conduct systematic observations and to engage in participatory learning experiences in a number of jointly supervised field settings, with ample opportunity for individual reflection and shared experiences with peers, is the ideal. In the process of initial preparation, becoming at ease with information technology and its application is a vital set of skills for the school system executive to acquire. The use of intuition and creativity should be given equal emphasis with the use of rational models of decision-making. As well, school system executives of the future require the most creative minds on campus as mentors. Thus the reward system for professors of education, currently based almost exclusively on research publications, is no longer tenable. Under a professional studies rubric, rewards accrue according to how the quality of one's work in developing school leaders, and of being identified with the sort of executive one turns out. Scholars who model creative, intuitive and entrepreneurial leadership are needed to realize this ideal.

Current university admissions criteria require strengthening in order to attract potential leaders of the highest caliber. The model being suggested is that faculty, in concert with an advisory committee of practicing administrators, should justify the knowledge base to be taught and administrative skills to be acquired and refined; construct verifiable performance indicators; and determine the minimum criteria for admission to, placement in, and completion of, the program. In this regard traditional admissions criteria might be operationalized within the concept of the 'assessment center' (see Chapter 7).

As mentioned elsewhere in this book, the derivation of a set of national standards for the profession is another area of evident need. When formulated and set at an appropriate level they could exercise enough leverage to upgrade the curricula of schools of education striving to adopt national standards. According to Clifford and Guthrie (1988) enforceable national standards for certification would leave individual schools of education little choice but to alter their course offerings and instruction. To be effective this strategy would require a sensitive combination of pressure and support on the part of implementers (McLaughlin, 1990).

Effective implementation of the new model requires the support of increased funding and the injection of resources, both human and material, into reform efforts. It is clear that the interdisciplinary and clinical components of the professional studies model will make it more expensive than traditional preparation programs. Policy makers must realize, or be brought to understand, that an investment outlook is needed because high-quality schooling is inextricably linked to the economic, cultural, and social well-being of society. The health of a state's university system is logically contingent upon that of the public school system.

Structural change of the proportions advocated here will not come easily. The research 'industry' remains well-founded, well-connected and entrenched. Initiating significant change increases workloads, creates anxiety and stress, and may induce a backlash if it does not appear to be working well. Change facilitators need to be ready to cope with resistive factors so as to realize the implementation of the professional studies model, with some bold and new perspectives applied to the preparation programs of school leaders that are both visionary and compensatory. The Cooperative Superintendency Program (CSP) at the University of Texas at Austin exemplifies these considerations and is the focus of the next section.

## Administrator Preparation Program in Texas

Texans have become increasingly aware that their prosperity and societal well-being lie largely in their educational system. The key to its success is effective leadership, as well as being part of the larger state reform movement (Murphy, 1991). The Cooperative Superintendency Program located at the University of Texas Department of Educational Administration at Austin is a response to earlier national and state imperatives to restructure preparation programs for school system administrators. As is evident from national trends, the need for effective preparation programs is intensified by the knowledge that a large number of superintendents in Texas will approach retirement in the next five to ten years.

In developing an appropriate model, faculty at the University of Texas reviewed research describing what superintendent work activity entails. They also conducted further independent research to verify the knowledge and skills identified by Hoyle, English and Steffy (1985), and similarly, the National Association of Secondary School Principals' (NASSP) identification of skills required of school administrators in order to be effective (Collier, 1987; Sclafani, 1987). Faculty used these data, together with the essential components for administrator preparation identified by the National Commission on Excellence in Educational Administration (1987), as the basis for considering graduate program redevelopment. As a starting point in the process of reforming the school executive curriculum four major components were addressed:

(i) the knowledge base and administrative skills required of school managers and leaders were identified, using the available research on the superintendency;

(ii) a situational review of the (then) formal course offerings and resources was conducted. This was in order to determine in which units the application of relevant research findings and methods to the solution of school problems might be most appropriately applied;

(iii) the optimal location of supervised practice activities was reviewed and revised and integrated into the University's doctoral program; and

(iv) considerations regarding the assessment of school executives' competence within the revised frameworks were addressed.

### The School Executive Leadership Program

To give it its full title the Cooperative Superintendency Executive Leadership Program is a faculty response to criticisms emanating from community concerns in Texas about weak program conceptualization, lax recruitment/selection/admissions procedures, poorly articulated program structure, and abstract content divorced from the world of practice. The success with which the CSP initiative has corrected perceived deficiencies is reflected in the national recognition accorded to it by AASA, in 1987, as an exemplary program for administrator preparation. Its uniqueness lies in the cooperative approach adopted between a council of Texas superintendents for public schooling, the Texas Education Agency, and the Department of Educational Administration at the University of Texas at Austin. A major feature of the design is its advanced professional 'resident-in-training' component. Since its original inception, the design has been refined and its program elements renewed over ten cycles of cooperation by the partnership. Latterly this has also included graduating fellows from previous cycles.

The purpose of the Cooperative Superintendency Program is to identify a prospective pool of applicants from a national talent search, and to screen candidates using assessment center methods and the application of other scientifically-based rigorous selection criteria for entry to the program. After successfully completing a program of intensive study and research involving the application of innovative learning activities, combined with a lengthy internship in a management position, fellows are awarded a PhD degree. They then return to the profession of educational administration with expectations that they will rapidly rise to senior executive positions in the superintendency or as central office staff.

Mindful of the previous discussion concerning the upgrading of admissions standards to preparation programs for potential administrators, the remainder of this chapter describes the selection processes and summarizes the main features of the Cooperative Superintendency Program, with which the fellows (i.e., successful candidates in the selection and screening process) are engaged over a two-year cycle from selection to graduation. The purpose of detailing the program is to exemplify how the national agenda for restructuring and reform might be realized in practice. The Cooperative Superintendency Program is, of course, but one interpretation of the national agenda, providing an example of an innovative program in operation, which may possibly serve as a model for other colleges of education considering their own program reforms. It also models the translation and articulation of theory with practice under a professional studies rubric.

The CSP is completed over a twenty-four month period during which university-based coursework and assessment, field research and an internship are integrated with each other in order to develop successful and effective educational leaders. Vital components of the program are the establishment of long-term relationships between participants and experienced mentors from the university, education and business communities, and the development of a research-based plan for recurrent learning and professional growth.

*Screening and Selection of Candidates*

The key to a continually successful program is the selection of promising educational leaders in the first instance. The talent search for CSP candidates is vigorous. Initially, candidates are urged to nominate themselves by completing a standard application form. External nomination is not necessary and has no weight in the selection process. Nominations are encouraged irrespective of race, ethnicity and gender and these considerations apply overall in open competition.

More than 800 nominators within the state and some from interstate, who are in position to identify prospective talented school leaders, are requested to solicit promising candidates and make recommendations to faculty concerning specific individuals. Prospective candidates are then approached directly and invited to apply for entry to the program. Nominators are requested not to screen out prospective applicants because of their assumed non-availability.

A talent search commences in the year preceding the commencement of a new CSP cycle and the identification of finalists is usually completed by early March. They come to Austin for an appraisal seminar in mid-April after which the successful fellows are formally notified, and commence their two-year program in June.

After acknowledgement of an application, the applicant is requested to compile and submit a candidacy portfolio and is supplied with very specific guidelines in order to accomplish this task. The purpose of the portfolio is to allow for initial screening and provide baseline data for the assessment of prospective fellows.

A completed portfolio contains vital information about the candidate in addition to generating personal perspectives derived from a number of different sources. The contents of a candidacy portfolio are listed below:

* A professional/personal curriculum vitae, sufficiently comprehensive to portray the nature of the candidate's administrative career to date, and illustrative of his/her professional development. This goes beyond the simple statement of position and title held. The candidate is also asked to list professional certificates and provide specific information about recent self-development and/or professional development endeavors.
* Complete records of undergraduate and graduate courses taken.
* Professional referees: The names and address of three-five professional referees are required, together with the context in which each has been able to observe the candidate. At least one should be a university professor who can make a disinterested appraisal of the candidate's performance as a student, and at least two should be in a position to comment about the candidate's administrative performance. These reports are received unsighted by the candidate and treated confidentially by appraisers.
* Confirmation of Graduate School Admission Status to the University of Texas at Austin is a prerequisite to entry to the Cooperative Superintendency Program. Documentary evidence that admission to the Graduate School has been granted is also required.
* Evidence of administrative performance and developmental growth in the form of newspaper clippings, citations or awards, printed letters of commendation, employee sheets, authorship of published articles and reports, speeches, evaluation reports and miscellaneous materials produced under the candidate's leadership for use by others. The content, form and manner in which these data are presented is deliberately left open-ended to allow for creative interpretation and presentation.
* A written self-portrait for the benefit of the selection panels, providing each with a personal profile in which the candidate reflects on his/her personal accomplishments and achievements, strengths and weaknesses and an assessment of discrepancy needs when confronted with the prospect of being selected as a fellow. Profile components are provided to assist the candidate in achieving this task, but it is up to individuals to build the portfolio and provide evidence to support their own self-appraisal.

### The Process of Selecting a Fellow

Once a portfolio is received and checked for completeness, referees are approached for their evaluations that are then added to the documentation. Candidacy portfolios are circulated to multiple panelists who assess each applicant independently. Collectively each assessment panel determines a 'finalist' or 'non-finalist' allocation. Candidates who fall into the latter category are informed of this shortly after the decision is made. There is no formal quota on the number of finalists who qualify, but numbers are limited in order to maintain the integrity of the program and the resources needed to support it.

Finalists participate in the whole day appraisal seminar in mid-April. Here assessment center methods are used for selection purposes and include in-basket simulations, presentations on a previously prepared topic, panel interviews and paper-and-pencil tests. Multiple assessors are used throughout the appraisal procedure.

Data obtained from the appraisal seminar together with that contained in the candidacy portfolio are examined summatively by a selection panel consisting of from five-ten members. Individual panelists evaluate each candidate's personal data independently and present his/her judgments to the panel as a whole. The panels are convened for sessions lasting several days. Panel consensus is the general rule adopted for final selection; majority choice tends to be the exception and only occurs in extenuating circumstances. Again unsuccessful finalists are notified immediately and the nomination of successful candidates follows suit. For each cycle the number chosen is usually in the order of ten-fifteen fellows.

### Operation of the Cooperative Superintendency Program

After completing the comprehensive screening and selection process previously described above, all fellows admitted to the program initially undertake additional and varied diagnostic assessment activities. This is in order to determine each fellow's strengths and weaknesses with respect to leadership skills, competencies and the extent of his/her substantive professional knowledge. A combination of leadership assessment instruments drawn from business and industry, as well as instruments that focus on the professional skills of school instructional leadership, are employed in this diagnosis. Data derived from these appraisals are used formatively for developing individualized professional growth plans for fellows. Personal appraisal data greatly assist in the early formulation of an array of pro-fessional experiences of different scope and intensity for each CSP fellow.

Out of the individual growth plans a group plan is constructed to guide further interactive learning activities throughout the remainder of the semester. By this means fellows analyze their personal strengths and weaknesses and learn how to work cooperatively with others in the development and implementation of a plan to achieve mutually shared educational ends.

The cadre of fellows in each new cycle spend the first two semesters as a group in a 'block-of-time' core program. In this way individuals are exposed to theory and research by means of an innovative, holistic and comprehensive program of study and disciplined inquiry. Using personal and group data, a variety of learning opportunities are made available to fellows over the duration of the program in which each can acquire knowledge, skills and competencies matched to his/her needs, interests, background and unique composition of strengths and weaknesses. The program is underscored by a research-based spiral curriculum conceptualized at the University of Texas. The curriculum is organized around competencies and skills, identified and ordered into domains that provide a conceptual framework for leadership; the rationale for this is described in Chapter 7 where it is presented in a generic professional growth context.

There is a logic in the utilization of a research-based professional develop-ment model for use over an executive career span, suitably modified as a curric-ulum framework for preparation programs. A clear advantage of this is that it encourages a closer articulation of the work of the profession with that of the university. Lack of this feature in many programs has been previously alluded to in this chapter and it is a constant source of dissatisfaction with administrator preparation programs as they are currently structured.

During the first two semesters, every effort is made to ensure that theoretical knowledge is combined with 'real world' experiences. In the following two semesters, fellows move from theoretical to practical settings where they gain field-based experiences of several different types. Activities planned for each fellow are tailored to specific areas of need identified through the assessment process and requiring further attention.

Program content is drawn from a variety of disciplines in the liberal arts and social sciences, including their applied forms. Only infrequently are doctoral students in education exposed to the theory, concepts and empirical bases of the various disciplines subsumed under these headings. In the complex world of the superintendency, the intelligent use of knowledge drawn upon eclectically from a range of disciplines and applied to school and school community problems is of fundamental importance to the execution of effective leadership. While universities are especially suited to induct students to the coded forms of knowledge embodied in the disciplines, they are less able on their own to provide opportunities for the application of research findings to the solution of school problems, or to make adequate provision for supervised clinical practice in field settings.

Internship placements are an important aspect of the experiential learning opportunities provided by the Program. While enrolled as a CSP fellow, an individual may spend one-two years as an intern in the Texas Education Agency, Texas Association of School Administrators, or in a number of Independent School District central offices or Education Service Centers, concurrent with their attendance at formal classes. Presently fellows receive an annual salary of $25,500.

In addition to existing faculty, practitioner-scholars, identified as outstanding superintendents in Texas, join with professors to conduct seminars and classes on topics specifically related to their areas of expertise. A wealth of leaders from the local, state and federal levels of government, along with chief executive officers from business and industry, regularly participate as guest lecturers on a variety of subjects related to executive leadership. By this means, fellows are confronted with a range of perspectives on a topic, issue or area of concern. This contrasts with the perspectives offered by a single academic, as is more generally the case in traditional preparation programs. Additionally each fellow gains access to the collective experience of four mentors each chosen from the fields of government, industry, university and public education. At least one of the mentors is involved in the initial diagnostic process described earlier in the chapter, thus providing feedback and support to each fellow from the onset of the program.

During the field experience and dissertation phases, mentors continue to play a key role in the professional preparation and development of fellows via their participation in Peer-Assisted Leadership (PAL). This strategy is modelled along the lines of the program developed for principals by the Far West Laboratory. The PAL program pairs students with practicing superintendents. Partners learn how to collect information about each other by shadowing and conducting reflective interviews, thus PAL activities afford fellows the opportunity to become more intelligent about their own leadership behaviors and those of a peer. PAL participants attend six training sessions and also engage in follow-up activities between training meetings.

Vertical Team Problem Solving provides a further structured pathway for guiding fellows into the world of practice. The function of the vertical problem-solving team is to allow its members to plan and implement school improvement projects. It is a collaborative group comprising members of a school district that include the superintendent, central office administrator, a principal, a teacher, and classified employee, and a school board member. Composition of the team ensures that all levels of the school system are represented in discussions about school problems.

Fellows and faculty members alike join vertical teams as facilitators. In order to undertake this role, they receive specialized training during the first year of their full-time residency. During the second year of the CSP they are afforded opportunities to practice facilitator role behavior in vertical team problem-solving modes in 'live' situations. Engagement with vertical team problem-solving processes by fellows and university staff provides opportunities for training, support and assistance in the development and implementation of school improvement plans. The use of this strategy also serves to close the theory-practice gap by enabling students and staff, as facilitators, to develop, practice and refine interpersonal skills in communication and conflict resolution that are necessary adjuncts to effective leadership.

The Cooperative Superintendency Program is about to commence its twelfth cycle of operation. An index of its success is the high quality of graduating fellows, now in senior executive positions, who maintain contact with the institution and each current cycle of fellows. Collectively they testify to the success of the CSP publicly recognized by the American Association of School Administrators (AASA). The program is kept constantly under review and modified each cycle using the best available evaluation and research data. It is intended that this will continue to make it responsive to changing educational circumstances and professional requirements while going some way to meet the overarching needs of a complex, dynamic and democratic society.

# Chapter 9

# Leadership for Learning — Learning for Leadership

*David S.G. Carter*

The work of the superintendency has changed considerably since the beginning of this century. The early role of the superintendent was that of a single head of the school system, whose primary function was to plan and manage technical operations. The current role is that of administrator who must deal with the complex problems of the organization, at the same time meeting many diverse external needs of the community and dealing with societal pressures, not least those requiring the restructuring and reform of the education system *per se*. An increased press for accountability, competency testing, performance management and a plethora of new mandates has placed increasing and new demands on the already hard pressed executive.

Looking at the changing role requirements and new demands placed on the shoulders of those who are to spearhead necessary restructuring and reform, one point is clear. We cannot develop or evaluate the new leadership required for the next century by applying criteria which were developed for a time and place that no longer exists. Hand in hand with the challenge of rethinking the superintendency leadership role is a problem noted by both researchers and practitioners over the last decade — that the time-honored practices for preparing and selecting individuals for these work roles in school systems is inadequate (Pitner, 1982; National Commission on Excellence in Educational Administration, 1987).

This was both a theme taken up at great length in Chapter 8 and a focus for the total reconceptualization and restructuring of administrator preparation, described by the Cooperative Superintendency Program at the University of Texas at Austin, and also reported as a case study in that chapter.

In spite of ambiguities, contradictions and a general air of pessimism about the seemingly poor performance of the public schools, one positive outcome from our turbulent environment is that it presents a rare opportunity to be proactive. AASA, taking advantage of this as a responsible professional organization, is developing the enabling mechanisms to ensure that practicing school executives who have completed university-based preparation, either recently or in the distant past, have the resources available to diagnose their individual strengths and weaknesses and construct a personal profile of these. The executive would then develop a growth plan, identify resources and activities to be used in the treatment phase or growth period and self-monitor and validate the professional development process and its outcomes. By this means it becomes possible to refine school executives' diagnosed skills and capabilities in a highly focussed manner. The National Executive Development Center (Chapter 10) is the keystone of this renewed leadership effort focussing on current and emergent needs of the profession and especially those of the field-based practitioner. A speech presented to the American Association of School Administrators by Estes (1988) made explicit some of the underlying assumptions attendant to the formation of the NEDC and its modus operandi as follows:

> Our focus will be formative and developmental, procedures will be personalized based on the diagnosed needs of the individual, our efforts will address a core of executives, not just the superintendent. That is, we will recognize the importance of other members of the superintendents administrative team and those of equivalent status in central education agencies, and, we will address leadership through a world view — that is, we will look at a wide range of leadership skills, competencies, practices and underlying foundations. We include here, for example, the generally accepted dimensions of instructional leadership, general administration and suggest that leadership must be informed by the liberal arts. (Estes, 1988, p. 3)

The specific form adopted by the NEDC, which is evolving around the operations of a number of pilot sites, is the subject of the next chapter. In this chapter the focus is on aspects of leadership including a summary of leadership theories that seek to maintain the threads of continuity in the context of change, leadership behaviors and leadership training models. A major assumption is that the skills of leadership can be taught and competencies acquired and/or developed. Tichy and Devanna (1986) and Bennis and Nanus (1985) are advocates of the notion that leaders are made not born. This view has also guided and informed the work of the Meadows-funded project team at the University of Texas at Austin, the conceptual work of which is presented later in this chapter.

## Distinctions Between Management and Leadership

Given the tendency in the literature to confuse the term management with leadership, it is necessary to clarify some fundamental semantic and conceptual difficulties arising from the frequent interchange of the terms one with another. Confusion surrounding this was raised initially in Chapter 1. The problematic nature of 'management' has been the subject of close study by scholars, practitioners and others seeking to categorize its components and understand its meaning over a lengthy period of time. According to Drucker (1974), leadership is distinctly an American word. He captures the essence of this in the following statement:

> . . . even within the American usage, management is not adequate as a term, for institutions other than business do not speak of management or managers as a rule. Universities or government agencies have administrators, as have hospitals. Armed services have commanders. Other institutions speak of executives and so on. Yet all these institutions have

in common the management function, the management task, and the management work. All of them require management and in all of them management is effective, the active organ. (p. 5)

Reaching into antiquity, management has been the *sine qua non* of all organizations, public or private (Cribben, 1972). The pyramids stand today in mute testimony to the managerial acumen of the ancient Egyptians, while Socrates discussed the subject of management with his students in the following terms:

Do not, therefore . . . despise men skillful in managing a household; for the conduct of private affairs differs from that of public concerns only in magnitude; in other respects they are similar; but what is most to be observed, is, that neither of them are managed without men; and that private matters are not managed by one species of man, and public matters by another; for those who conduct public business make use of men not at all differing from those whom the managers of either private or public affairs use judiciously, while those who do not know, will err in the management of both. (George, 1972, p. 17)

A contemporary definition of management circumscribes it as '. . . composed of those activities concerned with procuring, coordinating and deploying material and the personnel needed to accomplish the goals of the organization (Ubben and Hughes, 1987, p. 6). In more specific school-focussed terms Sergiovanni (1987) asserts that it involves the allocation of financial and other resources; the planning and implementing of organizational features; and the provision of actions, arrangements and activities needed for the school to reach its goals. Bennis and Nanus (1985) aptly make the distinction between managers and leaders in the following terms:

To manage means to bring about, to accomplish, to have charge of or responsibility for, to conduct. Leading is influencing, guiding in direction, course, action, opinion. The distinction is crucial. Managers are people who do things right and leaders are people who do the right thing. (p. 21)

Leadership, according to Guthrie and Reed (1986), is considered to be a quality that enables an individual within a given setting to motivate and inspire others to adopt, achieve and maintain organizational and individual goals, while Sergiovanni (1987) considers that it entails defining the mission and purpose of the school, identifying and setting goals, marshaling and directing human resources, solving problems and making decisions creatively, and motivating staff. The National Commission on Excellence in Education placed heavy emphasis on the need for and role of leadership in eliciting community support for the proposed transformation of American schools:

Principals and superintendents must play a crucial leadership role in developing school and community support for the reforms we propose, and School Boards must provide them with the professional development and other support to carry out their leadership role effectively. The

Commission stresses the distinction between leadership skills involving persuading, setting goals and developing community consensus behind them, and managerial and supervisory skills. (National Commission on Excellence in Education, 1987, p. 78)

The 1980s has placed a premium on leadership skills that go well beyond management to encompass transformational leadership behaviors. In so doing new challenges for the superintendency that are instrumental to the much needed deep seated reform of our schools and school systems have been presented. A visionary and futures orientation is a crucial element to be developed in the new breed of school administrators and school system executives. Perhaps the most widely accepted distinction between managers and leaders is that offered by Burns (1978), where the former are regarded as transactors and the latter as transformers. Whereas the manager negotiates fair exchanges or transactions with employees, providing rewards or punishment in exchange for their effort, leaders transform the organization in accordance with a vision of where it should be heading.

Transformational leaders, then, are people who exhibit leadership skills beyond those of managing the system in order to move the system toward achieving its next stage of evolution. They help others share in their vision of where the system should be heading to such an extent that it becomes the fused purpose of the organization. In communicating this vision, both formal and informal channels are used to provide up-to-date information on the status of the organization for sharing, and for further use by participants.

To accomplish a mission based on a shared vision requires the conceptualization of a desired alternative future, engaging in risk-taking behaviors to facilitate and give effect to change in the desired direction(s), empowering others in this process and communicating the vision to every level in the organization. Thus the idea that one can use others in shared decision-making, and that their empowerment to be effective in this area produces results, has opened up a new range of possibilities for superintendents quick to see and utilize the possibilities this creates.

In this regard Hoyle (1989b) asserts that . . . 'Administrators who cannot project themselves into the future can only respond to the immediacy of the present and cannot imagine an array of possible futures' (p. 252). He goes on to list the skills required by administrators for the twenty-first century as:

* the ability to view the big picture of the future;
* the ability to cope with stress created by personal, societal, and technological change;
* the ability to select, maintain, and provide growth for professional staff and support personnel;
* the ability to manage information systems;
* the ability to be humane and create humanistic environments;
* the ability to relate and communicate with leaders in other agencies.

It is not enough, however, just to have a vision for the future; you have to own it too, you have to believe in it and you have to live it. Not only do great school leaders have great vision, not only are they committed to it; they also have a concern for, and a skill in creating a climate in which instructional and school improvement can take place. This ability to create a climate where there is openness and trust is critical to success. As mentioned in Chapter 2, Sclafani (1987) surveyed 1000 superintendents around the country and separated the 100 most exceptional from the others. The single difference on 144 items that distinguished the effective superintendents from the others was their concern for climate.

At a personal level the transformational leader is concerned about individuals, committed to the ongoing development of all players in the organization and, thereby, to move each individual to realize his/her full potential. In spite of uncertainties in the larger environment, the leader demonstrates a positive attitude toward overcoming difficulties and steadfastly exhibits a well-developed values set that motivates him/her to be a strong advocate for excellence in education, pursuing an education of high quality for all students within the school district. The transformational leader is a self-directed learner who seeks continually to further improve him/herself both personally and professionally.

In reality it is relatively rare for an individual to be characterized wholly as either a transactional or a transformational leader. Most are likely to exhibit elements of both in varying degree over time. This assertion is supported by the research of Buck (1989), who showed that there were some leaders in her sample of superintendents who were considered to be 'movers and shakers' and others who were functioning quite well within the *status quo*. Indepth interview data also showed that those exhibiting clear transformational leadership behaviors were not simply content to superintend the *status quo* in situations where the organization, board of trustees and local community wanted things to remain fairly constant from year to year. When transformational leaders cannot promote and implement change throughout their district, they will frequently seek another position elsewhere at their own request.

## Leadership Forces Promoting Excellence in Education

Excellence in education is a pervasive concern that has served to place the nation's schools and school systems high on the public policy agenda. The phrase 'in search of excellence' is now widely known via the title of the book by Peters and Waterman, *In Search of Excellence: Lessons from America's Best Run Companies.*

Gubernatorial elections have been heavily oriented to education platforms in a number of states driven by a perceived dissatisfaction with existing conditions. A renewed interest in quality and excellence in education has impacted a number of early studies within the school effectiveness movement resulting in their extension and refinement. But what do we mean by excellence in education and how can it be characterized?

A concise yet comprehensive notion has been propounded by the National Commission on Excellence in Education from the points of view of the learners, the school or college and society at large:

> At the level of the individual learner, it means performing at the boundary of individual ability in ways that test and push back personal limits, in school and in the workplace. Excellence characterizes a school or college that sets high expectations and goals for all learners, then tries in every way possible to help students reach them. Excellence characterizes a society that has adopted these policies, for it will then be prepared through

the education and skill of its people to respond to the challenges of a rapidly changing world. (National Commission on Excellence in Education, 1983, p. 16)

Excellence is clearly concerned with the achievement of outcomes at the highest possible level and success in this area is not necessarily referenced back to any individual person. Today it is becoming commonplace to speak of 'leadership forces' since leadership need not, and perhaps should not, be focussed on a single individual — at least within school settings. Sergiovanni (1984), drawing on the school effectiveness literature, has identified five leadership forces that can be arranged in a hierarchy. Each of the forces '. . . can be thought of as the means available to administrators, supervisors and teachers to bring about or preserve changes needed to improve schooling' (pp. 6–12). They are:

**Technical** — derived from sound management techniques. Examples include the capacity to plan, organize, coordinate and schedule to ensure optimum effectiveness.

**Human** — derived from harnessing available social and interpersonal resources. Examples include building and maintaining morale, encouraging growth and creativity, providing needed support and using participatory approaches to decision-making.

**Educational** — derived from expert knowledge about matters of education and schooling. Examples include the capacity to diagnose problems, counsel teachers, provide supervision and develop curriculum.

**Symbolic** — derived from focussing the attention of others on matters of importance to the school. Examples include touring the school, visiting classrooms, presiding at ceremonies, knowing students and providing a unified vision.

**Cultural** — derived from building a unique school culture. Examples include the articulation of a unique school mission, socializing new members, telling stories and maintaining myths, and the rewarding of those who reflect the culture.

The symbolic, rather than the behavioral, aspects of leadership are key factors in the research indicating that leaders make little difference to organizational effectiveness when paying too much attention to the instrumental and behavioral aspects of leadership and not enough to its symbolic and cultural aspects. A problem of identifying leadership in schools stems from the limited conception that schools are naturally rigid and thus leadership comes to be viewed narrowly as being concerned with 'facts' as objectives, behavioral outcomes, and measurable effectiveness. Schools in reality are rather adaptive and realize or infer their goals from the direction(s) they take. The substantive nature of leadership, in effect therefore, is much more concerned with the social meanings that are embedded in the organization's culture, and the chief aspects of this sort of symbolic leadership include the notion of 'leadership selectivity'. According to Sergiovanni, this means communicating priorities by the attention the leader pays to different things; leadership consciousness, involving the leader's espousing and modeling of purposes, standards and beliefs; and leadership fidelity, involving the building of staff loyalty to the organization's norms and aspirations.

Following Katz (1974), technical and human leadership forces are important for routine competence but insufficient to achieve excellence. Their absence results in ineffectiveness. Educational leadership forces are essential for routine competence and are linked to, but are not sufficient for, excellence. Deficiencies in this dimension also result in ineffectiveness. Symbolic and cultural leadership forces are essential to excellence but their absence may not affect routine competence.

### Leadership Theories

Research on leadership has been conducted systematically since the turn of the century. Through the decades of trying to understand what makes a person a leader several theories have emerged about leadership, each of which has implications for the development and training of leaders.

**Trait Theory of Leadership** — The first forty years of research focussed on leadership as a set of character traits. The approach was one of identifying those traits that were believed to be characteristic of good leaders and then selecting leaders who had these traits. In essence, this exemplified the idea that leaders are 'born' not 'made'. It lay beyond training and education, at least in the short term, to develop the desired character traits and their potential in this area lay unrealized for leadership development.

**Leadership as Specific Behaviors** — The trait theory of leadership was followed by an opposing point of view within which behaviors associated with leadership were isolated. Behaviors associated with leadership were considered to be reasonably consistent throughout most work environments and could in most cases, be promoted and developed through training.

**Theory of Leadership Styles** — A more sophisticated understanding of leadership which evolved dealt with the concept of leadership style, focussing on the interaction between the leader and the follower. A range of 'styles' was identified in this theory, based on such factors as consideration of followers, initiating structures and autocratic vs. democratic decision-making. Attempts were made initially to identify and then initiate training that would produce an optimum leadership style. Again, the contemporary view was that an optimum style would be appropriate for all situations.

**Situational Leadership** — Following accumulated research findings, as problems with each of these theories became evident, a theory developed that was more situational in nature. This theory holds that effective leadership varies from situation to situation, and that what is viewed as effective leadership is contingent upon the situation in which that leadership is effected. This theory has achieved wide acceptability accounting as it does for greater complexity in explaining the phenomenon than do earlier ones. Those who identify with this approach to leadership have attempted to identify either the conditions under which certain traits or capabilities are effective, or the kinds of behaviors that effective leaders would use under certain conditions. Training is focussed partially on skills and partially on the identification of which type of leadership is called for under what contingencies. It is this last theory that dominates current research on leadership and is the focus of much leadership development in both the private and public sectors.

Each of the theories listed above goes some way to helping us understand the phenomenon which, in its totality, still remains as elusive as it ever was. Each theory and approach to understanding leadership behaviors, however, presents only a partial picture and a partial explanation of leadership phenomena. What is common to each theory is that leadership is regarded as a subset of human action, encompassing the six views described above but, reaches beyond each of them. A more comprehensive view of leadership is that it is more than the sum of its parts. It embraces, for example, a moral involvement which means that actors do what they do because they believe it is the right thing to do. This idea, according to Greenfield (1991), is central to understanding the challenge of leadership in schools. It is in sympathy with Terry's view, when he asserts:

> . . . it is grounded in traits, yet the required skills are not exhausted by traits. It is sensitive to shifting situations, yet it recognizes complexities beyond situational theory's reach. It is shaped by roles and position, yet it is greater than any organizational hierarchy. It is activated by power, yet challenges the primacy of power. It is driven by vision, yet is not satisfied with just any direction. It is ethical, yet always tempered by an awareness of existence, ambiguities and unforeseen consequences. Therefore leadership is a kind of social ethical practice. (Terry, 1988, p. 15)

This aspect of the phenomenon is recognized and addressed in the first of the six leadership domains initially described in Chapter 7. The six domains are tentative in nature and the model advanced is open ended in order to allow for the inclusion of other domains that may emerge at a later date, if further research and conceptualization of the nature of leadership should warrant it.

### The Superintendent as Instructional Leader

Given the literature on effective schools, it seems that a superintendent must also sustain a greater involvement in the district's instructional program (Wallace, 1987). A voluminous literature exists concerning the topic of instructional leadership, that is leadership toward educational achievement as it applies to the role of the principal. This perspective was initially taken up in Chapter 1 and we return to it again here seeking to clarify its nature, scope and efficacy, *vis-à-vis* the role of the superintendent at the district level.

Much of the research to date has focussed on the relationship between principal's behaviors and student achievement, while very little has investigated the relationship between the superintendent and student achievement. Cuban (1985) observes that research has neglected the superintendent's role as instructional leader noting '. . . the broader perspective of district administrators is often missing from the researchers' analyses of effective schools' (p. 132). According to Bridges (1982), 'Irrespective of the variables adopted in studying the impact of the administrator, there is a pronounced tendency to study the impact of the elementary school principal and to neglect the impact of the superintendent' (p. 22).

From a normative perspective, Schlechty and Joslin (1986) maintain that 'the superintendent is or should be the chief teacher in the school system — the person who defines problems and inspires others to solve them. Leadership, then, is more important than managerial skill though managerial skill is not to be discounted' (p. 159). If this view is accepted then the outcomes of schooling are unequivocally the bottom line responsibility of the chief executive officer.

Cuban (1988) states that the leaders of today are symbolic leaders whose instructional role is broadened through the shaping of the district's mission, establishing a district climate that signals a seriousness of purpose, and designing rituals and structures that infuse life into both the mission and the climate through the exercise of good communication skills. He adds that in the 1980s the instructional role of superintendents emerged cast in terms of what superintendents should do. In other words, a newer and somewhat broader role emerged for the superintendent where '. . . intentions and strategies become lesson plans and units of curriculum invented to achieve desired ends . . .' (p. 254). Thus a superintendent from this point of view can be regarded as a teacher both in and out of the classroom guiding staff and community to new understandings and strategies for improvement and renewal.

At a practical level, in the past few years, there has been an expenditure of a lot of effort on the part of professional associations, practicing superintendents, and professors of educational administration to identify and delineate the competencies and skills that are needed in order to be an effective superintendent (see Appendix for example). Much of the work done in this area has involved identifying competencies and skills based on the perceptions of superintendents themselves and includes the views of significant others. As these have been identified and confirmed, further research suggests that *inter alia* the skills of instructional leadership required of superintendents should be validated against their role in promoting school effectiveness.

Muller (1989) undertook to investigate the relationship of specified superintendent instructional leadership competencies and elementary principal effective instructional leadership behaviors to school effectiveness. He concluded, like Peterson *et al.* (1987), that superintendents of effective school districts were highly involved in the instructional and curricular affairs of the school district. In a related study, the findings of Stott (1991) showed that the superintendents regarded instructional issues as important to the well-being of a district. It is also noteworthy that the critical incidents most frequently described by superintendents, were those in which they were actively engaged in instructional leadership, and which they considered largely to have eventuated in successful outcomes.

While public school superintendents are charged with instructional accountability, they have been historically unprepared to deal with past and contemporary critical instructional problems. Herman (1989) conducted a study into the dynamics of this with a view to identifying the personally and situationally impacted competencies and skills accruing to the superintendent's instructional leadership role. She used a reputationally identified sample of forty-eight Texas school superintendents who were interviewed in the field by a team of researchers. The team employed a cooperatively designed and field tested instrument structured to capture the skills and strategies of the superintendents as they described critical events drawn from their experiences.

From these data, responses that fell within the ambit of an operational definition

*Table 9.1: Personal variables related to the Effective Schools Correlates*

| Correlate | Personal Variable |
|---|---|
| Focus on Instruction | Maintains Academic Focus |
| Focus on Evaluation | Focuses on Measurement and Evaluation |
| Instructional Leadership | Demonstrates Instructional Leadership |
| High Expectations | Communicates High Expectations |
| Climate | Provides Climate |

to be instructionally related were selected for systematic analysis of instructional behaviors. Five hundred and eight behaviors derived from the data were sorted by means of content analysis into twenty-four instructional competencies and five instructional skill areas were derived. Attitudinal behaviors described by the superintendents were sorted into five categories of personal variables each impinging on instructional competencies and skills, while analysis of the contexts of instructionally related questions were resolved to form ten situational variables which also impact on the previously identified competencies and skills.

The Effective Schools Correlates appeared as a strand throughout the interviews and analysis of data and their terminology is reflected in Herman's findings. She reported that one of the most striking derivatives of the instructional leadership categories was the strong alignment with the correlates that occurred during the construction of the personal variables. This feature is summarized in Table 9.1.

From Herman's data, and reinforced by Wallace (1985), the profile of a skilled and actively involved dynamic leader emerged, whose instructional acumen and sense of the technical core function is a clear departure from the typical role that is described in the literature. Going beyond the identified competencies, skills, personal and situational variables, there was also a sense of effectiveness and self-efficacy in acting out the role.

While the model of the superintendent as an instructional leader is rather uncommon in the recent literature, the findings of Herman are not without historical precedent. This is captured by Cuban's (1988) expansion of his tridimensional role model of the superintendent as a managerial, political and instructional leader. In this regard he observed that the instructional role of the superintendent has once again re-emerged as a central issue concerning what superintendents should do, and guidance for this has become clearer in an emerging body of coherent research concerning 'effective schools'.

Paralleling efforts to increase the instructional role for both teachers and principals, the focus has also expanded to include the district superintendent in which Cuban observes that, 'Setting goals, establishing standards, selecting and supervising staff, insuring constancy in curricula and teaching approaches have become benchmarks of instructionally active superintendents' (1988, p. 136).

### Learning for Leadership

*The Contemporary Scene*

In the flux of educational change, much is going on in the public schools concerning both in-service training and the advanced preparation of individuals for leadership positions and leadership roles. Harris *et al.* (1992) note that as pressures continue to mount for reforms and the restructuring of our schools, leadership behavior comes under close scrutiny even more than the practices of teachers. See also Giroux, 1992, for a critical theory perspective on this.

The pre-service preparation of leadership personnel continues to be a crucial aspect of leadership training within the broader context of educational reform and with the spotlight clearly focussed on school and school system administrators. This has brought to light a number of problem areas currently being addressed in which local school districts, professional associations and private interest groups have all engaged in improving education through leadership training.

The graduate preparation of leadership personnel has been, and still tends to be, somewhat mistakenly regarded as the unique responsibility of university degree programs. It has not proved possible though for such programs to fully serve the leadership training needs of elementary and secondary education in certain respects. Even the finest pre-service programs for administrators and supervisors are widely acknowledged to be preparatory at best, and, as is evident in other parts of this book, criticisms by practitioners are commonly reported of many existing approaches to graduate preparation. There does appear to be a wide and growing agreement emerging under the influence of the University Council for Educational Administration (UCEA), several professional associations, and the National Policy Board for Educational Administration (NPBEA) that graduate preparation must be up-graded and collaborative relationships improved upon.

As has frequently been mentioned in the earlier chapters of this book, many graduate programs are primarily degree oriented, staffed by small faculty groups, and poorly funded. Selective admissions criteria tend to be low and related to academic criteria to the exclusion of other professionally relevant concerns. Part-time study programs allow few opportunities for field study and intern experiences (but see Chapter 8). These defects in graduate preparation in most universities and colleges have long been recognized. As Murphy (1991) observes, '. . . the reform movement has, in many ways, provided the momentum needed for a reexamination of the structures, content and processes common to the schooling of administrators' (p. 50), providing the impetus for most graduate preparation programs to be dramatically restructured; not in this case to prepare transactional 'coping' administrators, but to provide an entirely new breed who can lead the nation's schools into a future conceived out of a shared vision.

Professional associations are increasing their involvement in leadership training. A wide variety of different kinds of training activities are being made available to members and non-members on a fee paying basis. Much of this activity appears in well recognized and traditional forms, such as conference speakers, the provision of short courses, workshops and seminars. While these types of training activities have their limitations in promoting all round professional competency development, they do provide the vehicles for generating an awareness of new concepts, new information technology, emerging issues, and practices. Perhaps their greatest value is in creating a mindset in the practitioner for more sustained and meaningful training, building on initial consciousness raising activities. This is not to devalue the intrinsic nature of the sorts of activities mentioned above which, on other occasions, might also be usefully employed as resources for more sequentially structured and longer term programs of leadership training.

LEAD Center grants, to assist in establishing training organizations addressing the in-service training needs of administrators and supervisors, were provided out of federal funds in the late 1980s. Some of these centers became associated with universities while others were organized in line with professional associations or state departments of education.

The National Academy of School Executives (NASE), subsumed under the American Association of School Administrators, has made regular provision for numerous and wide ranging workshops and seminars to meet the needs and interests of school superintendents. While these training activities tend to be brief and discontinuous, they do offer an extensive variety of topics of current interest that collectively raise professional awareness. A similar program of workshops is also available under the direction of the Association for Supervision and Curriculum Development (ASCD), and referred to as the National Curriculum Study Institutes (NCSI). These provide for the current interests of school principals and supervisors, rather than the explicit concerns of superintendents.

The production of materials specifically for use in leadership training has become a booming industry for private vendors, as well as becoming an area of endeavor for various professional associations. The publication of tapes, study guides, video-cassettes, and computer software now serve to augment the traditional publications of some professional associations, and hence have the potential to be used selectively in training programs. As a result of burgeoning growth in both the number and variety of multi-media learning materials, their increasing availability through media centers and professional collections in large districts, association headquarters and college libraries, there now exists a bank of artifacts holding a vast potential for contributing to more innovatory approaches to leadership training.

It is virtually impossible to gain a completely clear and accurate view of the current scene in leadership training in all its aspects and nuances. However, to the informed and persistent observer, the impression to be gained is the availability of plentiful, if not massive, quantities of both material and human resources, numerous organizations and a range of media. These appear to have an almost casual and incidental engagement with a receptive corps of educational leaders as they are utilized at present. The problems of providing a better alignment of resources with the needs and aspirations of executives are both strategic and logistical in nature.

*Basic Model Types for Leadership Training*

On-the-job leadership training continues to suffer from a very limited use of the most promising of practices. The obstacles facing busy administrators and supervisors are not dissimilar to those faced by teachers. Demanding jobs, characterized by fast pace, leave neither time nor energy for extensive professional development activities. Peterson (1984) analyzed problems associated with the use of an experiential learning model applied to the work of school principals. He showed that 'task brevity', a non-sequential variety of demands on time, and fragmentation of the work flow are such that there is little opportunity for reflection, analysis, dialogue, or generalizing about one's own practices. These sorts of work practices in schools can logically be transposed to some degree to all leadership personnel, and they may explain, in part, their limited engagement with in-service education evident in the professional lives of most administrators. The realities of the situation suggest the need for models that have a much greater power of engagement for developing leadership under such difficult work practices as those referred to above.

Four basic model types, with a currency for on-the-job training in different contexts, are summarized in the next section of this chapter. While they are described separately for the purpose of exposition, different variations and combinations of two or more models are sometimes utilized in practice. The model types are:

(i)    independent study;
(ii)   diagnostic-prescriptive analysis;
(iii)  study groups; and
(iv)   mentoring/coaching/networking.

### Independent Study

This approach to the development of leadership competencies tends to be widely used on an informal basis. Within this model, individuals elect to read, attend professional meetings, and even try out an occasional new technique or procedure. The more formal use of independent study involves the selection of a goal or objective and pursuing it via the more systematic allocation of time encompassed by a planned program of readings and related activities designed to achieve intended outcomes.

This type of on-the-job training draws its strengths from its foci on the personal needs of individuals, providing for flexibility in the scheduling of the use of time, and placing control of learning processes in the hands of those individuals undertaking responsibility for their own ongoing professional development. The model's robustness is due to its attention to personal needs, providing for the flexible use of time, and allowing the individual to retain control of the nature, substance and pacing of his/her own learning. These strengths at the same time provide some serious limitations in undertaking this type of approach to executive development, especially when utilized informally in the absence of carefully structured action plans.

### Diagnostic-Prescriptive Models

These rely on some sort of informal testing or assessment program to provide feedback to the executive regarding his/her strengths, weaknesses and suggestions for remediation. The use of diagnostic procedures can take many forms, ranging from the elaborate assessment center operations (Chapter 7) of the NASSP Assessment Centers (Hersey, 1989) and the DECAS Executive Diagnostic Workshop described in Chapter 6 and by Carter, Estes, Loredo, and Harris (1991), to the simple self assessment inventories such as the Educational Administrator Effectiveness Profile (AASA, 1984 and 1988).

Irrespective of the instrumentation or the process employed, diagnostic analysis providing feedback on strengths or weaknesses can be informative and motivational to those undertaking it when sensitively and appropriately applied. Realistic prescriptions, following the preliminary diagnosis, tend not to be readily catered for in practice. The strengths of these types of models lie in their focussed diagnostic power using pre-structured instrumentation and analytical processes as a precursor to action planning. Their weakness lies in the fact that the 'client' is essentially dependent on the assumptions, rationale, philosophy, and frames of those who designed the diagnostic materials in the first place. Because of this, the intrinsic motivation for initiating action for growth and improvement tends to be rather limited.

### Study Group Models

The rather solitary features of the two model types described above are avoided with the group study approach to professional development in which group activity can take many forms. Groups can also vary in size, task, length of time for which they are constituted, kind of leadership, activities employed and locale (Harris, 1989). The inherent strengths to be found in study groups include further professional socialization, the sharing of knowledge and experience, and the multiplicity of activities which can be utilized because they are particularly amenable to group processes. While too much reliance tends to be placed on expository methods such as lecture and discussion modes, study groups make excellent vehicles for such things as quality circles, demonstrations, role-playing, buzz sessions, brainstorming, simulations and laboratory training activities. Cooperative learning arrangements can also be utilized, so that a group study can have a uniquely powerful effect on participants (Blake and Mouton, 1982).

The main weakness in this mode lies in the loss of a certain amount of personal identity through being bound to the social norms of the group and some attendant ambiguity over meeting explicitly defined individual needs. While groups can develop requisite knowledge, skills and attitudes, the transfer of these to the social realities of individuals working in specific contexts and undertaking particular roles are not clearly provided for.

### Coaching/Mentoring/Networking Models

At present these are still somewhat ill-defined in practice, as well as in the relevant literature. Generally these terms are used to circumscribe training arrangements in which two or more individuals team up to observe, discuss, share and provide support and assistance to each other on some sort of a reciprocal basis. It is noteworthy that *peer coaching* has become popular in the last decade. This concept embraces a modified form of clinical supervision as the last phase in a training program sequence.

The term *mentoring* is nowadays used to refer to dyadic relationships between professionals where direct observation is not necessarily involved as it is, for instance, in coaching. Mentor relationships are almost always voluntary, are usually but not necessarily peer-based, and the relationship entered into by the dyadic pair may or may not be a reciprocal one. The purposes and associated activities of mentoring are not very well reported but seem to cater for a wide variety and range of alternative interpretations.

*Networking* has much in common with both mentoring and coaching but involves a wider array of participants. It may also involve the use of telephones and assorted telecommunication devices over a range of distances. Mentoring, on the other hand, relies heavily on face-to-face communication between individuals.

All of these approaches are subsumed under small scale group interaction support models. Their effectiveness in promoting and facilitating training outcomes is probably most likely to occur in the area of effecting transfer to on-the-job situations, although these effects are not yet clearly understood. Given the relative weaknesses of most models in effecting transfer of training to field situations it seems that coaching, mentoring and networking are at least as deserving as any other of the models, in the design and formulation of training programs.

What is now clear to the professor and the practising superintendent is that if administrative positions are redesigned in terms of their work agendas, functions and performance standards, then preparation and retooling of school managers and future leaders should change and change quite dramatically. Initial learning and continuous learning of a recurrent nature is now an integral part of the role requirements for excellence in the superintendency. Schema for achieving the necessary changes are developed in the sections that follow.

### A Continuous Professional Development System

In an effort to design a prototype operating model for executive training, the Meadows Project Team at the University of Texas has been engaged in trialing various combinations of all the models mentioned in the preceding section. These have been synthesized into a flexible open system that seeks to capitalize on the strengths of all the model types while minimizing their weaknesses. Under the guidance of AASA's National Executive Development Center Advisory Committee such a system is currently being tested with some encouraging signs. Figure 9.1 delineates the major components of the system as well as indicating a logical flow of events.

Performance descriptors, volunteer leaders, and professional commitments from individuals and organizations are all necessary prerequisites for the system's functioning. The LEAD Resource Bank is designated in this figure as one concrete example of an extant organization that can supply training materials and other resources to individuals and groups.

In Figure 9.1, the large rectangle in bold borders represents an operating system. Four sub-systems are shown with arrows indicating a sequence of events for any given participant leader. Diagnostic assessment is followed by planning for improvement. The sub-system labelled 'Experiential Delivery System' represents any of a variety of training programs, utilizing the models described above. The last of the four sub-systems in the operating system is labelled 'Outcome Review'. This component provides for either formal or informal review of training experiences related to plans for improvement as a basis for making decisions for another cycle of diagnostic assessment, preceding yet further professional development of an ongoing nature. This notion is central to the continuous nature of this professional development system.

Conventionally, any identified need for an individual or group tends to be responded to in an *ad hoc* fashion, using any of the model types described in the

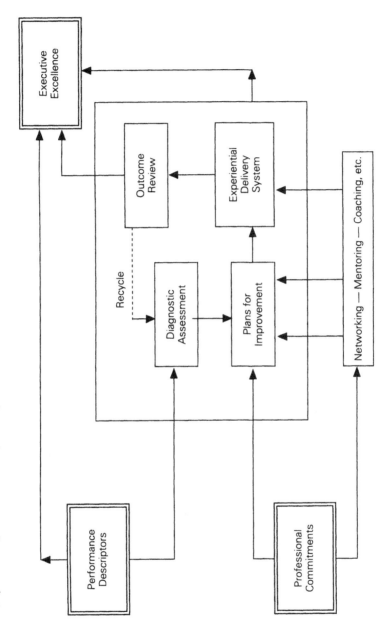

*Figure 9.1: Components of professional development system*

previous section. In the system currently being tested and described here, the diagnostic assessment sub-system is designed to be responsive to a broad array of potential needs. Under operational conditions the experiential delivery subsystem must similarly respond, with the individual improvement plan providing the necessary linkage between diagnosis and training. In this regard the networking-mentoring-coaching sub-system (figure 9.1) represents an organized effort to relate associated processes to the operating system in order to facilitate improvement planning, training experiences, and outcome reviews. By these means the system is able to keep the control of action planning and prioritization in the hands of individual executives.

The learning approaches first described in Chapter 8 provided more concrete examples of the visualization of generic learning models outlined in the previous section of this chapter. The application of state-of-the-art technology to specific learning opportunities that can be related to executives' preferred learning styles is a basic requirement for maximizing accessibility to practitioners in the field regardless of their context and location.

### Leadership Conceptualization for the NEDC

In the concluding part of this chapter we return to the leadership domains introduced in Chapter 7 and relate these to a particular conception of leadership developed out of the collaborative research, development and training activities of the American Association of School Administrators and a pilot site at the University of Texas at Austin. The relationship of leadership conceptualization to learning for leadership is the basis for the Diagnostic Executive Competency Assessment System, DECAS, comprehensively described and referenced in earlier chapters. The assumption is clearly that leadership preparation and development is based on a diagnosis of strengths and weaknesses leading to continuous, cyclic, ongoing and self-energized development of leadership competencies over the course of an executive's career span. These take place within the substantive base of leadership domains, currently believed to be six in number, but with provision for others to be added at a later date if warranted.

The call for a reconceptualization of leadership with consideration of culture, conflict, structure, and uncertainty is timely. An emphasis on leadership as it affects teaching and learning echoes a basic mission of the association captured by the AASA 'Leadership for Learning' programs. The call for examination of the relational aspects of leadership with emphasis on the perceptions and sense making structures employed in followership suggest a fruitful avenue for improving the practice and application of leadership.

Examination of the relational nature of leadership implies the need to envisage school leadership within a broad conceptual framework that takes into account the interrelatedness of district and site leadership forces. Issues concerning the co-ordination and control of principal behaviors by district leadership have been identified by Peterson (1984) and Murphy and Hallinger (1986) and also treated somewhat speculatively in the first chapter of this book.

Two developmental thrusts have occurred in the conceptualization of an operational view of leadership adopted by AASA. The first builds on scholarly descriptions and operational patterns of leadership drawn from the disciplines of psychology, political science, sociology, philosophy, management science and education with which to construct a framework for school leadership. This has been on the premise that far more is known about conceptualizing leadership than is being used to inform the art and craft of school leadership. Thus through scholarly reflection and synthesis, scholar-practitioner dialog, and descriptive research of superordinate and subordinate perceptions of effective school leadership, six domains have been used to provide a conceptual framework of school leadership comprising liberal education, instructional leadership, interpersonal relations, general administration, personal capabilities and multicultural perspectives.

Liberal education is regarded as the basis for recognizing the relation of the cultural context to leadership in which the latter is embedded. Instructional leadership is viewed as a basis for identifying the relations between a technical core of expertise to school leadership. Interpersonal relationships are regarded as fundamental to identifying certain human interactions as a function of leadership. General administration is seen as a basis for identifying the relation of individual traits, capabilities and characteristics to leadership. Finally, the domain of multicultural perspectives has been added in recognition of the fact that leadership is exercised within and in behalf of an ethnically complex and rich society requiring cross-cultural insights, skills and sensitivities, without which a conceptualization of leadership would at best be only partial and necessarily incomplete. In the final chapter of this book responsibility for operationalizing and giving form to each of these is reviewed.

While it is a widely shared belief that leadership makes a difference in the operation of schools, there has been, until recently, little convincing and compelling research to lend credence to this assumption. Pitner and Ogawa (1981) have suggested that the educational system at both policy and operational levels tends to function on the plausible belief that superintendents do in fact affect school district performance. Further, Pitner and Ogawa note that superintendents attribute this responsibility to themselves for improving instructional outcomes as a function of their leadership.

In building the knowledge base to understand what outstanding executives actually do in their work, as compared with those who are less effective, it has been possible to reconceptualize the intrinsically esoteric and elusive nature of leadership so that it becomes more instrumental in principled ways for the purposes of improving practice in the field, and for preparing our future school system leaders. This has been both a recurrent theme and a guiding principle for the work undertaken and reported in this book.

*Chapter 10*

# The Future: Mapping the Multisite Executive Development Center

*David S.G. Carter and Thomas E. Glass*

In concluding this book on the American superintendency, we have been through several iterations to work to the best approximation we could in order to 'capture' our work as it has evolved. Given that the R&D work at the University of Texas at Austin is now but one part of the work being conducted by a network of six pilot sites — the prototype of the National Executive Development Center — the perspective presented in this volume forms only a partial picture of the overall design for the future of a national center.

We felt it necessary, therefore, to add an epilogue to bring a Janus perspective to bear on the research and its products that we've achieved to date, and to describe how this is likely to be developed in the immediate future, in a coordinated way, to realize the NEDC ideal. This chapter, therefore, presents our current conceptions of the emergent plan and strategies for a network of pilot sites. In so doing, our orientation at this point becomes prospective in nature, recognizing that when innovating on a large scale, things may adapt to changing and changed circumstances and situations. The projections described in this chapter are those existing at the time of going to press.

### Background and Rationale for an Executive Development Center

It is now abundantly evident, and has been so for a number of years and is a recurrent theme in this book, that the composition, nature and societal expectations concerning educational reform are in a great stage of flux. Turbulence is a feature of the educational environment in which the superintendent has to conduct the district's routine operations as well as envisage, plan and lead the community toward a shared vision of alternative futures.

Out of an intensive flurry of research and professional activity over the last five years or so some gains are beginning to emerge (Murphy and Hallinger, 1989; Miskel, 1990). The exponential rate of change becomes apparent not only in technological advance but also in the rate at which society is striving to meet its historical but largely unrealized goal of providing equal educational opportunity for all. The new industrial age in which information is a major commodity calls for a new kind of leadership. This does not mean that we have done poorly in the past, but it does mean that what we are doing now needs to be improved upon. In order to effect this we must restructure the workplace and reshape roles. Education ultimately must be justifiable in its own right and on its own terms, but as new imperatives emerge, such as the economic drive for increased productivity, innovation, and international competitiveness, it becomes self-evident that an appropriate response is required from all levels of the educational system.

An examination of the implications of changing role requirements and demands of superintendents reveals an important fact. We cannot develop or evaluate the new leadership required for the next century by applying criteria which were developed for a time and place that no longer exists. Hand in hand with the challenge of rethinking the superintendency leadership role is a problem noted by both researchers and practitioners over the last decade, namely, that time-honored practices for preparing and selecting individuals for existing work roles in school systems are inadequate to meet current and projected societal needs (March, 1977; National Commission on Excellence in Educational Administration, 1983; Pitner and Ogawa, 1981). What is increasingly evident to both the professor and the practising superintendent is that, if we dramatically redesign administrative positions in terms of their work agendas and role profiles, functions and performance standards, then commensurate preparation and retooling of future school leaders will also have to change in line with this.

An optimistic view of human nature in our turbulent educational and sociopolitical environments prompts us to be proactive and exercise control over future educational directions and outcomes. The American Association of School Administrators (AASA), as a responsible professional organization, is striving to develop programs to ensure that practicing senior school executives have the necessary resources, human and material, and can take advantage of opportunities with no or minimal disruption to daily routines to retool and refine their capabilities. The strategy adopted by the AASA for achieving this is outlined in the subsequent sections of this chapter.

For a number of years AASA's National Executive Development Center has been addressing leadership across a broad front through an array of leadership skills, competencies, practices and underlying foundations. In addition to including the traditional aspects of instructional leadership and general administration, a platform is also adopted that leadership must be guided and informed by the liberal arts.

Members of the NEDC network have incorporated leadership within the parameters of six broad domains which are:

* General education
* Instructional leadership
* Administrative leadership
* Human relations
* Personal capabilities
* Multicultural perspectives

NEDC is currently faced with trying to define these domains with sufficient clarity and specificity in order that they may contribute to an understanding of,

*Figure 10.1: Leadership Domains and Task Area*

| Domain 1:<br>General<br>education | 1.1 Scientific/technological issues<br>1.2 Ethics/logic themes<br>1.3 Social/political issues<br>1.4 Humanistic themes |
|---|---|

| Domain 2:<br>Instructional<br>leadership | 2.1 Instructional planning<br>2.2 Staffing for instruction<br>2.3 Organizing for instruction<br>2.4 Human resource development<br>2.5 Evaluating instruction |
|---|---|

| Domain 3:<br>Administrative<br>leadership | 3.1 Strategic and operational planning<br>3.2 Board/administrative relationships<br>3.3 Community relations<br>3.4 Organizational climate/culture<br>3.5 Team building<br>3.6 Employee performance evaluation<br>3.7 Organization of central administration<br>3.8 Financial resource management<br>3.9 Facilities development |
|---|---|

| Domain 4:<br>Human<br>relations | 4.1 Communications<br>4.2 Influencing/motivating<br>4.3 Empathy<br>4.4 Conflict management<br>4.5 Managing change<br>4.6 Empowerment<br>4.7 Trust building/team building<br>4.8 Wellness<br>4.9 Non-adversarial bargaining |
|---|---|

| Domain 5:<br>Personal<br>capabilities | 5.1 Intelligence<br>5.2 Positiveness<br>5.3 Drive, energy, courage<br>5.4 Openmindedness<br>5.5 Altruism |
|---|---|

| Domain 6:<br>Multi-<br>cultural<br>perspectives | 6.1 Cross-cultural value differences<br>6.2 Intra-cultural value differences<br>6.3 Socioeconomic value differences<br>6.4 Staff perceptions/attitudes/ behaviors<br>6.5 Home perceptions/attitudes/behaviors<br>6.6 School structure and expectations<br>6.7 School/community interactions |
|---|---|

and also guide, personal leadership behavior (See Figure 10.1). This, it is believed, is the starting point for designing an effective 'self-energized' diagnostic system that identifies and confirms executive strengths while concurrently providing diagnoses of areas where improvement is needed, and presenting constructive feedback to the individual in a form that empowers him or her to take appropriate action for further self-improvement. A set of procedures for achieving this has been developed and refined at the Texas pilot site and is described in Chapters 6 and 7 of this book.

## The Mission: System Development

Developing competent and creative senior executives to lead schools in the twenty-first century demands a new system for facilitating their continuing professional development, along a career path of indeterminate length. In seeking to achieve this an evident need has emerged for the development of an operating delivery system for executive professional development both now and in the foreseeable future. A National Executive Development Center network can meet this goal, and be available to and serve a dynamic pool of some 50,000 school system executives.

*NEDC's Mission*
To develop competent, creative school executives who will lead schools into the twenty-first century by evolving a system that can facilitate the voluntary, continuous and personalized development of effective educational leaders.

The system offers opportunities for diagnostic assessment and professional development as well as being responsive to current and long-term needs. In addition, the system envisaged would serve the general restructuring of higher education programs for educational executives and the upgrading of allied administrator preparation programs.

The diagnostic and development process is unique in many ways because it is:

* individualized;
* transportable to many places;
* flexible in response to a wide array of needs and interests;
* open-ended, assuring continuing opportunities for career-long improvement; and
* research-based with a futures orientation.

## Basic Design Assumptions

Listed below are some of the basic characteristics of the continuous professional development system being evolved. It is:

**a developmental system** rather than a summative, decision-making or reward system that is being developed. The assumption is that development is the most effective approach to excellence in the leadership of our schools;

**a future-oriented, visionary system** rather than a remedial, static, narrowly focused system that is being developed. The assumption is that executive leadership in schools is extremely complex, changing, and not fully understood. Hence, a developmental system must be change-oriented and broadly conceived;

**a personalized system** that is being developed. The assumption is that situational factors, personal styles, and career stages are so numerous that the system must allow for personal choice in both diagnostic and improvement processes. A single instrument, procedure or set of experiences will not suffice to promote development of executives;

**an executive corps,** rather than the superintendent of schools, that is the focus of the system being developed. The assumption is that executive level leadership is nearly always a shared responsibility, especially in its more complex and effective forms. Hence, the system is designed with a restricted range of senior executive positions and leadership roles in mind. The superintendency team in local districts, executives in state and federal agencies, intermediate unit officers, and others in educational institutions responsible for the executive functions represent the 'target audience';

**leadership development,** a diagnostic/feedback improvement process that can be made systematic and be facilitated by an organized program of services.

Self-selection, diagnosis, and profiling of feedback data are presumed to be essential components of the system. Similarly, a professional development plan, followed by self-improvement efforts and alternative training resources are proximate goals for design considerations within this project. Finally, validation of outcomes with provision for further cycles are specified in order to assure a continuous ongoing process of professional growth and development.

## The Strategy: A Consortium of Pilot Development Sites

Six pilot sites have been designated to act in concert as a consortium in order to develop a system for diagnostic assessment and continuing professional development of school executives. This infrastructure when fully evolved will encourage the design, development, field testing and implementation process in order to make it essentially a participatory and collaborative as well as a developmental effort. Each pilot site is currently individually oriented to working toward an integrated and comprehensive system of staff development accessible to superintendents and other senior level school executives.

The pilot sites that have been selected include:

* Arizona State University
* Association of California School Administrators/University of Pittsburgh
* Iowa State University
* New England School Development Council
* Northern Illinois University/ University of   Alabama
* The University of Texas at Austin

Materials and procedures are currently being field tested, with performance descriptors detailed for each domain and validated against the relevant literature, expert opinion and professional wisdom (Harris and Wan, 1991). Developmental materials are both tentative and open ended, taking cognizance of alternative futures in these formative stages of development. The comprehensive system aims to diagnose professional capabilities in any of six or possibly more domains as the system matures, in order to provide individuals with continuing professional development experiences, based on personalized and thoughtful action planning. The resources developed by pilot sites should augment those already widely available. Most importantly, the professional development program is designed to access resources for upgrading and extending performance, utilizing information technology and resources such as the National Academy of School Executives (NASE) workshops, Texas Leadership in Educational Administration Development (LEAD's) Resource Bank, AASA's annual conference and publications, and extant college, business and government sources and programs.

The delivery system for continuous professional development utilizes mentoring, coaching and networking strategies to assure practicality and individualization of professional development efforts. Each pilot site will have primary responsibility for developmental work within the limits of a single domain (see Figure 10.1).

AASA has oversight of coordination, communication dissemination and diffusion activities concerned with planning and development of the NEDC, thus ensuring that the needs and interests of the profession are addressed in a balanced way across all domains. Overall management responsibility assures that dissemination and allied operations are put in place in an orderly, economical and logical manner.

## The Overarching Goals

The project is also being guided by a set of operational goals that apply to all pilot sites. Figure 10.2 specifies nine goals organized under three phases of development. Each goal is related to one or more phases that are overlapping rather than being rigidly sequenced.

### *Design and Development Goals*

The design and development phase gives primary emphasis to goals 1, 2 and 3. Goals 4, 5 and 6 are also involved in this phase to a lesser extent.

Design and development activities are already underway in several pilot sites, and substantially advanced in the Texas pilot supported initially by the Meadows Foundation and LEAD Project funding.

### *Testing and Evaluation*

Materials, instruments, procedures and operating sub-systems are being rigorously tested, and further evaluated for validity, utility, practicality and outcome effect(s). Goals 5 and 6 guide attention explicitly to testing for validity and reliability generally and field testing in particular. Teams at each pilot site place a special emphasis on field testing in order to assure system utility and practicality. Validation and field testing necessarily require the contemplation of goals 2 and 3.

*Figure 10.2: Overarching goals for NEDC system development*

Design and development
 1 Build and maintain a consortium of pilot sites for collaborative development of a
   system for the continuing improvement of school executives in America.
 2 Develop performance criteria and related descriptors for each domain.
 3 Develop and adapt instruments, materials, and processes for use in each component
   of a comprehensive system for executive development.
 4 Organize and make available training materials and resources, providing for retrieval
   technology and continuous updating and review.

Field test and evaluation
 5 Design and operate a comprehensive delivery system for field testing and evaluating
   of both processes and products.
 6 Test the applicability of NEDC materials and processes for improving administrator
   preparation programs.

Implementation and dissemination
 7 Develop mechanisms for monitoring, coordinating and directing executive development programs.
 8 Develop plans and materials for identifying and training personnel to implement continuous executive development programs.
 9 Disseminate and market a nationwide program to reach 50,000 executives.

*Implementation and Dissemination*

Developing mechanisms for monitoring and directing the NEDC Continuous
Professional Development Program when in operation involve training personnel, developing dissemination strategies, and utilizing marketing techniques. Goals
7, 8 and 9 focus attention on the main features of the development efforts aimed
at reaching the target group of executives. AASA is regarded as the agency
responsible for overseeing this phase of the project in toto. A special staff group
will eventually implement and disseminate strategies, processes and products
probably under the direction of the NEDC Advisory Committee and the Executive
Director.

**Pilot Site Plans**

*Domain 1 — General Education — New England School
Development Council*

*The New England site plan*
The New England School Development Council (NESDEC) is capitalizing on its
prior work in the area of school executive assessment/development as well as the
academic richness of the region to undertake the lead role in the general education
domain. NESDEC plans to parallel the prior efforts in the corporate sector of
providing a humanistic dimension to the continuous development of top executives.
  NESDEC, throughout its nearly forty-five years as a school study council,
has been known for its role in development and delivery. Highly regarded
by superintendents in the region, it hosts meetings of the executives of state

superintendent associations in New England as well as meetings of professors of educational administration from throughout the region. The proposed activities, however, will extend far beyond New England. Linkage with other pilot sites, institutions of higher education outside New England and major corporate training centers throughout the country will be important to this effort.

*Site focus*
The complexities of managing even relatively small school districts have resulted in almost two decades of attention being paid to knowing the law, building budgets, long and short range planning techniques, human relations skills, managing change, organizing work. All of these components are important for the success of the educational enterprise, and they consume the time and energies of most school executives.

If, however, superintendents of schools are to fulfil their role of interpreting the purposes and processes of education to the public domain and be eloquent spokespersons for the schools of America, their technical skills must be informed by an understanding of the political, economic, social and ideological changes which are influencing education today and will continue to an even greater degree in the future. To maintain congruity with anticipated changes in professional knowledge and skills, the focus of the project team is on the humanities, logic and ethics, the social/behavioral sciences, the physical sciences and the relatively new world of information science.

General education is comprehensive and contrasts with the narrow focus of most existing preparation programs concerned with school administration. The former is more concerned with the skills of inquiring, hypothesizing, problem solving and valuing than with detailing specific and prescribed factual content. This is not to devalue the professional knowledge base, but rather to highlight the often ignored process as well as substantive dimensions of knowledge. It is the latter which is often embodied in the narrower view of conventional executive preparation, articulated above. From an epistemological point of view, the substantive knowledge to be acquired has tended to be selected for its potential to provide insights and cultural understanding and to directly assist administrators dealing with current realities and future problems. Like most things in education the selection of knowledge in achieving aims is intensely problematic in complex areas of endeavor and should not be taken for granted.

*Domain 2 — Instructional Leadership*

*The Texas site plan*
The University of Texas at Austin has been engaged in preliminary design, development and testing activities related to the NEDC project, under a grant from the Meadows Foundation. These preliminary efforts have subsequently provided the underpinnings for a substantial portion of the comprehensive plan for an executive development system, presented here.

The Department of Educational Administration, the Texas Association of School Administrators and the Texas LEAD Center have collaborated in preliminary efforts to define executive performance, identify research and training programs and explore assessment alternatives. Initially under the umbrella of the

Meadows Foundation, the project team took responsibility for conducting a series of studies to isolate and analyze the performance characteristics of school executives. This enabled the domains which seemed to best capture executive leadership performance to be identified in the first instance. The Texas site then began an intensive effort directed toward explicating the Instructional Leadership domain in detail.

Design and development work undertaken by the project team includes designing a diagnostic assessment process, developing a preliminary set of instruments, and testing the diagnostic process in a workshop format. Computer-based data processing techniques and simulation materials have similarly been developed and tested. The Texas site, operating with the support of the Meadows Foundation and the University of Texas at Austin, is extending field testing and instrument development activities, concurrent with design and testing of a state-wide delivery system.

*Site focus*
The AASA/NEDC concept of a system for the continuous professional development of school executives guides current and projected initiatives at the Texas pilot site. Accomplishments of the project team to date include the identification of leadership domains and testing a task analysis approach for defining performance criteria. A set of instruments has also been developed and tested for use in a diagnostic process.

Professional development planning materials and procedures are being tested, including the development of plans for a computer-based storage and retrieval system for the identification and recovery of appropriate training materials. The next steps involve extending the system to include the design of a delivery system that will provide a variety of experiential alternatives to executives seeking to improve their current performance.

The Texas project team is seeking to have a truly comprehensive system in operation to permit the early testing of outcomes, determine cost/benefit ratios, and offer guidance to the other pilot sites. Much development work will be done at other sites for utilization at the Texas site in subsequent years. Notwithstanding the foregoing, a comprehensive system can be tested in the absence of other work across the pilot sites, utilizing a limited set of performance criteria, a fully developed diagnostic process and a number of delivery components (products and processes) to facilitate professional development of executives.

*Domain 3 — Administrative Leadership*

*Iowa State University site plan*
As a member of a consortium of universities and agencies involved in development activities for the National Executive Development Center of the American Association of School Administrators, Iowa State University's College of Education has assumed responsibility for the Administrative Leadership Domain. Prior to being selected as a pilot site, professors at ISU's College of Education have done a great deal of developmental work in the areas of: (i) employee performance evaluation; (ii) climate/culture; and (iii) strategic/operational planning. Not only are further efforts being made to design, develop, test and validate assessment and

training materials in these three areas; but efforts are also being made to design, develop, test and validate assessment and training materials in six additional areas.

This project is conceived as a cooperative protracted effort during which time ISU will closely coordinate its activities with those of the other pilot sites. ISU expects to utilize appropriate materials developed by the other sites, and the project team will make its materials available to the other pilot sites once they have been tested and validated.

*Site focus*

The focus of ISU's project is to develop the processes and artifacts required to diagnose and develop the human, technical and conceptual skills of school executives in nine areas. The nine areas are: (i) strategic/operational planning; (ii) board/administrator relations; (iii) community relations; (iv) organizational climate/culture; (v) team building; (vi) employee performance evaluation; (vii) organization of central administration; (viii) financial resource management; and (ix) facility development.

In each of the nine areas, ISU will first identify the key knowledge, skills and competencies required to promote executive effectiveness; second, determine whether or not there are adequate existing instruments to diagnose the degree of the executive's proficiency in each of the nine areas studied; third, identify the key knowledge, skills and competencies identified or being developed at other National Executive Development Center's sites to determine cross-over areas between and among sites that can be shared and integrated; and fourth, examine the universe of existing assessment and development materials for each of the nine study areas, integrate concepts and materials from the other NEDC's project sites, and widely disseminate the diagnostic and staff development materials created during the life of the project.

### Domain 4 — Human Relations

*The University of Pittsburgh site plan*

Human relations is the focus of the pilot site at the University of Pittsburgh. Education is a people-oriented profession; human relations skills are essential to effective leadership. Major emphases at the University of Pittsburgh pilot site are on the design, development and testing of materials and activities that (i) increase the participants' understanding of the relationship between successful leadership and human interaction skills; and (ii) expand his/her repertoire of human relations skills.

Over an extended period, the Pittsburgh site will work in close association with the other sites. Since the California site also focusses on human relations, the Pittsburgh site intends to maintain ongoing contacts with California. Integration across sites and between the California and Pittsburgh sites will expose the research at each site to a wider community of scholars, practitioners and critics and will provide a mechanism for ideas to flow from the regional, grass-roots level to the state and national level.

*Site focus*

The components of the human relations domain addressed by the University of Pittsburgh pilot site include:

— Communication
— Motivation, leadership
— Conflict management
— Managing change
— Participatory management and team building
— Alternatives to traditional collective bargaining techniques
— Wellness

## Association of California School Administrators

*Site focus*
The focus of the California School Administrators' executive development center is on improving the way superintendent-level administrators think about their job and the way they appear to treat others in the job setting. Participants, through diagnostic self-reporting instruments and structured activities in training seminars, learn to manage and balance their concern for satisfaction and security, and their concern for people and the job.

## Domain 5 — Personal Capabilities

*Northern Illinois University/University of Alabama site plan*
The focus for this site is to provide information about the personal capabilities of the executive in forms that will promote an understanding and appreciation of themselves and others, and enable individuals to grow personally and professionally.

Acknowledgment of the existence of structural (educable and unchangeable) and dynamic (educable and changeable) forces assist in making decisions about optimal sequences for education and training experiences. The immediate priority for accomplishing the mission statement is for the executive to gain self-knowledge. Assessment of the executive's inherent unchangeable and structural qualities, therefore, assume the status of an imperative. Through formative assessment the executive acquires an awareness of the tools, strengths and qualities that she/he possesses and can utilize in order to create a foundation of self-knowledge, upon which to make best use of available training opportunities.

An important distinction is made between the concepts of change and concepts of growth, considered to be crucial to an understanding of what actually *can* be accomplished by education and training. As stated previously, certain structural areas of personal capabilities are not changeable. Thus, for example, we cannot teach or train someone to be more intelligent or how to gain particular traits as part of their natural personality core. That is *not* to say, though, the individual cannot grow.

In this domain, reliance is placed on aspects of traditional university methods to impart knowledge as well as some innovative alternative approaches in order to answer questions that are central to leadership roles, such as:

What kind of personal feedback is important to the individual leader?
Which aspects of leadership are the individual's 'best fit'?
Given who they are what kind of *other* people does a particular leader need on the team?

*Domain 6 — Multicultural Perspectives*

*University of Arizona site plan*

The College of Education at Arizona State University is a member of a consortium of institutions and agencies involved in the creation of an executive development system for central office school executives. The focus of the Arizona executive development site is on the preliminary design, development, and testing of training and assessment materials for school executives related to the administration of schools in 'multicultural' settings. The project is conceived as a collaborative effort in which the Arizona site will be working closely with the others in all phases of the venture. Cooperation is especially significant for the Arizona site because some elements of the Arizona materials will be integrated into the materials developed at the other sites. Other elements will have 'stand-alone' capabilities and characteristics.

*Site focus*

The focus of the Arizona site is on the impact of 'multicultural perspectives' as these affect school executives in the operation of schools. Arizona State University (ASU) has a long commitment to improving education in 'multicultural' settings. The Arizona site intends to focus its activities on the development of instruments and materials related to the knowledge, skills, and competencies associated with the successful administration of schools and school districts in the 'multicultural perspectives' domain. Significantly this means the focus will be on:

* Cross-cultural value differences
* Intra-cultural value differences
* Socioeconomic value differences
* Staff perceptions, attitudes, beliefs and behaviors
* Student perceptions, attitudes, beliefs and behaviors
* Home perceptions, attitudes, beliefs and behaviors
* School structure and student expectations
* School/community interactions

The Arizona project team rejects the notion that 'a school is a school is a school' irrespective of its sociodemographic characteristics. The contention is that successful school leaders in 'multicultural' settings must demonstrate not only the typical administrative skills and competencies but also an additional and more complex set of knowledge, skills, competencies and sensitivities related to multiculturalism. From the standpoint of school policy and practice, it is essential for leaders to become knowledgeable about the way that schools can be perceived differently and can affect different groups of students in different ways. In line with this perspective, school executives must develop the analytical skills needed to identify and study those factors associated with cultural, ethnic, and social class differences within and among schools. These data can be used to develop an understanding of the reasons for, and responses to, problems of differential school achievement. This platform is especially relevant in those schools and school districts exhibiting 'multicultural' alongside low socioeconomic status (SES) conditions. Students in these schools are more likely to be classified as 'at-risk' of being underachievers, presenting behavioral problems to schools and dropping-out of school.

*David S.G. Carter and Thomas E. Glass*

Many culturally-different and/or low-SES students feel a sense of conflict with and estrangement from institutional norms and rules. Thus, the school executive needs to focus attention on sensitive communication if the student is to derive maximum benefit from the school.


## Conclusion

We started earlier in this volume with the metaphor of a map, in initially setting out the territory of the superintendency and using the former to explore its multifaceted nature. The major foci of earlier chapters have been organized around what are still in many cases the surface features, the contours, shown on the map. Putting these in place required us to take a retrospective look at the nature of the field, albeit from the unique perspective of members and associates of the Texas pilot site project team, working within the guidelines of AASA's National Executive Development Center. It also allowed us to engage in some 'crystal ball gazing' based on an extrapolation of selected contemporary trends, in order to map out the routeways showing the connectedness and interconnectedness of things. Here we took a prospective look at where these might lead with respect to promoting excellence in executive leadership for an uncertain set of alternative futures in the broader context of educational reform.

To the metaphors of map and explorer might now be added that of a compass. The AASA's conception of a National Executive Development Center provides the profession with at least one direction in which it might go; the means to achieve some vision of the future needs of our schools and those who populate them; and the wherewithal to know when we've arrived. If this volume contributes to the realization of this ideal then our purposes will have been well served.

Readers may wonder whether in fact the NEDC and its vision will ever fully materialize into a national coordinated and validated program of professional preparation for the nation's superintendents in the form and manner intended. It is a tenuous innovation which may not be sustainable due to a number of factors. First, the strange fragmented world of educational administration programs and the professoriate make it extremely difficult to communicate with both professional organizations such as AASA and superintendents in the field due to a lack of infrastructure. To develop a nationwide system of preparation there must be a high level of communication from both within and across the institutions of higher education, state agencies, and professional associations such as AASA, NASSP, NSBA and ASCD and this does not exist at the present time. Currently, communication links to practising superintendents are mainly through their professional associations. There are no communication links between the educational administration programs which touch more than perhaps 25 per cent of programs or professors. There is no single journal that is read by the educational administration professoriate designed explicitly to meet their needs. Perhaps the most pervasive education journal read by the professoriate is the *Phi Delta Kappan* which is not an 'ed admin' journal as such. The professional associations do have better inter-agency communication links of both a formal and informal nature. The state agencies which, through their certification standards, dictate the content of current educational administration preparation programs to a significant extent, have neither direct communication links with the associations and practitioners, and only very infrequently communicate with the higher education programs (usually during a five year review process).

When the NEDC does have its model fully field tested how will it be disseminated across the nation? This is highly speculative, but if proposals for national testing are accepted, and some form of national curriculum is put in place the logical extension of this is national standards for teachers with national preparation standards for administrators to follow. In our view it also seems logical in this scenario that those most responsible for implementing this alternative future of American education should be adequately prepared, among other things, to move public education away from its traditional roots of 'localism'. This may seem to lie in the realms of fantasy for some and be 'un-American' to others, but the signs at this time, as elsewhere in the world, point to some types of centralizing tendencies at work.

The intractability of American public education to change is well documented and it comes as no surprise to those social scientists who are concerned to examine the infrastructure of the organizations. School organizations are constantly trying to find and maintain consensus with many different client and interest groups. The current emphasis by reformers on measures of production (achievement scores) is a quasi-industrial profit model that works against the grain of the societal mission given the schools of 'being all things to all people' as much of the time as possible (but note Thomas and Moran, 1992). To move forth on a 'profit' model, decisions have to be made to fully maximize the resources of the 'business' which is, of course, moving away from being all things to all people. It is possible that achievement scores may raise for some schools but the number of 'losers' might well increase, contrary to the claims of some reformers. What is the part to be played out by the school administrator (i.e., superintendent) in this radical reorientation of the traditional role of the school — facilitator, maintainer of the status quo or obstructionist.

For the superintendent to be a facilitator of change he/she must possess the skills, knowledge and aptitudes necessary to dramatically change the nature of the school as an institution. The current school reform movement basically seems to portray the superintendent and school board as elements obstructing reform and restructuring (Finn, 1991; Chubb and Moe, 1990). On occasion they have been declared to be part of the problem rather than part of the solution, although this drastically over-simplifies a complex phenomenon. Superintendents and board members can block 'top down' reform in local districts even when it is mandated. Obversely, they can greatly facilitate its implementation if they see it is in the best interests of their district to do so. The role of the superintendent in convincing the board of the desirability of planned change is well documented in the AASA Ten Year Study (Glass, 1992). Superintendents initiate district policy more than three-fourths of the time. They are the key facilitators of change and reform in school districts, directly, if not indirectly. There is a case to be made that school reform efforts will flourish or fail depending on the opinions and actions of superintendents that they attract. The argument extends to the implementation of site-based decision making as well. The majority of school districts have a student enrollment of well under 3000 and here the superintendent remains the link with the school system and the local community that ultimately makes the executive decisions in most states.

Given these realities, the bottom line is that the emergent NEDC in its form and scope reaches far beyond current constraints affecting the skills and knowledge of the current generation of practicing superintendents. Its potential transformative power already reaches into the reform movement itself in influencing indirectly how schools will be restructured.

Hopefully, the task of developing a knowledge base and set of skills that define the effective superintendent will soon be developed and can be agreed upon by both practitioners and professors of educational administration. One of the lessons learned by those participating in the NEDC in the past several years is that professors of educational administration seldom agree with each other so that workable compromises can be established. Why this is the case is a bit baffling.

It will be interesting to note the outcomes of the 'knowledge base' projects presently being developed by UCEA institutions, and the 'professional standards' for the superintendency being developed by AASA. In recent years, NASSP (National Association of Secondary School Principals) and NAESP (National Association of Elementary School Principals) have developed lists of essential skills and competencies through committees populated by both practitioners and academics. However, to what degree these compendiums of skills and competencies are being integrated into principal preparation programs is not substantially known at this time.

A troubling question is how do the outcomes of the NEDC, AASA, UCEA, NASSP and NAESP become integrated into preparation programs? With so many hundreds of institutions in the 50 states conducting certificate programs, what vehicle exists to ensure reasonable conformity among programs? No workable authority exists to ensure that principals and superintendents are appropriately prepared for their important roles in school leadership. Thus, the professional development program described and encouraged in this book is a response.

If the NEDC as an entity is allowed to lapse, the work it has accomplished thus far will still survive and provide the fulcrum for future efforts designed to insure the effectiveness of the nation's educational leaders. It has been the most intensive expenditure of effort in partnering professional associations with institutions of higher education in decades to bring professionalism and effectiveness to the superintendency. Indeed, it has been insightful to us to chronicle both the superintendency and the NEDC in benchmarking what has been achieved to date.

Our collective aspiration is that we have made some contribution to an understanding of the current state of play with respect to the superintendency, its current and future needs, and its accomplishments. By sharing our knowledge, we hope that new and better knowledge can be developed on how best to prepare leaders for the nation's schools.

# Appendix

The following index provides to the reader a listing of the skills and components of knowledge needed by superintendents in order to effectively lead the *instructional system* of their districts through staffing. These skills and knowledge components have been translated into self-administered diagnostic instruments so that aspiring and present superintendents might gain a view of their competency levels in *Staffing for Instruction.*

PERFORMANCE CRITERIA — STAFFING FOR INSTRUCTION

DOMAIN 2: INSTRUCTIONAL LEADERSHIP

TASK AREA 2.2: STAFFING FOR INSTRUCTION

**Task 2.2.1**  The executive maintains adequate staffing levels while anticipating future changes in staffing needs.

**Sub-Task 2.2.1.1**  **Monitors to maintain staff adequacy**
2.2.1.1.1  Analyzes staffing patterns to determine the status quo regarding class size, qualifications, and mis-assignments.
2.2.1.1.2  Analyzes staffing patters to project anticipated retirements, leavers and non-renewals.
2.2.1.1.3  Confers with administrators and instructional specialists regarding shortages and other discrepancies.

**Sub-Task 2.2.1.2**  **Assesses needs for staffing changes**
2.2.1.2.1  Reviews proposals for additions and changes in staffing patterns.
2.2.1.2.2  Determines special staffing needs for new instructional programs.
2.2.1.2.3  Recommends goals for meeting needs for minority and special teachers in scarce supply.
2.2.1.2.4  Projects staffing requirements for long-range planning.

**Task 2.2.2**  The executive oversees a thorough system of recruitment procedures that leads to the identification of qualified candidates for job openings.

**Sub-Task 2.2.2.1**      **Plans for systematic recruitment**

2.2.2.1.1      Reviews and updates a comprehensive file of recruitment sources — placement offices, churches, military bases, etc.

2.2.2.1.2      Designs recruitment strategies for both long-term and short term identification of applicants.

2.2.2.1.3      Produces media for use in recruitment — slides, brochures, videos, posters, etc.

2.2.2.1.4      Develops plans for active participation for parents, students, teachers, and others in the recruitment process.

**Sub-Task 2.2.2.2**      **Directs or coordinates recruitment efforts**

2.2.2.2.1      Budgets for planned recruitment efforts.

2.2.2.2.2      Orients participants to assure a unified approach to recruiting.

2.2.2.2.3      Directs special efforts to identify and motivate future teachers.

2.2.2.2.4      Coordinates efforts to prepare and promote teacher aides for regular teaching.

**Task 2.2.3**      The executive provides for a screening process that designates the most qualified applicants prior to final selection.

**Sub-Task 2.2.3.1**      **Analyzes job descriptions**

2.2.3.1.1      Identifies the unique requirements distinguishing positions from each other.

2.2.3.1.2      Determines specific documents required for completion of applicant files for positions.

2.2.3.1.3      Designates kinds of educational, professional and work experiences relevant to the positions.

2.2.3.1.4      Determines cutting scores or priority criteria for applicant consideration beyond initial screening.

2.2.3.1.5      Specifies the essential legal, professional, and personal requirements of positions.

**Sub-Task 2.2.3.2**      **Assembles preliminary data**

2.2.3.2.1      Establishes procedures for receiving applicants and facilitating the filing process with promptness and ease.

2.2.3.2.2      Monitors the system for periodic, clerical reviews of applicant files to assure their completion and updating.

2.2.3.2.3      Designs a system for both computer-based and paper file storage of applicant data.

2.2.3.2.4      Designs data reduction procedures for formatting, profiling or summarizing applicants for easy review.

2.2.3.2.5      Applies initial screening criteria and related procedures uniformly and objectively to all applicants.

2.2.3.2.6      Provides information to applicants regarding criteria to be used, the status of their applications, and time table for screening and selection.

2.2.3.2.7      Utilizes a carefully programmed scoring and retrieval system for screening out applicants not minimally qualified.

2.2.3.2.8    Uses certification, experience and legal requirements for eliminating applicants lacking essential prerequisites.

2.2.3.2.9    Utilizes test scores, grades, and rating in forms that prevent arbitrary elimination of applicants.

2.2.3.2.10   Establishes clear affirmative action guidelines to assure that applicants from under represented populations are included in the pool for further consideration.

**Sub-Task 2.2.3.3    Identifies most promising candidates**

2.2.3.3.1    Designates priorities for the use of criteria for each specific position.

2.2.3.3.2    Develops procedures for pre-selection processing of applications to limit further data gathering and conserve resources.

2.2.3.3.3    Monitors a set of standard procedures for reviewing applicant files, identifying a limited number for further data gathering and review.

2.2.3.3.4    Plans for careful, special reviews of non-traditional applicants with unique skills or experiences.

2.2.3.3.5    Provides for the inclusion of trainees, interns, and para-professionals in the applicant pool to be reviewed for selection.

**Task 2.2.4.**    The executive provides a process for selecting the most highly qualified candidates for each instructional position.

**Sub-Task 2.2.4.1    Makes formal presentations**

2.2.4.1.1    Resources are provided to assure released time, travel funds, and consulting services.

2.2.4.1.2    Schedules are developed for interviews, data analysis, reviews, and decision-making.

2.2.4.1.3    Target dates for final decisions are set along with back-up plans for reconsideration.

2.2.4.1.4    Applicants identified for further review are promptly notified, encouraged to provide further data, and informed more fully of the positions.

2.2.4.1.5    Involves a variety of personnel reflecting various interests and appropriate kinds of expertise.

**Sub-Task 2.2.4.2    Training and guiding selection personnel**

2.2.4.2.1    Orientation and procedural review sessions are planned with all personnel to be involved in selections.

2.2.4.2.2    Provides training for individuals in fulfilling individual staff members to assure proficient use of tests, inventories, application forms and other data sources.

2.2.4.2.3    Provides interviewer training to assure that relevant and reliable information is provided in usable form.

2.2.4.2.4    Evaluations of the screening and selection process includes analysis of individual staff objectivity and reliability.

**Sub-Task 2.2.4.3**     **In-depth data gathering**

2.2.4.3.1     Specifies explicit selection criteria for top priority in gathering data on selected candidates.

2.2.4.3.2     Structures interviews to assure focus on highly relevant information, avoiding interviewer drift, and superficialities.

2.2.4.3.3     Systematically records interview data using standard procedures, respecting the rights of applicants.

2.2.4.3.4     Requires special instrumentation and procedures to assure highly discriminating data is available for selection.

2.2.4.3.5     Systematically utilizes tests, inventories, reference calls and other sources of data to clearly focus on selection criteria.

**Sub-Task 2.2.4.4**     **Analyzing selection data**

2.2.4.4.1     Secures independent recommendations and ranking of candidates by individuals with different perspectives.

2.2.4.4.2     Establishes procedures for summarizing, weighing, comparing, scoring, profiling and otherwise analyzing a variety of information.

2.2.4.4.3     Makes tentative decisions regarding ranking of finalists.

2.2.4.4.4     Provides for the systematic review of all relevant data assembled on the most promising candidates.

2.2.4.4.5     Develops sets of supporting conclusions regarding each finalist.

**Sub-Task 2.2.4.5**     **Making recommendations**

2.2.4.5.1     Characterizes finalists for a position in terms of unique and comparative strengths of each.

2.2.4.5.2     Clarifies availability of each finalist prior to final ranking.

2.2.4.5.3     Reviews advantages and disadvantages produced when alternative assignments are considered.

2.2.4.5.4     Decides on a recommendation to present for action.

2.2.4.5.5     Formulates a back-up plan of action in the event recommendations are not implemented.

**Task 2.2.5**     The executive provides staff orientation and induction programs that assure new personnel the information and support needed to function in new surroundings.

**Sub-Task 2.2.5.1**     **Orientation of new personnel**

2.2.5.1.1     Develops plans for orientation of new personnel, meeting with them, reviewing local philosophy and ideals.

2.2.5.1.2     Reviews and coordinates orientation activities in schools and offices to be sure all materials and information sources are provided.

2.2.5.1.3     Develops differentiated orientation procedures for inexperienced and experienced new personnel.

**Sub-Task 2.2.5.2**     **Induction Programs**

2.2.5.2.1     Organizes a one or two year induction program for

| | personnel training designed to respond to diagnosed needs for professional development, and provide special support and supervision. |
|---|---|
| 2.2.5.2.2 | Coordinates work of principals and other supervisors in assisting inexperienced personnel, developing guidelines for assignments, classroom supervision, and special support. |
| 2.2.5.2.3 | Reviews formative evaluation reports on inexperienced personnel, analyzing anecdotal reports, and offering suggestions to supervisors. |

**Task 2.2.6** The executive implements a placement system that assigns and reassigns personnel to positions that makes the best use of talents.

**Sub-Task 2.2.6.1** **Planning for systematic assignment, reassignment and balancing of personnel**

| 2.2.6.1.1 | Develops a comprehensive plan for systematically assigning, reassigning and balancing personnel in grades, programs, and other operating units. |
|---|---|
| 2.2.6.1.2 | Develops specific guidelines for reassigning personnel to respond to various personnel and instructional needs. |
| 2.2.6.1.3 | Negotiates agreements regarding follow-through on reassignments with principals and others. |
| 2.2.6.1.4 | Guides principals and staff in making assignments that serve the needs of the instructional program. |
| 2.2.6.1.5 | Promotes innovative team arrangements by careful assignment of personnel. |

**Sub-Task 2.2.6.2** **Assigning and reassigning to meet high priority needs**

| 2.2.6.2.1 | Allocates personnel resources to make best use of individual skills, interests, and preparation. |
|---|---|
| 2.2.6.2.2 | Reassigns personnel as required to meet changing conditions within schools or programs. |
| 2.2.6.2.3 | Reassigns personnel to assure opportunities for renewal, or personal growth. |
| 2.2.6.2.4 | Allocates personnel resources giving priority to innovative team projects or proposals. |

**Sub-Task 2.2.6.3** **Balancing staff in programs and schools to assure appropriate competencies needed**

| 2.2.6.3.1 | Allocates personnel resources to assure balance in quality of personnel between schools and programs. |
|---|---|
| 2.2.6.3.2 | Reallocates personnel as needed to make efficient use of available talents. |
| 2.2.6.3.3 | Recommends new personnel assignments with both individual and instructional needs in mind. |
| 2.2.6.3.4 | Restructures or reallocates vacancies to improve balance among schools and programs. |

**Task 2.2.7**      The executive directs the personnel operations of the system function to assure a stable yet improving and well balanced work force.

**Sub-Task 2.2.7.1**      **Policy administration**
2.2.7.1.1      Coordinates standard staff grievance procedures, assuring due process to all.
2.2.7.1.2      Analyzes federal, state, and local polices, and contractual, constitutional, and liability issues related to teacher rights and responsibilities.
2.2.7.1.3      Analyzes the principles and procedures related to administering personnel policies.
2.2.7.1.4      Analyzes laws and regulations relating to contacts, certification, assignments, and personnel records.
2.2.7.1.5      Defines job requirements for each position in terms of instructional processes.
2.2.7.1.6      Recognizes and classifies minimum job entry qualifications and skills.
2.2.7.1.7      Develops and analyzes job descriptions to reflect the needs of the instructional program practices, salaries, and agreements.

**Sub-Task 2.2.7.2**      **Providing an adequate wage and benefit schedule**
2.2.7.2.1      Proposes salary advancement based on preparation and qualifications related to position.
2.2.7.2.2      Proposes recognition or other incentives that relate to improvement of instruction.
2.2.7.2.3      Proposes fringe benefits that encourage job satisfaction.
2.2.7.2.4      Advises with business and finance officers regarding effects of wage and benefit decisions on instructional personnel.

**Sub-Task 2.2.7.3**      **Staff retention**
2.2.7.3.1      Identifies strategies for retaining staff and faculty.
2.2.7.3.2      Works cooperatively with employee organizations to get agreements on improving instruction.
2.2.7.3.3      Provides for a system of incentives for experienced personnel.
2.2.7.3.4      Offers funding for study leaves and sabbaticals for employee self-improvement.

**Sub-Task 2.2.7.4**      **Reduction in force**
2.2.7.4.1      Prepares alternate plans for reducing instructional personnel as required.
2.2.7.4.2      Analyzes the effects of alternative reduction in staff plans.
2.2.7.4.3      Analyzes actions with respect to federal, state, and local policies, and liability issues.
2.2.7.4.4      Applies EEO guidelines in reduction-in-force procedures, adapting affirmative action plans as needed.

**Sub-Task 2.2.7.5**   **Minority staffing**

2.2.7.5.1   Establishes goals for the recruitment of minority teaching candidates.

2.2.7.5.2   Proposes innovative programs for accomplishing affirmative actions goals.

2.2.7.5.3   Develops both short and long term plans for securing minority personnel of top quality

# References

ALVEY, D.T. and UNDERWOOD, K.E. (1985) 'When boards and superintendents clash, it's over the balance of school power', *The American School Board Journal*, October, pp. 21–5.

AMERICAN ASSOCIATION OF COLLEGES OF TEACHER EDUCATION (1988) *School Leadership Preparation: A Preface for Action*, Washington, DC, AACTE.

AMERICAN ASSOCIATION OF SCHOOL ADMINISTRATORS NATIONAL EXECUTIVE DEVELOPMENT CENTER. Learning for Leadership: AASA's/NEDC Program. A Proposal for a Five Year System Development Project, Arlington, VA, AASA.

AMERICAN ASSOCIATION OF SCHOOL ADMINISTRATORS (1979) *Selecting a Superintendent*, Arlington, VA, AASA.

AMERICAN ASSOCIATION OF SCHOOL ADMINISTRATORS (1982) *Guidelines for Preparation of School Administrators*, Arlington, VA, AASA.

AMERICAN ASSOCIATION OF SCHOOL ADMINISTRATORS (1983) *The Role of a Consultant in a Superintendency Search*, Arlington, VA, AASA.

AMERICAN ASSOCIATION OF SCHOOL ADMINISTRATORS (1984 and 1988) *The Educational Administrator Effectiveness Profile*, Arlington, VA, AASA National Executive Development Center.

AMERICAN ASSOCIATION OF SCHOOL ADMINISTRATORS (1990) *National Superintendent of the Year Program: Application Packet*, Arlington, VA, AASA.

ANGUS, D. (1987) 'The Retirement Plans of Michigan School Administrators', *Bureau of Accreditation and School Improvement Studies*, Ann Arbor, Michigan, University of Michigan.

BAILEY, M.D. (1985) 'The relationship among supervisory competencies, job expectations and position types', unpublished doctoral dissertation, Austin, TX, University of Texas at Austin.

BENNIS, W. and NANUS, B. (1985) *Leaders: The Strategies for Taking Charge*, New York, Harper and Row.

BLACKLEDGE, B.J. (1992) 'Private groups launch search for new urban superintendents', *Education Daily*, **25**, 26, 10 February, pp. 1–2.

BLAKE, R.R. and MOUTON, J.S. (1982) 'A comparative analysis of situationalism and 9.9 management by principle', *Organizational Dynamics*, spring, pp. 20–43.

BLUMBERG, A. (1985) *The School Superintendent: Living With Conflict*, New York, Teachers College Press.

BOLTON, D. (1988) 'New approaches to administrator assessment procedures', Seattle, Washington, Center for Assessment of Administrative Performance, University of Washington (mimeographed).

BRAY, D.W. (1989) 'History of the assessment center in the United States', in WILSON, J.D, THOMPSON, O.B., WILLWARD, B. and KEENAN, A. (Eds) *Assessment for Teacher Development*, Lewes, Falmer Press.

BRIDGES, E.M. (1982) 'Research on the school administrator: The state of the art, 1967–1980', *Educational Administration Quarterly*, **18**, 3, pp. 12–33.

BUCK, J.T. (1989) 'Transformational leadership behaviors of exemplary Texas superintendents', Austin, TX, The University of Texas, unpublished doctoral dissertation.

BURKE, D.L. (1990) 'An Analysis of Self-Perceived Operational Authority for Certain School District Decisions', by Selected Superintendents and School Board Presidents, unpublished doctoral dissertation, Northern Illinois University.

BURNETT, Q.S. (1988) 'School superintendent selection procedures and the performance of the person selected', unpublished doctoral dissertation, Austin, TX, University of Texas.

BURNHAM, J.G. (1989) 'The career development experiences and career patterns of superintendents in the U.S.', unpublished doctoral dissertation, Austin, TX, Univeristy of Texas.

BURNS, J.M. (1978) *Leadership*, New York, Harper and Row.

CARTER, D.S.G., ESTES, N., LOREDO, J. and HARRIS, B. (1991) 'Evolving a diagnostic system for formative use by senior school system executives in the USA', *School Organization*, **11**, 1, pp. 53–63.

CARTER, D.S.G., ESTES, N., LOREDO, J. and WAN, Y. (1991) 'An assessment center approach to school-executive diagnosis and development', *The National Forum of Applied Educational Research Journal*, **4**, 2.

CARTER, D.S.G. and HARRIS, B.M. (1991) 'Assessing executive performance for continuing professional growth', *Journal of Personnel Evaluation in Education*, **4**, 1, pp. 7–19.

CHAND, K. (1983) *The Current Trend of the Job Description of School Superintendents in the United States*, report of a study (EA 016 323).

CHUBB, J.L. and MOE, T.M. (1990) *Politics, Markets and America's Schools.* Washington, DC, Bookings Insitution.

CLARK, D. (1989) 'Improving the Preparation of School Administrators: An Agenda for Reform', Charlottesville, VA., National Policy Board for Educational Administration.

CLIFFORD, G.J. and GUTHRIE, J.W. (1988) *Ed School: A Brief for Professional Education*, Chicago, IL, University of Chicago Press.

COLEMAN, P. (1986) 'The good school district: A critical examination of student achievement and per pupil expenditure as measures of school effectiveness', *Journal of Education Finance*, **12**, 1, pp. 71–96.

COLEMAN, P. and LAROCQUE, L. (1988) *Reaching Out: Instructional Leadership in School Districts*, Simon Fraser University and the Social Sciences and Humanities Research Council of Canada, Spring.

COLLIER, V.L. (1987) 'Identification of skills perceived by Texas superintendents as necessary for successful job performance', Austin, TX, University of Texas, (unpublished doctoral dissertation), May.

CRAIG, D.W. (1982) 'Career patterns of Michigan public school superintendents in districts with an enrollment of 5,000 or more students', unpublished doctoral dissertation, Ball State University.

CRIBBEN, J. (1972) *Effective Managerial Leadership*, American Management Association Inc, Alexandria, VA.

CROWSON, R.L. and GLASS, T.E. (1991) *The Changing Role of the Local School District Superintendent in the United States*, Champaign, IL, National Center for School Leadership (Occasional Paper).

CROWSON, R.L. (1987) 'The local school district superintendency: A puzzling administrative role', *Educational Administration Quarterly*, **23**, 3, August, pp. 49–69.

CROWSON, R.L. and MORRIS, V.C. (1987) 'The superintendency and school reform: An exploratory study', *Metropolitan Education*, 5, Fall, pp. 25–39.

Crowson, R.L. and Hannaway, J. (1989) 'Introduction and overview: The politics of reforming school administration', in HANNAWAY, J. and CROWSON, R. (Eds) *The Politics of Reforming School Administration*, The 1988 Yearbook of the Politics of Education Association, Lewes, Falmer Press.

CUBAN, L. (1985) 'Conflict and leadership in the superintendency', Phi Delta Kappan, **67**, 1, pp. 28–30.

CUBAN, L. (1988) *The Managerial Imperative and the Practice of Leadership in Schools*, Albany, NY, State University of New York Press.

CUBBERLEY, E.R. (1916) *Public School Education*, Boston, MA, Houghton-Mifflin.

CUNNINGHAM, L.V. and HENTGES, J. (1982) *The American School Superintendency: A Full Report*, Arlington, VA, The American Association of School Administrators.

CURCIO, J.L. (1992) 'Vulnerability of the school district superintendent', paper presented at the annual meeting of the American Educational Research Association, San Francisco.

DEWEY, J. (1929) *The Quest for Certainty*, New York, Minton, Balch.

DRZONEK, A. (1988) 'The AASA performance goals as priortized by Illinois superintendents', unpublished research study. Northern Illinois University.

DRUCKER, P. (1974) *Management*, New York, Harper and Row.

DUTTWEILER, P.C. and HORD, S.M. (1987) *Dimensions of Effective Leadership*, Austin, TX, Southwest Educational Development Laboratory.

ESTES, N. (1988) 'Superintendent and principal: Roles for the 21st century', *Insight*, Spring, pp. 28–9.

EVANS, M.C., PALMER, R.L. and HARRIS, B.M. (1975) A diagnostic assessment system for professional supervisory competencies, Documents 12A and 12B. Special Education Supervisor Training Project, University of Texas at Austin.

EXECUTIVE EDUCATOR (1992) In search of 100 of North America's top executive educators, **14**, 3.

FARMER, N.J. (1983) 'Characteristics of women principals in North Carolina', unpublished doctoral dissertation, University of North Carolina at Chapel Hill.

FEISTRITZER, C.E. (1988) *Profile of School Administrators in the US*, Washington, DC, National Center for Education Information.

FINN, C.E. *We Must Take Charge: Our Schools and Our Future*, New York, Free Press.

FINN, C.F. and PETERSEN, K.D. (1985) 'Principals, Superintendents and the Administrators Art', *Public Interest*, **79**, 42.

FIRESTONE, W.A. (1990) 'Continuity and incrementationalism after all: State responses to the excellence movement', in MURPHY, J. (Ed.) *The Educational Reform Movement of the 1980s: Perspectives and Cases*, Berkeley, CA, McCutchan, pp. 143–66.

FRASHER, J.M. and FRASHER, R.S. (1980) 'Sex bias in the evaluation of administrators', *Journal of Educational Administration*, **18**, pp. 245–53.

FUQUA, A.B. (1983) 'Professional attractiveness, inside sponsorship, and perceived paternalism as predictors of upward mobility of public school superintendents', unpublished doctoral dissertation, Virginia Polytechnic Institute and State University.

GAERTNER, K.N. (1980) 'The structure of organizational careers', *Sociology of Education*, **53**, pp. 7–20.

GEORGE, C. (1972) *The History of Management Thought*, Englewood Cliffs, NJ, Prentice-Hall Inc.

GIBBONEY, R.A. (1989) 'Education of administrators: An American tragedy', *Education Week*, April, p. 28.

GLASS, T.E. (Ed.) (1987) *An Analysis of Texts of School Administration: 1820–1985*, Danville, IL, Interstate Press.

GLASS, T.E. (1990) 'Chicago's schools: Can they be reformed?', *Educational Management and Administration*, **18**, 2, pp. 59–64.

GLASS, T.E. (1992) *The Study of the American School Superintendency: America's Education Leaders in a Time of Reform*, American Association of School Administrators, Arlington, VA.

GLASS, T.E. and SCLAFANI, S.B. (1988) 'Here are the skills you need to succeed as a superintendent', *Executive Educator*, **10**, 7, pp. 19–21.

GRADY, M. and BRYANT, M. (1991) 'School Board Turmoil and Superintendent Turnover: What Pushes Them to the Brink?', *School Administrator*, **28**, 2 February, pp. 19–25.

GREENFIELD, W.D. (1991) 'Toward a theory of school leadership'. Paper Presented at the annual meeting of the American Educational Research Association, Chicago.

GRIFFITHS, D.E. (1959) *Administrative Theory*, New York, Appleton- Century-Crofts.

GRIFFITHS, D.E. (1966a) *The School Superintendent*, New York, Center for Applied Research in Education.

GRIFFITHS, D.E. (1966b) *The Superintendency*, New York, Center for Applied Research, New York.

GRIFFITHS, D.E., STOUT, R.T. and FORSYTH, P.B. (Eds) (1988) *Leaders for America's Schools: The Report and Papers of the National Commission on Excellence in Educational Administration*, Berkeley, CA, McCutchan Publishing Corporation.

GRIFFITHS, D.E. (1988) 'Educational Administration: Reform PDQ or RIP', Invited Lecture, Division A, American Educational Research Association, New Orleans.

GUTHRIE, J.W. (1990) 'Effective educational executives: An essay on the concept of and preparation for strategic leadership', paper presented at the annual meeting of the American Educational Research Association, Boston.

GUTHRIE, J.W. and CLIFFORD, G.T. (1989) 'A brief for professional education', *Phi Delta Kappan*, **70**, 5, pp. 371–5.

GUTHRIE, J.W.R. and REED, R.J. (1986) *Educational Administration and Policy: Effective Leadership for American Education*, Englewood Cliffs, NJ, Prentice-Hall Inc.

HALL, G.E. and DIFFORD, G.A. (1992) 'State administrators association director's perceptions of the exiting superintendent phenomenon', paper presented at the annual meeting of the American Educational Research Association, San Francisco.

HALL, G.E., RUTHERFORD, W.L., HORD, S.M. and HULING, L.L. (1984) 'Effects of three principals styles on school improvement', *Educational Leadership*, **41**, 5, pp. 22–9.

HARRIS, B.M. (1986) *Developmental Teacher Evaluation*, Boston, MA, Allyn and Bacon.

HARRIS, B.M. (1989) *In-Service Education for Staff Development*, Boston, MA, Allyn and Bacon.

HARRIS, B.M. *et al* (1992) *Personnel Administration in Education*, Third Edition. Boston, MA, Allyn and Bacon.

HARRIS, B.M. and HILL, J. (1982) *The Developmental Teacher Evaluation Kit*, Austin, Texas, Southwest Educational Development Laboratory.

HARRIS, B.M. and WAN, Y. (Eds) (1991) *Performance Criteria for School Executives — Instructional Leadership Domain*, Austin, TX, College of Education, University of Texas at Austin.

HAUGHLAND, M. (1987) 'Professional competencies needed by school superintendents, as percieved by school board members and superintendents in South Dakota', *ERS Spectrum*, **5**, 4, pp. 409–42.

HAWLEY, W.D. (1988) 'Universities and the improvement of school management: Roles for the states', in *Leaders for America's schools: Report and papers of the National Commission on Excellence in Educational Administration*, San Francisco, McCutchan.

HENTGES, J.T. (1986) 'The politics of superintendent-school board linkages: A study of power, participation, and control', *ERS Spectrum*, **4**, 13, summer, pp. 23–32.

HERMAN, J.L. (1989) 'Instructional leadership skills and competencies of public school superintendents', unpublished doctoral dissertation, Austin, TX, University of Texas at Austin.

HERSEY, P. (1982) 'The NASSP Assessment Center develops leadership talent', *Educational Leadership*, **39**, 5, pp. 370–1.

HERSEY, P. (1989) 'Identifying and developing superior principals', in WILSON, J.D., THOMPSON, O.B., WILLWARD, B. and KEENAN, A. (Eds) *Assessment for Teacher Development*, Lewes, Falmer Press.

HILL, P.T., WISE, A.E. and SHAPIRO, L. (1989) *Educational Progress: Cities Mobilize to Improve Their Schools*, Santa Monica, CA, Rand Center for the Study of the Teaching Profession.

HORD, S.M. (1988) 'The principal as teacher educator', *Journal of Teacher Education*, **39**, 3, pp. 8–12.

HORD, S.M. (1990) *Images of Superintendents' Leadership for Learning*, Austin, TX, Southwest Educational Development Laboratory.

HORD, S.M. (1992) 'Entering and exiting the superintendency: Preparation, promises, problems', paper presented at the annual meeting of the American Educational Research Association, San Franscisco.

HORD. S.M., RUTHERFORD, W.L., HULING-AUSTIN, L.L. and HALL, G.E. (1987) *Taking Charge of Change*, Arlington, VA, Association for Supervision and Curriculum Development.

HORD, S.M. (1991) 'District-level executives' perceptions and about their role as instructional leaders', *Texas Researcher*, **2**, pp. 58–73.

HOY, W.K. and MISKEL, C.G. (1991) *Educational Administration: Theory, Research and Practice*, (Fourth edition), New York, McGraw-Hill.

HOYLE, J.R. (1987) 'The AASA model for preparing school leaders', in MURPHY, J. and HALLINGER, P. (Eds) *Approaches to Administrative Training in Education*, Albany, NY, State University of New York Press, pp. 83–98.

HOYLE, J.R. (1989a) 'Preparing the 21st-century superintendent', *Phi Delta Kappan*, **70**, 5, pp. 376–9.

HOYLE, J.R. (1989b) 'Administering learning environments in the 21st-century', *Theory into Practice*, **20**, 4, pp. 250–4.

HOYLE, J.R., ENGLISH, F.W. and STEFFY, B.E. (1985) *Skills for Successful Leaders*, Arlington, VA, American Association of School Administrators.

JACKSON, C.B. (1981) 'Career development for women in public school administration: A study of women school superintendents in the United States', unpublished doctoral dissertation, Univerisity of Colorado at Boulder.

Jacobson, S.L. (1986) *Administrative Leadership and Effective Small-rural schools: A Comparative Case Study*, New York, State University of New York, Ithaca College of Agriculture and Life Sciences at Cornell University, September.

JOHNSON, J.M. (1979) 'A comparison of male and female doctoral and postdoctoral students of educational administration at universities in Pennsylvania', unpublished doctoral dissertation, University of Pittsburgh.

JUDGE, H.G. (1982) *American Graduate Schools of Education: A View from Abroad*, New York, Ford Foundation.

KALLOS, D. and LUNDGREN, U.P. (1975) 'Educational psychology: Its scope and its limits', *British Journal of Educational Psychology*, **45**, pp. 111–21.

KATZ, R.L. (1974) 'Skills of an "Effective Administrator"', *Harvard Business Review*, **52**, pp. 33–42.

KONNERT, W. and GARNER, J.B. (1987) 'Assessing and altering risk-taking propensity: Keys to superintendency success', *Catalyst*, Spring, pp. 7–12.

LEITHWOOD, K.A. and MONTGOMERY, D. (1982) 'The role of the elementary school principal in program improvment', *Review of Educational Research*, **52**, 3, pp. 309–39.

LEITHWOOD, K.A. and STEINBACH, R. (1989) 'Components of chief education officers' problem solving', paper presented at the annual meeting of the American Educational Research Association, San Fransisco.

LITTLE, S.H. (1980) 'Sponsorship and other factors in mobility of women in school administrative positions', unpublished doctoral dissertation, Austin, TX, University of Texas at Austin.

LUPINI, D. (1983) 'Educational leadership and the political fact', paper presented at the Annual Joint Conference of the Alberta School Superintendents and the Alberta Education Management Society, Edmonton.

MCCARTHY, M.M. (1987) 'The professoriate in educational administration: Current status and challenges ahead', *UCEA Review*, **28**, 2, pp. 2–6.

McCarthy, M.M. *et al.* (1988) *Under Scrutiny: The Educational Administration Professoriate*, Tempe, AZ, UCEA.

McCleary, P. and Ogawa, R.T. (1985) *Locating Principals who are Leaders: The Assessment Center Concept.* Educational Considerations.

McLaughlin, M.W. (1990) 'The Rand change agent study revisited: Macro perspectives and micro realities', *Educational Researcher*, **19**, 9, pp. 11–16.

March, J.C. (1977) 'Analytical skills and the university training of administrators', *Journal of Educational Administration*, **12**, 1, pp. 17–40.

Martin, R.V.R. (1981) 'Minority women administrators' perceptions of barriers in higher education', unpublished doctoral dissertation, University of Connecticutt.

Melvin, C.A. (1991) 'Translating Deming's 14 points for education', *School Administrator*, November, pp. 19–21.

Miklos, E. (1988) 'Administrator selection, career patterns, succession, and socialization', in Boyan, N.J. (Ed.) *Handbook of Research on Educational Administration*, New York, Longman.

Milstein, M.M., Bobroff, B.M. and Restine, L.N. (1991) *Internship Programs in Education Administration: A Guide to Preparing Educational Leaders*, New York, Teachers College Press.

Miskel, C. (1990) 'Research and the preparation of educational administrators', *Journal of Educational Administration*, **28**, 3, pp. 33–47.

Morris, M.P. (1980) 'Critical characteristics of top level women administrators in the overseas American sponsored school', unpublished doctoral dissertation, Univerisity of Denver.

Muller, R.W. (1989) 'Instructional leadership superintendent competencies related to student achievement', Austin, TX, University of Texas unpublished doctoral dissertation.

Murphy, J. (1991) 'The effects of the educational reform movement on departments of educational leadership', *Educational Evaluation and Policy Analysis*, **13**, 1, pp. 49–65.

Murphy, J. and Hallinger, P. (1986) 'The superintendent as instructional leader: Findings from effective school districts', *Journal of Educational Administration*, **24**, 2, Summer, pp. 213–31.

Murphy, J. and Hallinger, P. (1987) 'New directions in the professional development of school administrators: A synthesis and suggestions for improvement', in Murphy, J. and Hallinger, P. (Eds) *Approaches to Administrative Training in Education*, Albany, NY, State University of New York Press.

Murphy, J. and Hallinger, P. (1989) 'A new era in the professional development of school administrators: Lessons from emerging programmes', *Journal of Educational Administration*, **28**, 2, pp. 22–45.

Murphy, J., Hallinger, P. and Peterson, K.D. (1985) 'Supervising and evaluating principals: Lessons from effective districts', *Educational Leadership*, **43**, 2, October, pp. 78–82.

Murphy, J. (1992) *The Landscape of Leadership Preparation: Reframing the Education of School Administrators*, Newbury Park, CA, Corwin Press.

National Association of Elementary School Principals (1990) *Principals for 21st Century Schools*, Alexandria, VA, NAESP.

National Association of Secondary School Principals and National

ASSOCIATION OF ELEMENTARY SCHOOL PRINCIPALS (1990) *Principals for Our Changing Schools: Preparation and Certification*, Fairfax, VA, NASSP and NAESP.

NATIONAL COMMISSION ON EXCELLENCE IN EDUCATION (1983) *A Nation at Risk: The Imperative for Educational Reform*, Washington, DC, US Government Printing Office.

NATIONAL COMMISSION ON EXCELLENCE IN EDUCATION (1984) *A Nation at Risk: The Full Account. Report of the Commission edited and published by USA Research*, Cambridge, MA, NCEE.

NATIONAL COMMISSION ON EXCELLENCE IN EDUCATION (1987) *Leaders for America's Schools*, Tempe, AZ, University Council for Educational Administration.

NATIONAL GOVERNORS' ASSOCIATION (1986) *Time for Results*, Washington, DC, NGA.

NATIONAL POLICY BOARD FOR EDUCATIONAL ADMINISTRATION (1989) *Improving the Preparation of School Administrators: An Agenda for Reform*, Charlottesville, VA, NPBEA.

ORTIZ, F. (1982) *Career Patterns in Education: Women, Men and Minorities in Public School Administration*, New York, Praeger.

PACHECO, B.A. (1982) 'Barriers to advancement in educational administration as perceived by women administrators', unpublished doctoral dissertation, University of the Pacific.

PAULU, N. (1988) *Experiences in School Improvement: The Story of 16 American Districts*, Washington, DC, US Department of Education, Office of Educational Research and Improvement.

PETERS, T.J. and WATERMAN, R.H. (1982) *In Search of Excellence: Lessons from America's Best-Run Companies*, New York, Harper and Row.

PETERSON, K.D. (1984) 'Mechanisms of administrative control over managers in educational organizations', *Administrative Science Quarterly*, **29**, 4, pp. 573–97.

PETERSON, K.D. and FINN, C.E. (1985) 'Principals, superintendents, and the administrators art', *The Public Interest*, 79, Spring.

PETERSON, K.D., MURPHY, J. and HALLINGER, P. (1987) 'Superintendent's perceptions of the control and coordination of the technical core in effective schools districts', *Educational Administration Quarterly*, **23**, 1, pp. 79–95.

PITNER, N.J. and OGAWA, R. (1981) 'Organizational Leadership: The Case of the School Superintendent', *Educational Administration Quarterly*, **17**, 2.

PITNER, N.J. (1982) *Training the School Administrator: State of the Art*, Center for Educational Policy and Management. Eugene, OR, University of Oregon.

POLLACK, S., CHRISPEELS, J., WATSON, D., BRICE, R. and MCCORMICK, S. (1988) 'A description of district factors that assist in the development of equity schools', paper presented at the annual meeting of the American Educational Research Association, New Orleans.

POWELL, R.E. (1984) 'A comparison of selection criteria and performance evaluation criteria for Missouri school superintendents', unpublished doctoral disseration, University of Missouri-Columbia.

PRINGLE, P.G. (1989) 'Relationship of general administrative leadership skills to superintendent selection and contract renewal', Austin, TX, University of Texas unpublished doctoral dissertation.

RHODES, L.A. (1990) 'Beyond your beliefs: Quantum leaps toward quality schools', *The School Administrator*, **48**, 12, December, pp. 23–6.

RIST, M. (1991) 'Urban superintendents', *Education Week*, November.

ROBERTSON, M.C. (1984) 'A survey of the selection of school superintendents in Massachusetts', unpublished doctoral dissertation, Boston Univerisity.

RUTHERFORD, W.L. (1985) 'School principals as effective leaders', *Phi Delta Kappan*, **69**, 1, pp. 31–4.

SALLEY, C. (1979–80) 'Superintendent's job priorities', *Administrator's Notebook*, **28**, 1.

SARASON, S.B. (1990) *The Predictable Failure of Educational Reform*, San Francisco, CA, Jossey Bass.

SASS, M.L. (1989) 'The AASA performance goals and skill areas as seen in terms of importance by professors of educational administration', unpublished dissertation, Northern Illinois University.

SCHILLER, J.M. (1988) 'The relationship of principal interventions to teacher success in implementing computer education', paper presented at the annual meeting of the American Educational Research Association, New Orleans.

SCHLECHTY, P.C. and JOSLIN, W.A. (1986) 'Images of schools', in LIEBERMAN, A. (Ed.) *Rethinking School Improvement*, New York, Teachers College Press, pp. 147–61.

SCHWENK, C.R. (1988) 'The cognitive perspective on strategic decision-making', *Journal of Management Studies*, **25**, 1, pp. 41–56.

SCLAFANI, S. (1987) 'AASA Guidelines for Preparation of School Administrators: Do They Represent the Important Job Behaviors of Superintendents?', Doctoral dissertation, Austin, University of Texas.

SERGIOVANNI, T.J. (1987) 'The theoretical basis for cultural leadership', in SHIEVE, L.T. and SCHOENHEIT, M.B. (Eds) *Leadership Examining the Elusive. 1987 Year Book of The Association of Curriculum Development*, Alexandria, VA,

SERGIOVANNI, T.J. and CORBALLY, J.R. (1984) *Leadership and Organizational Culture: New Perspectives on Administrator Theory and Practice*, Urbana, IL, University of Illinois Press.

STEARN, G.E. (Ed.) (1968) *McCluhan: Hot and Cold*, Harmondsworth, Penguin.

STOTT, J.D. (1991) 'An analysis of personal and professional characteristics of superintendents selected as being exemplary', unpublished doctoral dissertation, Northern Illinois University, December.

TERRY, R.W. (1988) *Leadership — a Preview of the Seventh View. Preview: Action Leadership*, San Francisco, CA, Jossey Bass.

THOMAS, M.W. (1978) *A Study of Alternatives in American Education, Volume II: The Role of the Principal*, Santa Monica, CA, Rand Corporation.

THOMPSON, S.D. (1989) 'Troubled kingdoms, restless natives', *Phi Delta Kappan*, **70**, 5, pp. 371–5.

TICHY, N.M. and DEVANNA, M.A. (1986) 'The transformational leader', *Training and Development Journal*, July, pp. 27–32.

TROHOSKI, C.V. (1984) 'Principal's interventions in the implementation of a school health program', unpublished doctoral dissertation, University of Pennsylvania.

TUCKER, M.S. (1988) 'Peter Drucker, knowledge, work, and the structure of schools', *Educational Leadership*, **45**, 5, February, pp. 44–46.

UBBEN, G.C. and HUGHES, L.W. (1987) *The Principal: Creative Leadership for Effective Schools*, Boston, MA, Allen and Bacon.

UNIVERSITY OF TEXAS AT AUSTIN AND THE AMERICAN ASSOCIATION OF SCHOOL

ADMINISTRATORS (1987) *In Search of Excellence in the Superintendency: A Report to the Meadows Foundation*, Austin, TX, University of Texas.

WALKER, W.G. (1989) 'Leadership in an age of ambiguity and risk', *Journal of Educational Administration*, **27**, 1, pp. 7–17.

WALLACE, R. (1985) *The Superintendent of Education: Data Based Instructional Leadership*, Pittsburgh, PA, Learning Research and Development Center.

WALLACE, R. (1987) 'The role of the superintendent in promoting educational reform in the United States', in HOPKINS, D. (Ed.) *Improving the Quality of Schooling*, Lewes, Falmer Press.

WENDEL, F.C. and SYBOUTS, W. (1988) *Assessment Center Methods in Educational Administration: Past, Present and Future*, Tempe, AZ, University Council for Educational Administration.

WIMPELBERG, R.K. (1988) 'Instructional leadership and ignorance: Guidelines for the new studies of district administrators', *Education and Urban Society*, **20**, 3, pp. 2–12.

YOUNGS, B.B. (1988) 'Leadership: Is there a generation gap?', *The School Administrator*, **3**, 45, March, pp. 8–9.

# Contributors

**David S.G. Carter** is Visiting Professor to the Department of Educational Administration at The University of Texas at Austin, and Senior Research Fellow to the Meadows Project. He is based at the University of Notre Dame, Australia.

**Nolan Estes** is Haskew Centennial Professor of Public School Administration at The University of Texas at Austin and Director of the Meadows Project.

**Thomas E. Glass** is Professor of Educational Administration at the University of Northern Illinois.

**Shirley M. Hord** is Senior Research Associate at the Southwest Educational Development Laboratory, Austin, Texas, charged with fostering leadership and the school improvement process.

**Judith G. Loredo** is a team member of the Meadows Project and Professor at Huston-Tillotson College, Austin.

**Ben M. Harris** is Hage Professor Emeritus at the Department of Educational Administration in the College of Education at The University of Texas at Austin. He was the Coordinator of the Meadows Project.

# Index